••• **BULATS Edition**

Business
BENCHMARK

Upper-Intermediate

Student's Book

CAMBRIDGE UNIVERSITY PRESS

Guy Brook-Hart

CAMBRIDGE UNIVERSITY PRESS
Cambridge, New York, Melbourne, Madrid, Cape Town, Singapore,
São Paulo, Delhi, Dubai, Tokyo, Mexico City

Cambridge University Press
The Edinburgh Building, Cambridge CB2 8RU, UK

www.cambridge.org
Information on this title: www.cambridge.org/9780521672894

© Cambridge University Press 2006

This publication is in copyright. Subject to statutory exception
and to the provisions of relevant collective licensing agreements,
no reproduction of any part may take place without the written
permission of Cambridge University Press.

First published 2006
4th printing 2011

Printed in Dubai by Oriental Press

A catalogue record for this publication is available from the British Library

ISBN 978-0-521-67289-4 Student's Book BULATS Edition Upper-Intermediate with CD-ROM (Windows, Mac)
ISBN 978-0-521-67116-3 Student's Book BEC Vantage Edition
ISBN 978-0-521-67290-0 Teacher's Resource Book Upper-Intermediate/Vantage
ISBN 978-0-521-67291-7 Personal Study Book Upper-Intermediate/Vantage
ISBN 978-0-521-67659-5 Audio Cassette BULATS Edition Upper-Intermediate
ISBN 978-0-521-67660-1 Audio CD BULATS Edition Upper-Intermediate
ISBN 978-0-521-67292-4 Audio Cassette BEC Vantage Edition
ISBN 978-0-521-67293-1 Audio CD BEC Vantage Edition

Cambridge University Press has no responsibility for the persistence or
accuracy of URLs for external or third-party internet websites referred to in
this publication, and does not guarantee that any content on such websites is,
or will remain, accurate or appropriate. Information regarding prices, travel
timetables and other factual information given in this work is correct at
the time of first printing but Cambridge University Press does not guarantee
the accuracy of such information thereafter.

Introduction

Who this book is for

This book is intended to be an interesting and stimulating course for upper-intermediate students of Business English (Common European Framework Level B2). It provides a general Business English course both for students who have not yet worked in business and for people who are working and have experience of business environments.

It provides the practical reading, speaking, listening and writing skills necessary for people who need English for working in business. It also contains a wide range of essential business vocabulary and grammar.

For students who want to study for a Business English qualification, this book gives a complete preparation for the Cambridge Business Language Testing Service (BULATS) test. It is accompanied by a CD-ROM containing a complete past BULATS test supplied by Cambridge ESOL.

What the book contains

The book contains the following elements:

- **24 units for classroom study**. These units are organised in groups of four around a theme: human resources, marketing, etc. While each unit gives training and practice in a variety of skills, the first unit in each group mainly concentrates on reading skills, the second on listening, the third on writing and the fourth on speaking. Each unit contains essential vocabulary input for business students.
- **Grammar workshops**. For each group of four units, there is a two-page Grammar workshop. These explain and extend the grammar work introduced in the units. In the units, you will from time to time see, for example ▶ *page 26 (Comparison of adjectives)*, which indicates that there is supplementary material in the Grammar workshop.

- **Exam skills and Exam practice section**. This section, which starts on page 121, gives you detailed guidance on how to approach BULATS test tasks at your level, the skills required and what the task is testing. The Exam skills pages contain exercises to build up your skills for the test. The Exam practice pages contain questions/tasks from a past BULATS test for your level*, supplied by Cambridge ESOL.
- **Sample answers** to the writing exercises in the book.
- **Full answer keys** for all the exercises in this book.
- **Transcripts** for all the listening activities in the book.
- **CD-ROM** with a complete BULATS test.

Also available are:

- **2 audio CDs/cassettes,** containing a variety of recorded material, including interviews with business people and BULATS exam listening tasks.
- **Teacher's Resource Book**, containing guidance and suggestions on how to approach activities in the book, full answer keys plus extra photocopiable activities and case studies to supplement the units in the Student's Book.
- **Personal Study Book**, containing activities and exercises based on the vocabulary, grammar and skills covered in each unit. It is intended as reinforcement of material you have studied in class. The Personal Study Book contains keys to all its exercises, so you will be able to check your answers yourself. It also contains a Word list of vocabulary from the Student's Book.

* The BULATS test is designed to assess learners' level of Business English from beginners to advanced, so this book does not contain advice on how to approach BULATS tasks which are too easy for your level. See the information about the test on page 122.

Map of the book

	Unit	Reading	Listening	Writing
Human resources	**1** Staff development and training 10–13	Recruitment brochure Training at Deloitte Touche	Conversation about a training course	
	2 Job descriptions and job satisfaction 14–17	The management accountant	What people like about their jobs A human resources manager	Brief job descriptions
	3 Letters of enquiry and applications 18–21	Job satisfaction at EMI	Advice on job applications	A letter of enquiry about careers An email applying for a job
	4 Telephone skills 22–25	A telephone quiz Phone answering tips	Telephone language Enquiring about a job	
	Grammar workshop 1 (Units 1–4) 26–27 Comparison of adjectives and adverbs, Present perfect and past simple, Simple questions,			
Marketing	**5** Promotional activities and branding 28–31	Promoting AXE The power of brands	Supermarkets' own brands	
	6 New product development 32–35	Developing and launching 'chai'	Developing and launching a new product Launching and promoting a product	
	7 A stand at a trade fair 36–39	The International Food Exhibition Preparing an exhibition stand	Conversation with a trade-fair organiser	An email giving information An email asking for information A fax answering enquiries A memo informing staff
	8 Establishing relationships and negotiating 40–43	Asking questions about a product	Establishing a business relationship Negotiating	An email summarising an agreement
	Grammar workshop 2 (Units 5–8) 44–45 Countable/uncountable nouns, -ing forms and infinitives, The first conditional			
Starting new business activities	**9** Going it alone 46–49	Buying into a franchise A letter to a franchiser	Why start your own business?	A letter of enquiry to a franchiser
	10 Financing the start-up 50–53	Raising finance	Setting up a food consultancy Setting up a multimedia company What's important when starting a company?	
	11 Starting up in a new location 54–57	A new location in Scotland A proposal	A new location in Scotland	A proposal
	12 Presenting your business idea 58–61	Making the most of presentations	Signalling the parts of a presentation	
	Grammar workshop 3 (Units 9–12) 62–63 Tenses in time clauses, The second conditional, Comparing and contrasting ideas, Modal verbs			

Speaking	Vocabulary	Language work
Discussion: Who should pay for training? Preparing a staff training scheme	Job training: *bonus schemes*, *promotion*, *training budget*, *learning goals*, etc.	Expressing personal opinions Comparison of adjectives Making suggestions
Saying what you like/dislike about your job/studies Describing your job Discussion: How to handle job interviews	Acronyms for job titles Job titles Job descriptions	Forming questions
Discussions: What makes a great place to work? How best to apply for jobs	*Perks*, *colleagues*, etc. *Approachable*, *fulfilling*, etc.	Asking complex questions Formal/informal style
Discussions: Problems using the phone Telephone skills training Role-plays: Booking a hotel; Recruiting an assistant Talking at a business meeting		Structuring a talk
Complex questions		
Discussions: Advantages and disadvantages of promotional activities; Brands Role-play: Promoting a shampoo	Promotional activities Marketing terms: *brands*, *logo*, etc.	Brainstorming
Discussion: New products Launching a product Role-play: Promoting a new service	*Entrepreneurial*, *upmarket*, etc. Marketing vocabulary	Expressing purpose
Discussion: Trade fairs		Forming questions
Discussion: new products and negotiating Role-plays: Establishing a business relationship On a stand at a trade fair Negotiating a deal	*Stock*, *mark-up*, *sale or return*, *overheads*, etc. Terms and conditions	Asking questions about a product First conditional
Discussion: Why start your own business? Advice on buying a franchise Questions to ask a franchiser	*Make a go*, *expertise*, *premises*, *mortgage*, etc. Financial terms	Tenses in time clauses
Discussion: What business would you start? Role-play: Getting advice about starting up Mini-presentation: Starting a business	Collocations for starting companies Ways of financing start-ups	Second conditional
Discussions: Extra information; What is important when starting in a new location?; Which city? Agents vs. distributors vs. joint ventures		Making recommendations Contrasting ideas
Structuring a presentation A brief presentation Role-play: Presenting your business idea	Equipment for presentations	Modal verbs

	Unit	Reading	Listening	Writing
Business travel	**13** Business hotels and sales conferences 64–67	Business accommodation Planning a lively sales conference	Conference problems	The results of a survey
	14 Business conferences 68–71	A conference programme	Arranging conference facilities Networking at a conference A destination management company	
	15 Reports 72–75	The Forest Conference Centre	A report on the use of private company jets	A report on the use of private company jets
	16 Business meetings 76–79	Think before you meet	Talking about meetings A business meeting	A report about meetings An email agreeing to a meeting
	Grammar workshop 4 (Units 13–16) 80–81 *While* and *whereas* for contrasting ideas, Modal verbs: perfect forms, Passives 1 & 2, *Too/enou*			
New technologies, innovation, and change	**17** New technologies and change 82–85	The Internet and change Change at Adobe Systems	Changes at work	
	18 Using the Internet 86–89	Website design	E-shopping at Tesco.com Websites and business	Email requesting an upgrade to a website
	19 A staff survey 90–93	Reading a report	A working party	Report on staff survey to modernise office
	20 Offshoring and outsourcing 94–97	Can outsourcing work for small businesses?	What should we offshore? Offshoring from Britain	
	Grammar workshop 5 (Units 17–20) 98–99 *Used to*, Articles, Reported speech			
Customer relations	**21** Customer loyalty 100–103	From satisfaction to loyalty	A supermarket and customer loyalty	
	22 Communication with customers 104–107	Turning complaints to your advantage Training in customer communication skills	Communicating with customers at Espresso Customer communication at Not Just Food	
	23 Corresponding with customers 108–111	A letter about a new service A letter from a dissatisfied customer	Preparing a letter of complaint	A letter about a new service A letter of complaint
	24 A business seminar 112–115	Advertisement for a business seminar	Speakers at a business seminar A short talk	
	Grammar workshop 6 (Units 21–24) 116–117 Relative pronouns, Expressing causes, Expressing results			

Sample answers for writing exercises	118
EXAM SKILLS AND EXAM PRACTICE	121–150
Contents of exam section	121
Answer keys	151
Transcripts	167

Map of the book

Speaking	Vocabulary	Language work
Discussion: The needs of the business traveller Mini-presentation: business travel Planning a conference	Hotel vocabulary; *subscribers*, *chain*, etc. Conference vocabulary: *keynote speech*, *tailor*, etc.	Expressing criticism (modal perfects) Contrasting ideas
Role-play: Networking Discussion: Choosing a conference destination	*Networking*, *reinventing*, *enhancing*, etc.	
Saying what charts show Discussion: Private jets	Vocabulary for expressing changes	Using the passive
Discussion: Meetings A survey of meetings; Speaking at a meeting Role-play: A finance meeting	Types of meeting; Meeting vocabulary Verbs for meetings; *cornerstone*, *set out to*, etc.; Expressing opinions	*Too* and *enough*
Discussions: New technologies and change What is important when making changes? Role-play: Introducing new technology	New technology, *customer base*, *knowledge worker*, *licence fees*, *applications*, etc.	*Used to* for past actions/habits The definite article
Discussions: Your favourite websites; What is important when buying over the Internet?	Computers; Internet *Straightforward*, *target audience*, etc.	
Discussion: The results of a survey	Flexible working; Expressing numbers	Reported speech Reporting verbs
Discussion: Advantages/ disadvantages of offshoring Role-plays: Offshoring parts of a clothing manufacturers Outsourcing to reduce risk	Discussion phrases *Make redundant*, *assurance*, *shareholder*, etc.	Expressing causes
Discussion: What makes you a loyal customer? Role-play: A staff meeting	*Bond*, *revenue*, *vendor*, etc.	Relative pronouns
Discussion: Effective methods of communication Advice on dealing with complaints Role-play: Dealing with losing customers	Customer collocations *Rapport*, *retain*, etc.	
Discussion: Communicating new products and service, keeping customers happy		Expressing results
Discussion: What you can learn from other people in business Speaking at a business seminar	Discourse markers for short talks	Expressions followed by *-ing* forms

Map of the book

Acknowledgements

The author and publishers would like to thank the following for agreeing to be interviewed for this book:
Lewis Bronze, Christina Bunt, Amanda Hamilton, Maxine McPherson, Jane Milton, Charlotte Weston.

The author and publishers are grateful to the following for permission to reproduce copyright material. It has not always been possible to identify the sources of all the material used and in such cases the publishers would welcome information from the copyright owners.

Text
pp.12–13: Deloitte for adapted material from www.graduates.deloitte.co.uk; p.16: *The Independent* for the adapted article 'Constant quality in a changing world' by Virginia Matthews, 25 September 2003, © Independent News and Media Limited; p.19: EMI for the text 'Our People' taken from the EMI website (www.emimusic.co.uk); p.25: About, Inc. for adapted material 'Phone answering tips to win business', 2004 by Susan Ward. Used with permission of About, Inc. which can be found on the Web at www.about.com. All rights reserved; p.28: Unilever for text on company background, © Unilever 2005; p.31: *The Economist* for the adapted article 'Who's wearing the trousers', 6 September 2001; p.77: *The Economist* for the adapted article 'Think before you meet – too many meetings are a waste of time', 23 October 2003; p.134: *The Economist* for the adapted article 'How 51 gorillas can make you seriously rich', 19 August 2004, © *The Economist* Newspaper Limited, London; p.33: Sharon Smith for the article adapted from *The Financial Times*, 3 July 2004, with permission of Sharon Smith; pp.42–43: Dynamic Living for the descriptions of the CorkPops Wine Opener and the Battery Operated Peeler; p.67: Kimberly McCall for text adapted from 'Radical Rendezvous' from *Entrepreneur* Magazine, July 2003, © 2005 Kimberly McCall; p.85: The Wharton School for adapted text from 'Getting reorganisation right: How Bruce Chizon drove change and innovation at Adobe Systems' from Knowledge@Wharton, with permission of The Wharton School, University of Pennsylvania; p.87: *The Financial Times* for the screen shot of the FT.com home page, 7 December 2005 © The Financial Times Ltd; p.94: The Wharton School for adapted text from 'Can BPO Work for Small Businesses?', from Knowledge@Wharton, with permission of The Wharton School, University of Pennsylvania; p.101: LOMA for the adapted article 'Creating a customer-centric culture' by Stephen Hall, Reprinted from LOMA's Resource Magazine. Visit LOMA at www.loma.org.

Logos
p.11: the Flight Centre logo, with permission of Flight Centre Ltd; p.12: the Deloitte logo (www.deloitte.com), with permission of Deloitte, © Deloitte & Touche LLP 2005; p.16: the Norgren logo, with permission of IMI Norgren; p.17: the Tesco logo, with permission of Tesco PLC; p.18: the EMI logo (www.emimusic.co.uk), © EMI Music Publishing Ltd; p.28: the Unilever logo (www.unilever.co.uk), with permission of Unilever; p.32: the Tea UK logo, with permission of Tea UK Ltd www.drinkmechai.co.uk; p.51: the Not Just Food logo, with permission of Not Just Food; p.53: the Espresso Education logo, with permission of Espresso Education; p.67: the McCall Media & Marketing logo, with permission of McCall Media & Marketing; p.84: the Adobe logo, with permission of Adobe; p.94: the Hoyt logo, with permission of Hoyt Corporation; p.100: the Hay Group logo, with permission of Hay Group.

Photos
Cover photo: Getty Images
A1Pix Digital Picture Library for p.36 (br); AA World Travel Library for p.55 (l & r); About, Inc. for the photograph of Susan Ward, 2004 by Susan Ward. Used with permission of About, Inc. which can be found on the Web at www.about.com. All rights reserved p.25; Action Plus for p.28 (d); Alvey & Towers for pp.74, 112 (b); courtesy of Air New Zealand Group for p.69 (R. Poulton); Airsport Photo Library for p.61 (br); Alamy for pp.34 (tl) (Alex Serge), 61 (tl) (Jan Caudron/Anaklasis); Art Directors & TRIP for pp.22 (r), 96 (l & r); Bananastock.com for pp.68 (t), 72 (t); courtesy of Dr Bowden-Kirby for p.69; courtesy of Lewis Bronze for p. 15 (tr); courtesy of Christina Bunt for p.17; Car & Bike Photo Library for p.108 (r); courtesy of Celebrity Speakers (NZ) Ltd for p.69 (b); courtesy of Cobalt Systems Ltd for p.41; Corbis for pp.31, 46 (1), 43 (3), 56, 58 (m), 61 (bl), 68 (ml), 79, 82 (d), 90 (m), 104 (c), 106; courtesy of Cork Pops, Inc for pp.42 (l), 43 (l); Jim Cummins/Corbis for p.40 (t); courtesy of Catherine DeVyre for p.69; Dynamic Living for pp.42 (l & r), 43 (l & r); John Feingersh/Corbis for p.36 (t); courtesy of Flight Centre Ltd for p.11; Getty Images for pp.20, 50 (a, c, d, e), 68 (b), 85, 113; courtesy of Amanda Hamilton for p.15 (bl); HartMcLeod for pp. 28 (a, b, c, e, f, g, h, i), 30, 58 (1–9), 82 (a, b, e, f, g), 104 (a, b, e, f, g); courtesy of Hoyt Corporation for p. 94; ImageSource/Rex Features for p.50 (t); Imagestate for pp.52, 59; Andre Jenny/Alamy for p.28 (t); Ronnie Kaufman/Corbis for p.14 (t); KD Photography for p.34 (bl); Brian Lee/Corbis for p.94 (t); Jean-Pierre Lescourret/Corbis for p.76 (t); Yang Liu/Corbis for p.108 (t); courtesy of Maxine Macpherson for p.15 (br); The London Marriott Hotel, Kensington courtesy of Marriott for p.65; courtesy of Kimberly McCall, © 2005 Kimberly McCall for p.67; Mediacolours/Alamy for p.32 (t); courtesy of Jane Milton for pp. 15 (tl), 51; courtesy of Not Just Food for p.89; courtesy of Oil & Vinegar for pp.47, 48; John Phillips/Photofusion Picture Library/Alamy for p.56 (t); Pictor International/Image State/Alamy for p.86 (t); Steve Prezant/Corbis for p.22 (r); Punchstock for pp.13 (Photodisc), 16, 66, 78 (Bananastock), 21, 104 (d) (Imagesource), 43 (2) (Blend), 50 (b), 70 (image100), 68 (mr), 92, (Digital Vision), 76 (b) (Goodshoot); Reuters/Corbis for p.36 (t); Rex Features for pp.34 (tr), 36 (m); Royalty Free/Corbis for pp.10 (t), 82 (t); Pete Saloutos/Corbis for p.100 (t); Skyscan/A Sanger-Davies/www.photographersdirect.com for p.73; courtesy of Tea UK Ltd www.drinkmechai.co.uk for pp.32 (br), 33; courtesy of Tesco PLC (www.tesco.com), © tesco.com, 2005 for pp.86, 103; TIPS Images for pp.82 (c), 108 (l), 110; Topfoto for p.19; courtesy of Tourism New Zealand for p.69 (W. Stone); Unilever © Unilever 2005 for p.29; Bill Varie/Corbis for p.112 (t); courtesy of Susan Ward for p.25; Henry Westheim Photography/Alamy for p.58 (t); courtesy of Charlotte Weston for p.71; William Whitehurst/Corbis for p.18 (t); Rob Wilkinson/Alamy for p.90 (t); Jeff Zaruba/Corbis for p.104 (t).

Every effort has been made to trace the copyright holders, and we apologise in advance for any unintentional omissions. We would be pleased to insert the appropriate acknowledgement in any subsequent edition of this publication.

Photo research: Kevin Brown
Text design and layout: Hart McLeod
Project management: Jane Coates
Edited by: Catriona Watson-Brown
Production controller: Gemma Wilkins

Thanks

The author would like to thank all the editorial team for their help, advice, guidance, enthusiasm, feedback and ideas throughout the project, especially Charlotte Adams (Editorial Manager), Sally Searby (Senior Commissioning Editor), Jane Coates (Series Editor), Catriona Watson-Brown (Freelance Editor), Gemma Wilkins (Production Controller) and Marie Allan (Permissions Controller). Special thanks also to Susie Fairfax-Davies for using her compendious list of contacts to search out and interview business people for the book, and thanks to the following people for kindly giving up time and agreeing to be interviewed: Christina Bunt (Tesco), Amanda Hamilton (Tea UK), Lewis Bronze (Espresso), Jane Milton (Not Just Food), Maxine Macpherson (Allied Europe) and Charlotte Weston (Pacific World).

The author would also like to thank his Business English students at the British Council, Valencia, from 2003 to 2005, who patiently and good-humouredly worked through and trialled the materials and, consciously or unconsciously, pointed out faults and inconsistencies.

The author would like to give his warmest thanks and love to his wife, Paz, and his children, Esteban and Elena, for their patience and encouragement during the many long hours spent in the back room working on the book.

The author dedicates the book to his mother, Mary Brook-Hart, whom he thinks of with much love and great pride.

The publishers would like to thank the following people for their invaluable feedback when reviewing this course material: David Booth and Hugh Bateman from Cambridge ESOL; Elaine Allen, Paul Bress, Rachel Connabeep, Philip Dover, Rosemary Richey, Roger Scott, Thiruvenkataswami, Chris Turner, Bruce Warburton, Julian Wheatley, Dr Bob Wright.

Recordings by James Richardson at The Soundhouse Studios (sound engineer: Mark Oliver).

Staff development and training

Getting started

1 Work in pairs. Look at these benefits of working for a company and discuss the following.
 - Which benefits do you think would be most attractive to someone who has just finished their studies and is looking for their first job?
 - Put the benefits in order from the most attractive to the least attractive.

   A bonus scheme ☐
   Responsibility ☐
   A high salary ☐
   An in-house training scheme ☐
   The opportunity to travel ☐
   A permanent contract ☐
   Long holidays ☐
   Rapid promotion ☐

2 Change partners and summarise what the attractions of a company training scheme would be for a new member of staff.

Useful language

Giving opinions: agreeing and disagreeing

I think …… would be the most attractive because …… .
I'm not sure about that. For me, …… would be more useful than …… because …… .
Perhaps you're right. And I don't think …… is as important as …… .

▶ page 26 (Comparison of adjectives)

Recruitment brochure

Vocabulary

Check the meanings of these words, then use them to complete the sentences below.

| ability certificate course degree development |
| experience hands-on knowledge qualifications |
| ~~skills~~ trainee training |

1 Our school-leaver trainee programme aims to teach you key *skills* such as word processing and bookkeeping.
2 Although he lacks formal ……… such as a university degree, he came through the ranks due to his ……… to take on new ideas and to manage people. Now he's one of our best managers.
3 The degree ……… you study at university is likely to decide the sort of job you do afterwards. However, whatever you study, it's always useful to have a university ……… .
4 At the end of the four-week training course, you will receive a ……… . The course aims to give you a thorough ……… of the company's activities and the skills to do your job competently. However, there are a lot of things which you can only learn with ……… , and this takes a lot of time.
5 He has excellent qualifications, and with our policy of professional ……… and on-the-job training, he will almost certainly become one of our high fliers. In fact, next week he's going on a management ……… course.
6 As a ……… computer technician, his training course is much more ……… than theoretical.

10 Staff development and training

Reading

1 You are going to read an extract from a recruitment brochure for graduate trainees. Before you read, match these expressions from the text (1–6) with their definitions (a–f).

1 day one
2 throw you in at the deep end
3 promote from within
4 come through the ranks
5 become a high flier
6 shuffle up the ladder

a achieve great professional success
b get promotion slowly
c have to learn something difficult with little training or experience
d move people inside a company to higher positions
e rise to higher positions from the bottom of an organisation
f your first day at work

2 Read the text below quickly to find out why Flight Centre Limited thinks staff training is so important. When you have finished, discuss your answer with a partner.

Company background — **FLIGHT CENTRE**
Flight Centre Limited is one of the world's largest independent travel retailers, employing more than 5,500 people worldwide.

Go anywhere
YOU WANT TO GO

We believe in giving you a lot of responsibility from day one – but that doesn't mean throwing you in at the deep end. One of our major priorities is to **1** _B_ you get the training and support you need to gain the skills which will allow you to succeed personally and professionally.

The training starts as soon as you **2** ...... – and it never stops. The initial programme is **3** ...... partly at your office and partly in our dedicated Learning Centre. For the first 12 months, you'll have a regular programme of training **4** ...... topics as diverse as Advanced Sales, Goal Setting and Time Management, as well as Airfares and Packages.

After that, you can develop in any direction you choose by **5** ...... a range of courses and events in four key development areas: Sales and Service, Product and Airfares, Systems, and Personal Development. All this is provided at no **6** ...... to you – which is exactly the way it should be. We have a consistent **7** ...... of promoting from within; currently about 90 per cent of our Team Leaders have come through the ranks, and we want to keep it that **8** ....

We're also keen to train the leaders of the future with our Leadership Development programme. It's an intensive set of training courses **9** ...... up by specialist project work. After all, becoming a high flier in any company shouldn't be about just waiting to shuffle up the ladder. Here, the best people develop as far as they like, as fast as they like. We hope you'll be one of them. And it's a measure of the success of our philosophy on cultivating personal and **10** ...... development, as well as promoting from within, that earned us the Training and Development award for excellence, as voted by our employees, in the latest *Sunday Times* '100 Best Companies to Work For' 2004 UK survey.

Adapted from http://www.therecruitmentcentre.com

3 Read the text again and choose the best alternative for each gap.

1 A want   B make sure   C hope   D prepare
2 A join   B recruit   C contract   D employ
3 A introduced   B done   C based   D fixed
4 A dealing   B covering   C learning   D working
5 A going   B assisting   C training   D attending
6 A money   B payment   C cost   D price
7 A record   B reputation C activity   D standard
8 A type   B sort   C kind   D way
9 A set   B backed   C held   D kept
10 A life   B work   C career   D profession

4 Compare your answers with a partner and discuss whether you would like to work for a company like this.

Talking point

Work in small groups and discuss the following.

- Companies should pay for training to do the job, but staff should pay for training which gives them qualifications.
- Training should be done in employees' free time.
- If a company trains you, you should agree to work for that company for a number of years afterwards.
- All staff need continuous training – not just new recruits.
- It doesn't matter what you study. The important thing is to get a good degree.

Staff development and training **11**

Training course

Listening

02 1 Listen to a short conversation about a training course.

2 Match these phrases from the recording (1–6) with their definitions (a–f).

1 tailor-made
2 learning goals
3 training budget
4 hands-on training
5 computer literate
6 core skills

a practical, not theoretical training
b able to use a computer
c basic essential skills
d money reserved for training staff
e specially designed to meet your needs
f your objectives when doing the course

3 Check your answers by looking at the transcript for Track 2 at the back of the book.

4 Discuss these questions with a partner.

1 What are the advantages of a course which is tailor-made?
2 How can trainers design courses which meet the learning goals of their trainees?
3 How much of a company's budget should be used for training?
4 What sort of courses are suited to hands-on training?
5 Why is it important nowadays to be computer literate?
6 In your job, or a job you know about, what are the core skills?

Training at Deloitte Touche

Company background — **Deloitte.**
Deloitte Touche Tohmatsu is a worldwide company offering management consultancy, auditing and financial advisory services.

Reading

In business, it's important to be able to follow the structure and arguments of the texts (articles, reports, letters and emails) you are reading. This type of exercise, where sentences are removed, helps you to focus on this skill.

1 Read the article *A great start to a promising career*. What is the subject of each paragraph?

A GREAT START to a promising career

Sally Shoesmith, aged 23, reports on how she's getting a flying start as a management consultant.

I've been with for Deloitte for nearly two years now. I was originally attracted to this company in my final year at Cambridge. I was looking for a company which would put me in the fast lane to promotion and I realised that, in my case, this meant an organisation with a policy of on-the-job training and development. **1** ..F.. As I discovered at my first recruitment interview, they also place a lot of emphasis on getting professional qualifications, which really impressed me.

Deloitte actually helps employees to reduce the conflict between work and study. In my case, this means I've always been allowed to give exam preparation priority over my client work. Right from the beginning, my boss, Neil, has gone out of his way to help and encourage me. **2** ...... I find it's a good moment to discuss solutions to any problems I have with him.

Task tip
- Consider the subject of each paragraph.
- Look at clues in the sentences (e.g. in sentence B, what is this an example of? In sentence C, who does *he* refer to?).
- Read the text again when you have finished to check that your answers are logical.

2 Choose the best sentence for each gap. There is one extra sentence.

A At Deloitte, there's a national 'first time, every time' culture, which makes sense because the sooner you pass exams, the sooner you get down to real work.
B For example, there is a course I did quite early on in the job called *Introduction to Client Services*, which concentrated on presentation, interview, teamwork and writing skills.
C He monitors my progress formally, but apart from that, we usually have lunch together once or twice a week.
D It is pretty tough, as I have to fit the academic work in around my daily workload.
E Naturally enough, much of what I've learnt has been taught me informally by the people I work with.
F On their website, Deloitte talked about job satisfaction and giving employees the chance to grow and develop throughout their careers, so it seemed a company worth applying for.
G The firm has agreements with local training colleges, who provide many of the courses graduate trainees follow.

12 Staff development and training

Apart from professional qualifications, we're also given plenty of internal training. This includes courses intended to help develop one's organisational, delivery and leadership qualities. **3** ...... This gave me a really confident and practical start to my work with the firm, as so much of my work involves using exactly these skills.

Another thing which attracted me to Deloitte was that you can choose your training method to suit your individual learning patterns. This is because they want us to pass our exams at the first attempt. **4** ...... Also, I think, when you've got your professional qualifications you're treated with much more respect by both your colleagues and your clients.

When I arrived at Deloitte, we went through an initial three-day programme to develop our core skills and introduce us to the firm and our new colleagues. **5** ...... In the near future, I expect to be passing on the knowledge I have acquired to next year's intake of graduate trainees. We are given formal six-monthly appraisals and, what is more, we are given plenty of advice by peers, managers and partners.

Fully funded study towards professional qualifications is a vital part of many careers in Deloitte, and at the moment I'm starting on a Masters degree in Business Management with the London School of Economics. **6** ...... On the other hand, we are provided with very generous study leave, and the firm has a great track record of success. I can see myself working here for many years to come, as they're providing me with all the opportunities I need.

Adapted from Deloitte: Training and Development (http://graduates.deloitte.co.uk)

Vocabulary

1 Find words or phrases in the text which mean the following.

1 getting a higher position in the company quickly (paragraph 1) *in the fast lane to promotion*
2 training while you are working (paragraph 1)
3 has made a special effort (paragraph 2)
4 supervises (section C)
5 training inside the company (paragraph 3)
6 essential basic skills (paragraph 5)
7 people who have studied at university and are learning the job (paragraph 5)
8 assessments, evaluations (paragraph 5)
9 people at the same level in the company as the writer (paragraph 5)
10 completely paid for (paragraph 6)
11 amount of work to do (section D)

2 Work with a partner. Talk about:
- how long you have worked in the same company / studied in the same college where you are now
- what training courses you have done, and when you did them.

▶ **page 26** (Present perfect and past simple)

Staff training scheme

Talking point

Work in pairs or small groups. Your company has decided it needs to provide more training for staff. You have been asked to help prepare a staff training programme. Discuss the situation together and decide:
- what kinds of courses would be most useful
- how to choose who should go on the courses
- whether the courses should happen during working time or free time.

Task tip

If you don't work for a company, or you don't work for the same company, quickly invent a company before you start.

Useful language

Making suggestions

Why don't we + *infinitive* ?
 (e.g. Why don't we run a computer skills course?)
Why not + *infinitive* ?
 (e.g. Why not ask for suggestions from staff?)
How about + *-ing* form ?
 (e.g. How about running a computer skills course?)
What do you think?
Do you agree?

Staff development and training 13

UNIT 2

Job descriptions and job satisfaction

Getting started

1 With a partner, decide what job title each of these abbreviations stands for.

1 CEO *Chief Executive Officer*   3 PA   5 Director R&D
2 CIO   4 HRM   6 PRO

2 Check your answers by looking at the list of job titles in the box in the next exercise.

Vocabulary

1 Match each of the statements (a–g) below to the job title they describe (1–7 in the box).

a 'I have to supervise and know about what's going on in all the different parts of the company. I have to represent the company in all important decisions.'

b 'I am a qualified accountant and a member of the management team. I monitor my company's financial performance, as well as supervising the budgets for various projects and controlling their costs.'

c 'My job is around the development and training of the managers in the store where I work, and making sure they do their jobs well. Also, I'm responsible for the recruitment of new staff.'

d 'I give advice about all sorts of different things connected with food, such as advice on how to market it, developing new recipes; I also write articles about it.'

e 'My job? It's our computer systems and information technology (IT) in general, and how they affect all parts of our organisation, from customer relations to accounting to recruitment.'

f 'In the past, a job like mine would have been much more secretarial – typing and so on. Now, I'm very involved in every aspect of her work, setting up meetings, organising her travel, dealing with her routine correspondence and generally easing her workload.'

g 'We've got a very big project on at the moment, for a new product, and I have to build up the project teams, provide them with the resources they need, check they're meeting targets and working within their budgets, and particularly that they're meeting deadlines, so that the product is launched on time.'

1	Finance Manager	b
2	Human Resources Manager	
3	Chief Executive Officer / Managing Director	
4	Chief Information Officer	
5	Director of Research and Development	
6	Personal Assistant	
7	Marketing Consultant	

14 Job descriptions and job satisfaction

2 Find words or phrases in the statements which mean the following.

1 how well parts of the company are doing   *performance*
2 put new products on sale
3 finding new staff for the company
4 person who looks after financial records
5 reducing, making easier
6 groups of people who work together on a project
7 objectives which a company or team decides it wants to reach
8 money which is reserved for a particular activity
9 doing things within the correct time

3 Work in groups. Write one or two sentences like the ones you read in the previous activities. Read your sentence(s) to the rest of the group. The other students should guess what job you are talking about.

What I like about my job

Listening

1 Look at the following reasons why people might like their jobs. Underline the key words in each one.

a building <u>customer</u> <u>relationships</u>
b finding solutions for customers
c being my own boss
d learning from my job
e balancing working life with family life
f seeing the success of my company

2 Compare your answers with a partner.

03 3 Listen to four people talking about why they like their jobs. What reason do they give? Choose from the reasons a–f in Exercise 1.

1 Jane Milton ....   3 Amanda Hamilton ....
2 Lewis Bronze ....   4 Maxine Macpherson ....

> **Task tip**
> When you listen, you won't hear exactly the same words as in Exercise 1 – you have to listen for the same idea to be expressed.

4 Compare your answers with a partner. Can you remember the key words or phrases which gave you the answers?

Talking point

Discuss in small groups.

- What do you most enjoy about your job/studies?
- Is there anything you dislike?

Job descriptions and job satisfaction   **15**

Company background

NORGREN

IMI Norgren is an international engineering company, specialising in fluid technologies.

The management accountant

Reading

1 Write one word in each gap to complete questions you might ask at a job interview.

a How hard ...*do*... you have ...*to*... work?
b What .... you like .... your job?
c How long .... you .... in your present job?
d What .... your ambitions .... the future?
e What .... your job consist ....?
f When .... you first attracted .... accountancy?

2 Write each of the questions from Exercise 1 in the correct gap in the interview. (There is one extra question.)

▶ page 27 (Asking questions)

3 Are these statements true or false? Correct the false ones.

1 Gabriella came to the UK in order to work.
   False: she came to the UK to study English.
2 She has always worked for the same company.
3 She looked after the financial affairs of her class at school.
4 She is only involved in the financial aspects of her company.
5 She has more junior staff working for her.
6 She gives financial information to the top level of management in her company.
7 She believes that sometimes she is asked to work too hard.
8 Her ambitions include going to work for a different organisation.

Talking point

Work in pairs and ask each other similar questions to the ones which Gabriella was asked.

Talk about the job you do, or a job you would like to do in the future.

FORGET THE STEREOTYPE OF ACCOUNTANTS: THEY ARE NOW AMBITIOUS, SMOOTH-TALKING BUSINESS STRATEGISTS

We interviewed Gabriella Andrews, 29, a finance manager with IMI Norgren. Born in Hungary, she came to the UK at 18 to study English, but stayed on to study European Business and Technology with German at Warwick. Following her graduation, with a first-class BSc Honours degree, she joined IMI as a trainee accountant. After various jobs with the firm, she became a finance manager with the company in February. She passed the final accountancy examinations in July 2002.

Q1: ....
A: I first became interested in finance, or at least money matters. at school, where I was the class treasurer for four years.

Q2: ....
A: I'm mainly interested in management accounting, so the accountancy qualification gives me the chance to work in other areas of the business and allows me to work in a more commercial environment. I like the interaction between various departments. And I get the opportunity to be involved in non-finance projects, too.

Q3: ....
A: I have two divisional management accountants reporting to me. I'm a member of the local management team, so I get involved in regular discussions involving the performance of all three divisions. I have financial managerial responsibility for two of them. I'm involved in various other projects, as well as new product launches and new IT system introductions – both are high-profile projects within the Norgren Group. I produce reports and I supply financial information to all levels within the organisation, from local management to the board of directors.

Q4: *How hard do you have to work?*
A: The working hours vary in our area; our busiest periods in the year are the end of the financial year, plus auditing, forecasting and any project-work deadlines. We are expected to work longer hours than usual then, so there's never a good time to take holidays. We still manage it, though, and I think the extra work should be seen as something that comes with a managerial position, really.

Q5: ....
A: In the long term, I'd like to progress from a local office to a job at headquarters with responsibility for various offices. I would like to stay close to finance, but I'd consider a general business management role as well.

Adapted from independent.co.uk

16 Job descriptions and job satisfaction

A human resources manager

Listening

Company background

Tesco is Britain's largest chain of supermarkets and the biggest food retailer in the UK.

You will hear Christina Bunt, a human resources manager for Tesco, talking about her job.

1 Match these words and phrases (1–8) with their definitions (a–h).

1 challenging
2 firing
3 cashier
4 customer service
5 selling point
6 part-time job
7 supervisor
8 pull the wool over someone's eyes

a trick or deceive someone
b something which attracts customers
c person who makes sure a job is done properly
d job which is only for part of the working week
e giving customers good treatment
f employee who takes your money at a supermarket
g dismissing someone from their job
h difficult and demanding

04 2 Listen and choose the best answer for each question.

1 What part of her job does Christina enjoy most?
  A Teaching job skills
  B Challenging tasks
  C Maintaining discipline in the workplace
2 What, according to Christina, makes managing people easy?
  A Strong discipline
  B Recruiting the right staff
  C Training staff to be friendly and polite
3 How did Christina become a personnel manager?
  A Tesco recruited her as a personnel manager.
  B She trained in another company as a personnel manager.
  C She started at the bottom and came up through the ranks.
4 What would she like to be doing in ten years' time?
  A Opening new stores
  B Working as a store manager
  C Working in human resources
5 Which of these things does Christina recommend candidates should do when they go for a job interview at Tesco?
  A Dress very smartly
  B Behave in a friendly, casual way
  C Try to look relaxed
6 How does she know that interviewees will be good at the job?
  A They are interested in things not linked to the job.
  B They express interest in their other activities.
  C They are good at the other things they do.

Task tip

It's not always necessary to understand every word someone says at work, but it is important to understand the main ideas.

Human resources

Talking point

1 Work in small groups. Discuss whether you agree with these opinions.

- If you employ the right people, you don't have a problem managing them once they're in the workplace.
- If you try and teach people to be polite and to smile, it doesn't necessarily work.
- First impressions are really important … be totally natural and don't try to put yourself forward as something you're not.

2 What other interview advice would you give?

Job descriptions and job satisfaction 17

UNIT 3

Letters of enquiry and applications

Getting started

Work in small groups and discuss the following.

What, for you, would make a company or organisation a great place to work?

You can consider these points:

- working in teams
- challenging work
- friendly colleagues
- company's reputation
- good working atmosphere
- level of responsibility

Useful language

Talking about importance

I really like …
For me, …… is very important because …… .
One of the things I think is essential is …… because …… .
I don't think …… is so important because …… .

- opportunities for promotion
- perks/benefits
- salary
- opportunities to travel

Job satisfaction at EMI

Reading

You are going to read what four different employees say about job satisfaction at EMI Music.

1 Before you read, discuss with a partner what you think would be the main satisfactions of working for a record company.

2 Read the statements 1–8 below and what the four people say in the website on page 19. Which person does each statement refer to?

1 I share the artists' achievements.
2 You get plenty of chances to do new things.
3 The job has so much variety.
4 My colleagues are ready to listen to my suggestions.
5 I have a lot of responsibility.
6 I find the innovations fascinating.
7 I don't work to a fixed timetable.
8 I deal with musicians from when they are new to when they are famous.

Company background

EMI Music is the world's largest independent music company and also the oldest record company in the world, dating back to 1897.

3 Discuss the following with a partner.

- Which of the things mentioned by the four employees do you think are most attractive?
- Which of the four jobs would most interest you?

Vocabulary

Find words or phrases in the text which mean the following.

1 inside the company (Helen)
2 pleasant additional things (Mark)
3 person who likes work that begins at nine o'clock in the morning and finishes at five, Monday to Friday (Mark)
4 supervising (Mark)
5 start doing a job that another person did before (Mark)
6 lots of (Deby)
7 places where public events happen (Deby)
8 the lowest level of an organisation (Deby)

18 Letters of enquiry and applications

CAREERS

Mark, Area Sales & Promotions Manager

"The great thing about my job is just the music. I get CDs constantly pushed into my hand, and I go to loads of gigs, so if you love music, there are plenty of added bonuses. Although, if you're a nine-to-five kind of person, then this isn't for you; as I say, I never really break out of work mode. There's no one standing over me, and nobody there to take over, so it all rests with me. As I say, though, that's what I love about it!"

Helen, Business Affairs Director

"The best thing about my job is the people, I feel really comfortable and I can be myself. It's such an interesting environment because I'm working in-house, so I work closely with the music and the artists. You see things from the beginning when you sign the contract right to the release and the success. I worked on the original contract for Blue, and they've done really well, so that's really great for me to feel part of it."

Sally, IT Business Systems Manager

"I find IT in the music industry a really interesting area to work in, as there are lots of new developments in areas like digital music kiosks and online distribution. I love music, too, and it's just nice being at work and being surrounded by music. Another really nice thing about EMI is the people; everyone is really open and receptive of each other's ideas."

Deby, Touring & Production Manager

"The great thing about my job is that it's really diverse, so one day we could be doing a classical show, and the next a full-on rock show. Usually there are loads of projects going on at once, so I have to work closely with my colleagues, the venues and the artists. It's all about learning, and you have to work hard, but there are loads of opportunities for development. EMI allows its employees to grow and develop themselves, so it is a great place to come in at entry level."

Abridged from http://www.emimusic.co.uk/04/hr_ourpeople.htm

A letter of enquiry

Writing

1 Imagine you are writing to EMI Music to enquire about opportunities to work for their company. In what order would you do each of these things in your letter or email?

a Ask for information about how to apply
b Ask for information about opportunities in the company
c Explain in more detail your qualifications and background
d Say briefly who you are
e Say where you have heard about the company
f Say why you are interested in working for them
g Say why you are writing

2 Read this sample letter. In what order do the above items appear?

Dear Sir or Madam,

I am a 22-year-old student of Business Administration from the University of Fribourg in Switzerland and I am writing to enquire about career opportunities within your company. I have visited your website and I see that people working in your company combine an interest in business with a love of music. I am in my final year of a four-year course of studies and am interested in working for a multinational company like yours because you combine a range of business challenges with scope for the innovative promotion of music, which is what I have been studying as my special research project.

My particular specialisation has been the promotion of young classical musicians, both through live concerts and using the Internet.

I would be most grateful if you could send me information about what opportunities exist in EMI Music, either as a management trainee or a marketing assistant, in a year's time. Could you also tell me how I should apply?

Thanking you in advance.

Yours faithfully,

Pierre Schneider

Letters of enquiry and applications

3 Complete these ways of asking for information by putting the words in brackets in the correct order.

1 I would like to know ....*whether I have the right qualifications.*....
 (qualifications I the whether right have)
2 I would be most grateful ....
 (you information me about opportunities could exist if in what EMI Music send)
3 Could you also tell me .... ?
 (apply should I how)
4 I'd be interested to know ....
 (applications final for the when is date)

▶ **page 27** (Complex questions)

4 Write a letter of enquiry to a company or organisation you would be interested in working for. Follow the structure of the letter you have just read, but change the details to reflect your situation and background.

Talking point

Discuss these questions in pairs.

1 When you apply for a job, is it better to send a letter or an email?
2 How many pages should your application be?
3 What things should you mention in your application?
4 Should you write your application in a formal or an informal style?
5 How many pages should your curriculum vitae (CV) have?
6 Should you send a photograph as well?

Advice on job applications

Listening

1 Work with a partner. Read the following pieces of advice about applying for a job. Rewrite each one, giving a reason for the advice.

a Include a photograph with your application.
 ....*Attach a picture to your letter or email so they can see what you look like.*.... .
b Send your application by email.
c Your letter of application should not be longer than one page.
d Mention your hobbies and interests.
e Ask someone to check your application before sending it.
f Follow your application with a phone call.
g Tell the truth about yourself in your application.
h Include names, addresses and telephone numbers of referees.

2 Say which pieces of advice you agree with, and which you disagree with.

05 3 You are going to hear an extract from a television programme in which five human resources officers give advice about applying for jobs. For each speaker, decide what advice from Exercise 1 is being given.

1 Samuel .... 4 Yukari ....
2 Marta .... 5 Ivan   ....
3 Salim ....

Letters of enquiry and applications

An email of application

Writing

1 Emails are often less formal than letters. However, when applying for a job, your application should normally be formal, whichever way you send it. Read the email of application on the right and choose the more formal phrase in each pair of words in italics.

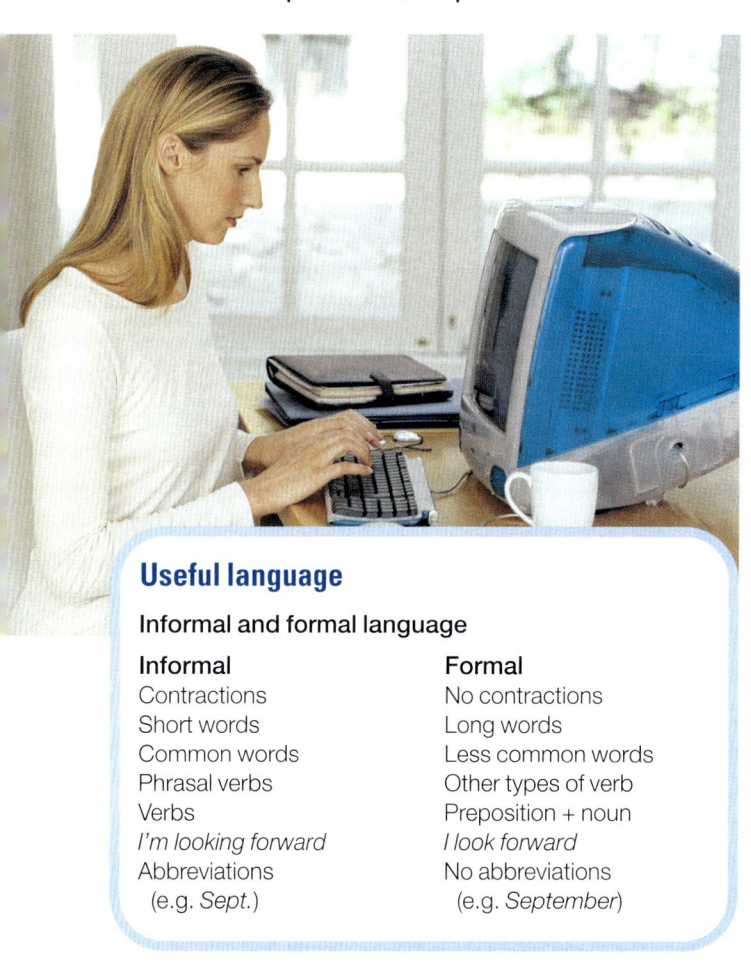

Useful language

Informal and formal language

Informal	Formal
Contractions	No contractions
Short words	Long words
Common words	Less common words
Phrasal verbs	Other types of verb
Verbs	Preposition + noun
I'm looking forward	*I look forward*
Abbreviations	No abbreviations
(e.g. *Sept.*)	(e.g. *September*)

Dear Sir or Madam,

a 1 *I'm* / *I am* writing 2 *to apply* / *in application* for the 3 *post* / *job* of North-Western Area Sales Manager, as currently advertised on your website.

b As you will see from my attached 4 *curriculum vitae* / *CV*, I am a 28-year-old graduate in Business and Marketing from Hamburg University, with five years of experience in marketing and sales with Audi AGF based in Bremen. My 5 *present job* / *current position* is Assistant Sales Manager for the Bremen and Neidersachsen region.

c Since leaving university, apart from 6 *working* / *practical experience* in the various posts I have 7 *held* / *worked in*, I have studied 8 *a lot* / *extensively* at night school, 9 *going on* / *attending* courses in Negotiating Skills, Personnel Management and Marketing. I have also 10 *attended* / *gone on* various internal courses in the same areas in the companies I have worked for.

d 11 *I am* / *I'm* interested in the post advertised because it seems to me to 12 *represent* / *be* the type of opportunity I am 13 *looking for* / *seeking*: to move into a large international producer of consumer products and to 14 *have the experience of managing regional sales* / *be a regional sales manager* myself.

e I hope my application and my 15 *curriculum vitae* / *CV* will be of interest to you. I am 16 *ready to come to an* / *available for* interview at any time, and my present 17 *employers* / *boss* would be happy to 18 *give* / *supply* a reference.

f I 19 *look forward* / *am looking* forward to hearing from you.

Yours faithfully,
Christa Schmidt
christaschmidt@fastmail.com

---

2 Read the email again and say in which paragraph Christa mentions each of these things.

Her CV ☐
A summary of relevant work experience ☐
Details of her academic background ☐
Her availability for interview ☐
Reasons for applying for this job ☐
References from her employers ☐
The reason for writing the letter [a]
Where she saw the advertisement ☐
The job training she has received ☐

3 Work in small groups and discuss the following.

- Is there anything extra you would put in an email/letter of application?
- Is there anything you would leave out?

4 Write an email of application for the next job you would like to do. Follow the structure of the email you have just read, but change the details to reflect your situation and background.

Letters of enquiry and applications 21

UNIT 4

Telephone skills

Getting started

Work with a partner and discuss these questions.

- Do you ever make telephone calls in English? When? What for?
- When is it better to make a phone call than send an email?
- What problems have you had when talking in English on the phone?
- In general, why is talking on the phone more difficult than talking face to face?
- How can you prepare for telephone calls, and what can you do to make sure there have been no misunderstandings?

Telephone language

Listening

1 Work in pairs, look at this form and say what type of information you think is missing.

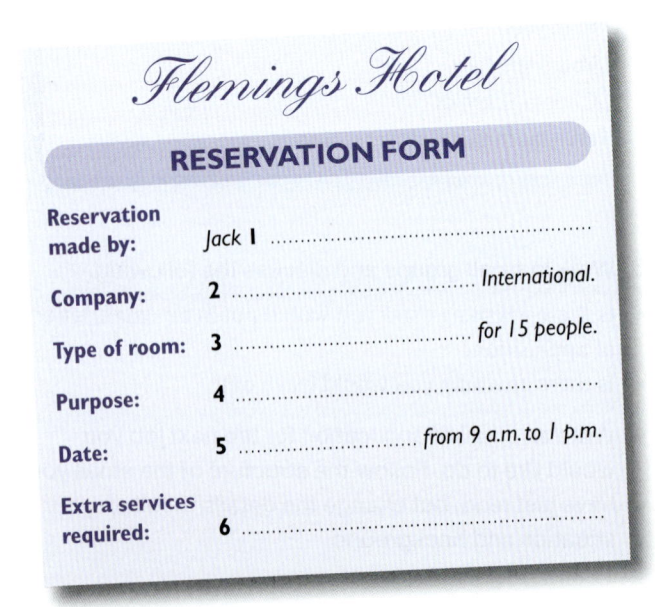

Flemings Hotel

RESERVATION FORM

Reservation made by:	Jack 1 ....
Company:	2 .... International.
Type of room:	3 .... for 15 people.
Purpose:	4 ....
Date:	5 .... from 9 a.m. to 1 p.m.
Extra services required:	6 ....

2 You are going to hear a telephone conversation between a customer and a hotel receptionist where they use some typical telephone language. Complete the notes in Exercise 1. For each gap, write one or two words or a number.

3 Read these extracts from the conversation and fill in the missing words.

- Flemings Hotel. How 1 .... you?
- Good afternoon. 2 .... Jack Rubenstein, and I'm 3 .... New York. I want to book a meeting room while I'm there in London.
- OK, sir. Let me get your details first. Could you 4 .... name again, please?
- Yes. My name's Jack Rubenstein, that's R-U-B-E-N-S-T-E-I-N.
- Fine, Mr Rubenstein. And 5 .... the name of your company, so I can put it on the invoice?
- No problem, the name of my company is Top Flight International.
- OK, and what size room 6 .... like?

- When 7 .... the room for?
- I was hoping for May 18 – that's in a month's time.

- Good. Could you 8 .... the rates, please?

4 Listen to the conversation again to check your answers.

22 Telephone skills

Role-play

Work in pairs and practise the language you have just studied for booking hotel rooms.
Each take one of the roles and prepare some of the language you want to use before you speak.

Student A: see below.　　Student B: see page 24.

Student A

You work as **PA to the Human Resources Manager**. Read this email which she has sent you, plan what you are going to say and make the phone call.

I want to hold interviews for the post of Marketing Manager (Scotland) on Friday 14 June in the morning. As you know, there are three candidates. Can you ring the Great Northern Hotel in Glasgow, please, and book two single rooms for the night of 13 June and one meeting room for the morning of 14 June? The Marketing Manager (Europe) will be accompanying me, and we will be interviewing together.

We want to start at 9.30 and finish at 1.00 with a half-hour coffee break at 11.00.

Also, can you find out the prices and let me know?

Thanks.

A telephone quiz

Reading

Work in pairs and answer these questions about how you should speak on the phone in English.
In many cases, more than one answer is possible.

1 Which do you think is the best way to answer the phone at work?
   A By saying *Hello!*
   B By saying your name.
   C By saying your name and the name of your department or company.
   D By saying the name of your company.

2 How do you think English people answer the phone when they are at home?
   A They say their phone number, e.g. *01 267 436636*.
   B They say the name of their town and their phone number, e.g. *Southampton 436636*.
   C They say *Hello!*

3 Which of these do you think would be the best way to reply when someone on the phone says *Can I speak to (your name)?*
   A *That's me!*
   B *Speaking.*
   C *Yes, I am.*

4 How should Alberto Costa introduce himself for the first time on the phone?
   A *It's Alberto Costa.*
   B *I'm Alberto Costa.*
   C *My name's Alberto Costa.*

5 How should Lucia Falcone introduce herself on the phone to someone who already knows her?
   A *This is Lucia Falcone.*
   B *I'm Lucia Falcone.*
   C *It's Lucia Falcone here.*

6 When you ask someone to wait on the phone, which of these is quite formal, which is informal, and which would you probably never say?
   A *Could you hold on a minute, please?*
   B *Hang on!*
   C *Wait, please.*

7 When you want to know who is calling you, which of these is formal, which is informal, and which sounds rude?
   A *Who's that?*
   B *Who are you?*
   C *Who's calling, please?*

8 Which of these is the most formal way to introduce the subject of your phone call?
   A *I want to talk about the sales conference in March.*
   B *I'm calling in connection with the sales conference in March.*
   C *Let's talk about the sales conference in March.*

9 Why is it especially important to use *please* and *thank you* on the phone?
   A The other person can't see your face, so you have to use these words more often to show you are being friendly and polite.
   B The British and the Americans both expect it.
   C It's not important.

10 Which of these would you say when you want to find some information on your computer while you're on the phone?
   A *Wait while I get it on my computer, please.*
   B *Just a moment while I get it up on the screen.*
   C *I'm just bringing up your details now.*

Telephone skills 23

Talking point

1 Discuss this question in pairs.

What's important when making a business phone call in English?

Use these ideas to help you if you like.
- Preparation
- Speaking clearly
- Checking understanding

2 Change partners. Imagine you are giving a brief talk at a business meeting. Take it in turns to explain what you think is important when making a business phone call in English. Try to talk for a minute. As in a business meeting, your partner should listen and not comment until you have finished.

Useful language

Listing and giving examples

I think there are three important things to remember when making a business call in English …
The most important thing is …… because …
For example, …
Another thing which is important is …
For instance, …
Finally, you should …

Student B (page 23 role-play)

You are a **receptionist at the Great Northern Hotel in Glasgow**. Study the information below and prepare to take a phone reservation.

Great Northern Hotel: room prices

Double room with bath: £165 per night
Single room with bath: £135 per night
Conference room: £50 per hour
Large meeting room (max. 25 people): £30 per hour
Small meeting room (max. 10 people): £20 per hour

Enquiring about a job

Listening

07 1 You are going to hear a woman phoning a company to enquire about a job. Listen and tick (✔) the phrases the speakers use from the quiz you have just done on page 23.

07 2 Listen again and complete the woman's notes below with one or two words or a number.

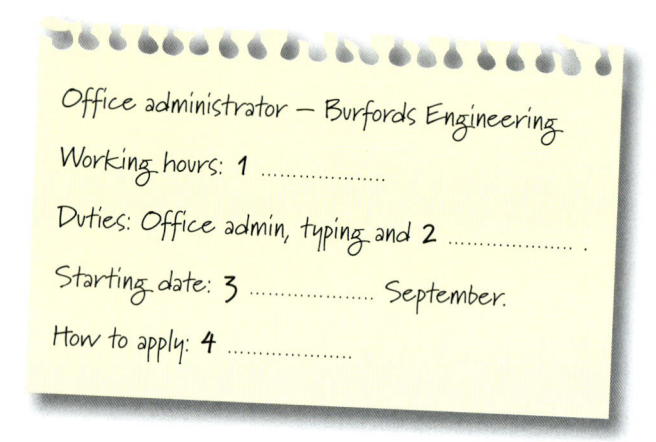

Office administrator – Burfords Engineering
Working hours: 1 ....
Duties: Office admin, typing and 2 ....
Starting date: 3 .... September.
How to apply: 4 ....

Role-play

1 Work in pairs. Jack Burford is also recruiting for the job of marketing assistant.

Task tip

Before speaking, spend a minute or two preparing what you want to say.

Student A

You are Jack Burford. Invent details of the post. Answer the phone and give information about the job. Use the conversation you have just listened to as a model.

Student B

You are interested in the job at Burfords Light Engineering. Prepare some questions and phone to find out details of the job. Use the conversation you have just listened to as a model.

2 Jack Burford also needs an office manager. Change roles and find out / give details about the post.

24 Telephone skills

Phone-answering tips

Reading

1 Work in pairs. You are going to read some advice about how to use the telephone to improve your business. One student should read Text A and the other should read Text B. While you are reading, make brief notes. Then, tell each other about the advice you read.

Text A

Phone-answering tips to win business

From Susan Ward,
Your Guide to Small Business: Canada.

How you answer the phone says a great deal about your business

Phone-answering skills are critical for businesses. The telephone is still most businesses' primary point of contact with customers. And the way you answer your company's phone will form your customer's first impression of your business. These phone-answering tips will ensure that callers know they're dealing with a winning business.

1 Answer all incoming phone calls before the third ring.
2 When you answer the phone, be warm and enthusiastic. Your voice at the end of the telephone line is sometimes the only impression of your company a caller will get.
3 When answering the phone, welcome callers courteously and identify yourself and your organisation. Say, for instance, *Good morning. Cypress Technologies. Susan speaking. How may I help you?* No one should ever have to ask if they've reached such and such a business.
4 Keep your voice volume moderate and speak slowly and clearly when answering the phone, so your caller can understand you easily.
5 Always ask the caller if it's all right to put him or her on hold and don't leave people on hold for longer than is necessary. If possible, provide callers on hold with progress reports every 30 to 45 seconds. Offer them choices such as *That line is still busy. Will you continue to hold or should I have Mrs Lee call you back?*

Adapted from http://sbinfocanada.about.com/cs/management/qt/telephonetips.htm

Text B

Phone-answering tips to win business

From Susan Ward,
Your Guide to Small Business: Canada.

How you answer the phone says a great deal about your business

Phone-answering skills are critical for businesses. The telephone is still most businesses' primary point of contact with customers. And the way you answer your company's phone will form your customer's first impression of your business. These phone-answering tips will ensure that callers know they're dealing with a winning business.

1 Train your voice and vocabulary to be positive when phone answering, even on a 'down' day. For example, rather than saying *I don't know*, say *Let me find out about that for you*.
2 Take telephone messages completely and accurately. If there's something you don't understand or can't spell, such as a person's surname, ask the caller to repeat it or spell it for you. Then make sure the message gets to the intended recipient.
3 Respond to all your calls within one business day. I can't emphasise this one enough. The early caller can get the contract, the sale, the problem solved and reinforce the favourable impression of your business that you want to circulate.
4 If you use an answering machine to answer calls when you can't, make sure that you have a professional message recorded. Update your answering machine message as needed. For instance, if your business is going to be closed for a holiday, update your message to say so and to say when your business will reopen.
5 Train everyone else who answers the phone to answer the same way. Check on how your business's phone is being answered by calling in and seeing if the phone is being answered in a professional manner. If they don't pass the test, go over this telephone-answering tips list with them.

2 In pairs or small groups, discuss what advice is very useful, and what is not so important.

Talking point

Work in pairs or groups of three. Your company has decided to run a one-day course on effective telephone skills at work. You have been asked to prepare the course. Discuss the situation together, and decide:

- which staff in a company would most benefit from this type of course
- what advice and training should be given during the course.

Use the Useful language on page 10 to help you.

Grammar workshop 1

Units 1–4

These exercises are intended to help you quickly revise in a business context grammar which you have probably studied before.

Comparison of adjectives and adverbs

> - These adjectives and adverbs use *-er* for the comparative and *-est* for the superlative:
>   - one-syllable adjectives,
>   e.g. *quick* → *quicker* → *quickest*
>   - two-syllable adjectives ending in *-y*,
>   e.g. *easy* → *easier* → *easiest*
>   - one-syllable adverbs,
>   e.g. *hard* → *harder* → *hardest*
> - These adjectives and adverbs use *more* for the comparative and *most* for the superlative:
>   - adjectives with two or more syllables,
>   e.g. *useful* → *more useful* → *most useful*
>   - adverbs ending in *-ly*,
>   e.g. *quickly* → *more quickly* → *most quickly*
>   NB Some two-syllable adjectives ending in *-y* can use *-er/-est* or *more/most*:
>   *healthy* → *healthier/more healthy* → *healthiest / most healthy*
> - These adjectives and adverbs are **exceptions**:
>   *good/well* → *better* → *best*
>   *bad/badly* → *worse* → *worst*
>   *much/many* → *more* → *most*
>   *little* → *less* → *least*
>   *far* → *further/farther* → *furthest/farthest*
> - *as* + adjective/adverb + *as*
>   He doesn't earn **as much as** I do.

1 Complete these sentences with the comparative/superlative form of each of the words below. Use each word once only and add *than* where necessary.

~~challenging~~ economical far friendly great hard highly impressive little long motivating strong

1 I'd like to have a *more challenging* job because this one doesn't stretch me very much.
2 Rents are so high that my company is moving its offices out of the city to somewhere .... Unfortunately, I'll have to travel .... to get there.
3 I got the job because I was .... qualified than the other candidates.
4 If they give me promotion, I'll have to work .... hours and have .... responsibility.
5 I'd have stayed in the job if my colleagues had been ....
6 Martin is undoubtedly the .... candidate because he has a much .... track record.
7 I really like my new job; the .... aspect is the opportunity to take my own decisions – something I couldn't do in my previous post.
8 There are still many places in the world where women earn .... men for the same work and where they have to work .... to get promotion.

2 Work with a partner, and say whether you agree or disagree with the above sentences. Why?

Present perfect and past simple

> - You use the **past simple** for things which started and finished in the past:
>   I **joined** my company three years ago.
> - You use the **present perfect**:
>   - for things which started in the past and are still happening now:
>   In the past three months, I'**ve been given** a lot more responsibility (which I still have).
>   I **have had** this job since I left university.
>   - for things in the past where the time is not stated:
>   I'**ve been** to New York three times on business.
>   - for things which happened in the past but which have a present result:
>   I'**ve lost** my job (and now I'm unemployed).

1 Look at these sentences from Unit 1. Say which use the past simple and which use the present perfect.

1 I've been with Deloitte for nearly two years now.
   present perfect
2 I was originally attracted to this company in my final year at Cambridge.
3 In my case, this means I've always been allowed to give exam preparation priority over my client work.
4 When I arrived at Deloitte, we went through an initial three-day programme to develop our core skills and introduce us to the firm and our new colleagues.

26 Grammar workshop 1

2 Put the verbs in brackets in the correct tense (present perfect or past simple).

1 I *have worked* (work) for the same company for only three years, but I'm already a senior manager.
2 I .... (go) on a training course during my first month at work, but I .... (not go) on one since then.
3 My first boss .... (be) very friendly, but she .... (leave) the company last year and I .... (not see) her since she .... (go).
4 They .... (change) the way we work completely in the last six months. Now we have flexible working, whereas before we .... (start) at nine and .... (finish) at five.
5 In 2004, they .... (post) him to Japan. He .... (be) there ever since, and during that time he .... (get) married and .... (start) a family.

Simple questions

> Questions are formed:
> - when the main verb is not *be*, by putting an auxiliary verb before the subject:
>   How long **have you** worked for Carrefour?
>   When **did you** graduate from university?
>   What **do you** like about your present job?
>   **Are you** prepared to work long hours?
> - when the main verb is *be*, by putting the main verb before the subject:
>   **Is** there a telephone near here?
>   **Are** you responsible for sales?

1 Complete the questions in this interview.

1 ....*Did you have*............ a good journey here today?
Yes, thanks, although there was a lot of traffic coming into the city.
2 .... be a problem for you?
Working in this city? I don't think so. I've always wanted to work here.
3 .... as an accountant?
Well, I finished my training three years ago, so as a fully qualified accountant, just three years.
4 .... most enjoy about your work?
Oh, I'm fascinated by figures, and especially how they reflect the performance of an organisation.
5 .... like to be doing in ten years' time?
In ten years' time, I'd like to have a post in senior management here, or in a similar organisation.

2 Work with a partner. Imagine you are interviewing him/her for a job. Ask similar questions. Then change roles.

Complex questions

> - Look at what happens to the word order of questions when you put a short phrase before them:
>   How long **have you** worked for Carrefour? →
>   **Can you tell me** how long **you have** worked for Carrefour?
>   When **did you graduate** from university? →
>   **I'd like you to tell me** when **you graduated** from university.
>   What **do you like** about your present job? →
>   **I wonder** what **you like** about your present job.
>   **Would** your present employer **be prepared** to give you a reference? → **Do you know if** your present employer **would be prepared** to give you a reference?
>   Can you see when to use question marks (?) and when not?

1 Rewrite these questions, starting with the words given.

1 How long have you been a product manager?
Could you tell me ......*how long you have been a product manager*......?
2 Have you studied abroad?
I'd like to know ....
3 When did you first become interested in this profession?
I wonder ....
4 What do you enjoy doing in your free time?
I'd like you to tell me ....
5 What will you be doing in ten years' time?
Can you predict ....?

2 Work with a partner. Ask these or similar questions about your partner's job/studies starting with *Could you tell me ..., I'd like to know ..., I wonder when ..., Do you know ..., I'd like you to tell me ...,* etc.

Grammar workshop 1   **27**

UNIT 5

Promotional activities and branding

Getting started

1 Work in pairs and match the promotional activities below with each picture.

1 direct mail
2 free gifts with every purchase
3 free samples
4 leaflets and brochures
5 newspaper articles
6 point-of-sales display
7 sponsorship
8 television and radio advertising
9 website

2 Say briefly what the advantages and disadvantages are of each.

Direct mail is expensive, but you can target individual customers.

3 Decide which promotional activities would be suitable for promoting a deodorant spray for men, and why.

Useful language

Discussing advantages and disadvantages

One advantage of (direct mail) is that …
Another good thing about it is that …
The main disadvantage of (a leaflet/leaflets) is that …
They also have the drawback that …

▶ page 44 (Countable/uncountable nouns)

Promoting AXE

Company background

Unilever is a large multinational based in Britain and Holland which produces foods, cleaning products and toiletries. It currently employs more than 223,000 people.

28 Promotional activities and branding

Reading

1 The text below describes how Unilever promoted their AXE deodorant spray in the USA. Read it very quickly to find out which promotional activities they used.

THE AXE EFFECT

When Unilever wanted to launch its AXE deodorant spray for men in the United States, it combined young men's natural interest in pretty girls with the attraction of a great house party. The idea was simple: boy buys AXE, boy meets girl, boy smells nice, girl likes boy.

The product, which was already popular in other parts of the world, was launched in the United States with a powerful promotional plan to make it appeal to American male youth culture. Using the slogan 'the AXE effect', the company used a number of marketing ploys to bring the product to the attention of the public. These included an online game, free samples of the deodorant, often given by attractive female models, in retail stores, point-of-sales displays, media advertising and public relations (PR), all of which hyped the centrepiece of the promotion: a once-in-a-lifetime party at a Florida mansion.

Unilever began the December before by direct-mailing millions of college students and young males aged between 11 and 24, who received free samples and information about the event, which was advertised as the AXE House Party: lots of girls, rock stars and a beach house. A radio advertising campaign and online publicity called for young men to log on to the Internet to play a video game on the AXE website. Participants had to apply their dating skills to score points. If the player reached a certain level, he entered a lottery to win a trip to the party.

AXE focused on the intrigue and discovery of the party. Leaflets similar to ones made for a party by a group of college students were posted in relevant locations such as men's toilets at nightclubs. There were also print ads in *Rolling Stone* and *Spin* magazines.

'It was all about getting into the mind of the 20-something guy,' says Mary Drapp, manager of strategic alliances and sponsorships for Unilever. And they succeeded in doing that. Their website received more than 943,000 hits, or 20% more than the goal. Some 100 lucky young men were flown in to attend the party, held near Miami. Hundreds of girls were invited to dance and enjoy musical acts from Nelly, Andrew W.K., Nicole and the Riddlin Kids. Guests could use the pool, go to a game room or play air hockey, cards or billiards.

The party was filmed and edited into an hour-long show broadcast on TNN in April. 'To our knowledge, nobody has ever taken a consumer promotion and turned it into a television show,' says Steve Jarvis, the marketing consultant for AXE. 'That was something completely original.' After the party, AXE continued to capitalise on the event. Some 500,000 special packs went on sale in retail stores, offering two cans of the deodorant spray with a free AXE house-party CD that featured songs from the artists who had appeared at the party.

Following the promotion, results included a 22% increase in general brand awareness among males aged 11 to 24 and a 3.0% to 3.7% increase in antiperspirant and deodorant market share.

Adapted from Promo

2 Read the article again and choose the best answer for each of the following questions.

1 Who were the target audience in Unilever's promotional campaign?
  A Young women
  B Young men
  C Men of all ages
  D Men and women

2 How did people get an invitation to the house party?
  A By receiving direct mail.
  B By answering an advertisement.
  C By applying through an Internet site.
  D By participating in a game.

3 What was aim of the publicity for the house party?
  A To show an exotic location.
  B To improve men's dating skills.
  C To excite people's curiosity.
  D To show people they needed AXE.

4 According to Mary Drapp, what was the aim of the promotional campaign?
  A To increase brand awareness.
  B To encourage people to visit the website.
  C To encourage a different type of customer to buy the product.
  D To show the effectiveness of the product.

5 What was unique about the promotion of AXE?
  A The house party.
  B The television programme.
  C The free disc.
  D The use of the Internet.

6 What was the effect of the marketing campaign?
  A Twenty-two per cent more people knew about AXE.
  B Sales of AXE increased by 22%.
  C There was an increase in the percentage of young men who knew about AXE.
  D Brand awareness rose to 3.7%.

Promotional activities and branding

Vocabulary

Match these words and expressions from the text (1–11) with their definitions (a–k).

1. launch (line 1)
2. ploys (line 10)
3. retail stores (line 13)
4. public relations (PR) (line 14)
5. hyped (line 14)
6. log on (line 22)
7. focused on (line 27)
8. hits (line 35)
9. capitalise on (line 46)
10. brand awareness (line 52)
11. market share (line 54)

a. build on an existing success
b. concentrated on
c. how much of the market is taken by a particular product
d. knowledge that a certain brand exists
e. the activity of keeping good relations between an organisation and the outside world
f. publicised strongly
g. shops, supermarkets, etc.
h. start using (your computer/the Internet)
i. tactics/tricks
j. visits (to a website)
k. start selling for the first time

Role-play

Work in groups of about four.

You work on the creative team in the marketing department of a large multinational company. The company has decided that it is time to launch in your country a shampoo which has been very successful in the United States and Canada. The target customers for this shampoo, called *Provocation* in the US and Canada, are young women aged 12–25.

Your job is to prepare a promotional campaign for the launch. You should:

- brainstorm ideas for possible promotional activities
- evaluate the ideas and decide which ones you want to use
- produce a plan of action
- compare your plans with other creative teams.

Useful language

Brainstorming

Brainstorming consists of thinking of as many ideas as possible, without deciding whether they are good or bad ideas until later. It is a common activity in advertising agencies.

How about ....? + -ing form
Why don't we ....? + infinitive
I think .... would be a good idea.
Have you thought of ....? + -ing form

> page 45 (-ing forms and infinitives)

Supermarkets' own brands

Listening

You are going to hear Christina Bunt talking about Tesco's own brands. An 'own brand' is a product which a supermarket sells with its own name on it, e.g. Tesco washing powder or Tesco bread.

1. Before you listen, discuss why supermarkets have own brands.

08 2. Listen and choose the best answer for each question.

1. Why did Tesco originally introduce their own brand?
   A To increase sales.
   B To reduce reliance on suppliers.
   C To reduce costs.
2. What is the main reason for supermarkets having own brands nowadays?
   A They bring customers back to their shops.
   B They have a higher profit margin.
   C They don't depend on outside suppliers.
3. Tesco can sell own value brands more cheaply than other brands because …
   A they pay their suppliers less.
   B they sell in large quantities.
   C they don't need advertising.

Promotional activities and branding

The power of brands

Reading

1 Look at these statements. Work with a partner and discuss whether you agree or disagree with each one.

1. When you buy a brand, you know the product will always be of the same quality each time.
2. Traditional methods of investigating consumers' tastes are often not effective.
3. The products we buy reflect the sort of people we want to be.
4. Sometimes the brand is invented before the product is developed.
5. People's loyalty to brands is decreasing.
6. People are willing to spend more on branded products.
7. Often the product itself is not as important as the feelings and ideas associated with it.
8. Nowadays, even strong brands have to deal with competition from other companies.
9. Some traditionally strong brands have found it difficult to remain attractive to consumers.
10. Brands save time and make shopping easier.

2 Read the following extracts from an article about brands, then say which extract each statement 1–10 in Exercise 1 corresponds to.

A Historically, building a brand was rather simple. A logo was a straightforward guarantee of quality and consistency, or it was a signal that a product was something new. For that, consumers were, quite rationally, prepared to pay a premium. 'Brands were the first piece of consumer protection,' says Jeremy Bullmore, a long-time director of J. Walter Thompson, an advertising agency. 'You knew where to go if you had a complaint.' Brands also helped consumers to buy efficiently. As Unilever's chairman Niall FitzGerald points out: 'A brand is a storehouse of trust. That matters more and more as choices multiply. People want to simplify their lives.'

B As shoppers have become more mobile and discovered more places to buy, including online websites, they switch products more often. Brands now face competition from the most unexpected quarters, says Rita Clifton, chief executive of Interbrand: 'If you were a soap-powder company years ago, your competition would come from the same industry and probably the same country. Now it could be anyone. Who'd have thought that Virgin would sell mobile phones, Versace run hotels or Tesco sell banking services?'

C The new marketing approach is to build a brand not a product – to sell a lifestyle or a personality, to appeal to emotions. But this requires a far greater understanding of human psychology. It is a much harder task than describing the virtues of a product. Clever, simple ads are dreamt up long before the product is produced. As one company president says of his product, it is its sense of humour, rather than its taste, that is the reason for its success: 'Our product is a personality,' he claims. 'We like certain people, but some people are just more fun and interesting.'

D The trouble is that most marketers have to struggle to create strong feelings for their brands. Firms such as Coca-Cola and McDonald's, complacent from past success, find it difficult to admit that their customers are changing to newer products. Yet others, panicking that they need to do something, reinvent themselves and, without realising it, lose the essence of their appeal. Old-fashioned market-research methods help explain such mistakes. Focus groups, for example, are poor at discovering the real reasons why people like brands, but they are still heavily used.

Adapted from *The Economist*

Vocabulary

Find words or phrases in the extracts which mean the following.

1. a design which represents a company/product (extract A)
2. spend extra (extract A)
3. increase (extract A)
4. change (extract B)
5. method (extract C)
6. job (extract C)
7. relaxed, satisfied and not worried about dangers (extract D)
8. change themselves radically (extract D)
9. attractiveness (extract D)

Talking point

Discuss in small groups. Choose a brand you are all familiar with.

- What image does it have?
- How do you feel about the brand?
- How is it marketed?

Promotional activities and branding   31

UNIT 6

New product development

Getting started

Work in pairs. Talk about two or three new products that have appeared on the market in the last ten years. Discuss:

- how you first heard about them
- if you think they are useful or desirable (if you would like to have them)
- where you can buy them
- how they are marketed
- how they are packaged.

Developing and launching 'chai'

Listening

You are going to hear Amanda Hamilton, managing director of Tea UK Ltd, talking about how she developed a new tea product called 'chai' for the British market.

Company background
Tea UK is a small family business based in the UK which specialises in developing and marketing tea-based products.

1 In small groups, briefly make a list of the steps you would take before launching a new drink on the market.

09 2 Listen and make a list of the steps that Amanda took. Are any of them the same as your list?

09 3 Listen again and choose the best answer for each question.
1 What was chai originally?
  A An Indian drink.
  B An American drink.
  C A drink Amanda invented.
2 Why did she start importing chai?
  A For selling to people travelling to work.
  B For herself.
  C For selling in shops.
3 Why did she decide to develop her own chai?
  A She couldn't afford to import it.
  B She couldn't depend on her suppliers.
  C She enjoyed experimenting with different flavours.
4 How did she test her product?
  A By using a market-research company.
  B By giving it to her own customers.
  C By trying it in the USA.
5 What was the supermarket buyer's reaction to her product?
  A He fixed another meeting for six weeks later.
  B He agreed to try selling it in a few stores.
  C He agreed to sell it in a large number of stores all over the country.

32   New product development

Reading

1 Read this article about how Amanda developed her product. (For the moment, ignore gaps 1–6.)

How to create a stir in the market

BY SHARON SMITH

When she was six Amanda Hamilton invited her friends to a mini sports day in her garden. **1** ..H.. 'I made a nice little profit, but then all the mothers rang mine to complain and I had to give the money back,' she recalls. Twenty-six years on, Hamilton is again using her entrepreneurial skills, but this time she aims to keep hold of any profits.

Hamilton is the co-founder of Tea UK, a company that introduced a decent early-morning cup of tea to commuters and launched the up-market Drink Me Chai Latte label. The idea for Tea UK came to Hamilton while commuting to her marketing job at the BBC. 'I found that getting a good cup of tea in London was a real struggle,' she says. 'You'd get a teabag thrown into a polystyrene cup full of milk. **2** ......' Hamilton decided to grab the opportunity by founding her own company.

Discovering that the costs of establishing a tea café in London were prohibitive – a £50,000 fee was demanded just to secure a site – she opted for a mobile tea-bar service. **3** ...... After two months of hunting, a site eventually arose at Lewisham railway station in south-east London. Hamilton was determined to build a reputation for quality; she infused the tea in hot water for each order and offered a variety of teas, including ginger.

Business soared, and within two months their takings covered the £350 monthly rent plus bills. She started serving chai latte, a spice-based tea from India she had heard was very fashionable in the US but had yet to take off in the UK. **4** ...... So, in March 2002, she flew to the US, visiting retailers and hanging around Los Angeles coffee bars to discover just how popular chai latte was and with whom. It was everywhere, and everyone was drinking it. It was more than just a niche product, it was the fastest-growing drink in the US.

Realising that it could take off in the UK, she decided to create her own version of chai latte which would cut costs and ensure a reliable supply chain. **5** ...... 'The tea bars were essential. I tested the different recipes on my customers. The day they finally announced they preferred my chai latte to the imported version was an utterly divine moment,' says Hamilton.

Drink Me Chai Latte was launched in July 2003, and in November of that year, Tesco started stocking it. Sales are promising, according to Tesco official Deborah Watson, who says that the product is already outselling some other new lines. Waitrose started selling it in April 2004. For Hamilton, Tea UK's future lies in Drink Me Chai Latte. **6** ...... The projected turnover for 2004 was £350,000.

Adapted from the *Financial Times*

2 Choose the best sentence (A–H) to fill each of the gaps in the article. There are two sentences you do not need.

A But it took a further 12 months of experimentation to produce the right recipe.
B However, it's her imagination and determination which have made the business a success.
C I realised that here was a gap in the market waiting to be filled.
D I knew that if I wanted something done properly, I'd have to do it myself.
E In the 12 months to September 2003, the tea bars produced sales of £55,000.
F The drink quickly snatched ten per cent of sales, but proved expensive to import, with an unreliable supply chain.
G They bought a customised three-wheel motorbike equipped with a coffee machine with £2,000 savings and a £5,000 loan.
H When they arrived, she charged an entrance fee of 5p each.

3 Discuss with a partner what extra information there is in the article which you didn't hear in the interview.

Vocabulary

Find words or phrases in the text which mean the following.

1 abilities needed to start a new business (paragraph 1)
2 expensive, high-quality (paragraph 2)
3 starting (a business) (paragraph 2)
4 too expensive (paragraph 3)
5 increased very fast (paragraph 4)
6 income/revenue from a shop (paragraph 4)
7 a product only bought by a small, specialised group of customers (paragraph 4)
8 become a popular product (paragraph 5)
9 selling it in their stores (paragraph 6)
10 selling more than (paragraph 6)
11 new types of product (paragraph 6)
12 expected or estimated sales (paragraph 6)

New product development **33**

Launching and promoting a new product

Listening

1 Work in small groups. Discuss and brainstorm ideas about what you think is important when launching a new product. When you have finished, work with a partner from another group and speak for about a minute about what you decided.

2 Listen to Amanda Hamilton talking about the same topic. Take notes on the following.

- What does she say is important?
- Why?
- How did she go about it?

3 Look at these promotional methods. Work in small groups and discuss how they could be used to promote chai.

1 article in the *Financial Times* ✓
2 articles in women's magazines ☐
3 sampling on television ☐
4 sampling at festivals ☐
5 advertising ☐
6 word of mouth ☐
7 website ☐
8 displays in shop windows ☐
9 samples in magazines ☐
10 stand at food fair ☐

34 New product development

11 4 Listen to Amanda Hamilton talking about how she has marketed chai. Tick the boxes in Exercise 3 to show which of the promotional methods she used.

11 5 Listen again and note down the reasons why she used/didn't use each promotional method.
For some of them, no reason is given.

Grammar workshop

Expressing purpose

1 Complete the following sentences and then compare your ideas with your partner.
   1 I sent samples to journalists on food magazines so that
   ....
   2 I used my contacts at the television company in order to
   ....
   3 Have you considered putting samples in magazines to
   .... ?
   4 Word of mouth is the most effective form of marketing, so ....
   5 It's important for a website to look good and be simple to use, so ....

2 Study these ways of expressing purpose (A–D) then answer the questions.
   A 'It's very important to keep momentum, **so** we had iced chai and I created a chill-out zone …'
   B We go to festivals **to** give people the chance to sample our product.
   C We had a stand at a trade fair **in order to** attract buyers from hotel and restaurant chains.
   D It's important to have a good website **so that** you can sell the product internationally.
   1 Which examples use an infinitive?
   2 Which examples are followed by a sentence?

Role-play

1 Work in groups of four. Read this situation.

> You work for an interior design company in your city (you decorate and furnish the inside of houses and offices) and until now, you have only worked with architects and builders. Now you would like to sell your services directly to the general public as well, and you are having a meeting to decide how to promote yourselves.

2 Each of you should take one of these roles and prepare what you are going to say at the meeting.

> **Managing Director:** You know you can find good staff and you are confident that there is a large market for your services, so you want to expand the business quickly. You would like to use some form of advertising and also direct mail. You are ready to invest heavily in promotion.

> **Finance Director:** You are cautious about expanding the business too fast, having a marketing budget which is too large, taking on too many new employees and having cashflow problems. You would like to distribute leaflets round shops and offices and also have some advertising posters at bus stops.

> **Marketing Manager:** You love promoting services in any way possible, and the more imaginative and unusual, the better. You especially favour events such as stands at trade fairs, or sponsoring a local sports team, but you are always happy to consider other ideas.

> **Sales Manager:** Until now, visiting companies and architects has always been very successful and you strongly believe in the personal touch. You would like the marketing budget to be spent on increasing the sales staff, who would then be involved in direct selling, either by telephone or by visiting potential customers.

3 Hold the meeting, and make sure you reach agreement on how to promote your services.

4 Report back to the rest of the class what you have decided to do.

New product development 35

UNIT 7

A stand at a trade fair

Getting started

Work in pairs and discuss these questions.

1. What is happening in the pictures?
2. How can companies promote their products by having a stand at a trade fair?

The International Food Exhibition

Reading

1. Frank O'Donnell works for Pop-the-Cork Ltd, a small company (about 50 employees) which produces and exports typical regional foods and meals from his country, the Republic of Ireland. Look at the memo and the email which he has received from his boss and answer these questions.

1. What is a memo?
2. How can you start and finish a memo?
3. How can you start and finish an email to someone in the same office?
4. What does Bill want Frank to do? Why?

Memo

From: Bill Cowley
To: All Staff
Subject: The International Food Exhibition

Following conversations with several of our suppliers, I have decided that next year we will take a stand at the International Food Exhibition in London in March. The objective will be to expand our customer base and hopefully find some new export markets for our products.

Preparing for the exhibition and manning the stand will require quite a lot of extra work from staff, especially as this is the first time we have done this. I shall be contacting individual members of staff to ask for their help in carrying out this new project successfully.

BC

From: Bill Cowley
To: Frank O'Donnell
Cc:
Subject: The International Food Exhibition

Frank

Can you get in touch with the organisers of the IFE and find out:

- how much it costs to have a stand at the exhibition
- when we would need to book the space.

This is their website: http://www.showfood.co.uk

Thanks

Bill

---

36 A stand at a trade fair

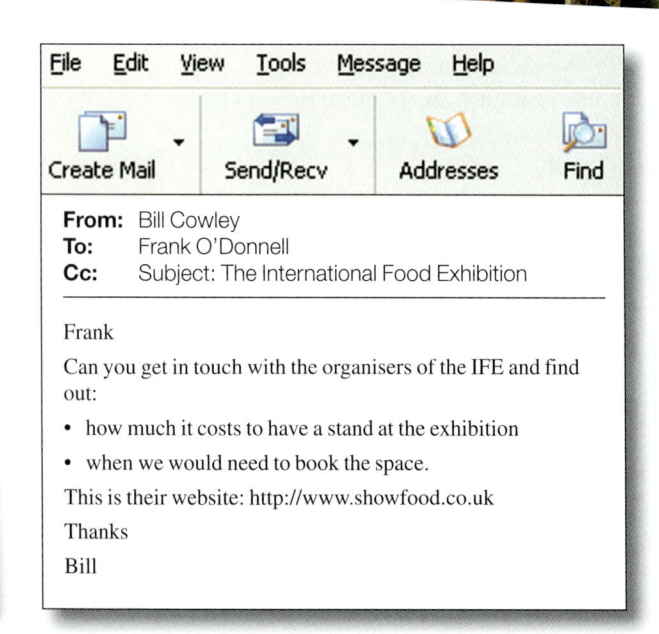

2 Frank has decided to contact Showfood by email. Which of these things should he put in his email?

a A brief description of his company's activities ☐
b A question about the price of spaces at the exhibition ☐
c Mention that his boss has asked him to write the email ☐
d A question about when it is necessary to reserve a place at the exhibition ☐
e His position in the company ☐
f The reasons for wanting a stand at the exhibition ☐
g Thanks for the information ☐
h The other trade fairs where they have exhibited ☐

3 Read the email which Frank sent them. Which of the things (a–h) from Exercise 2 did Frank include?

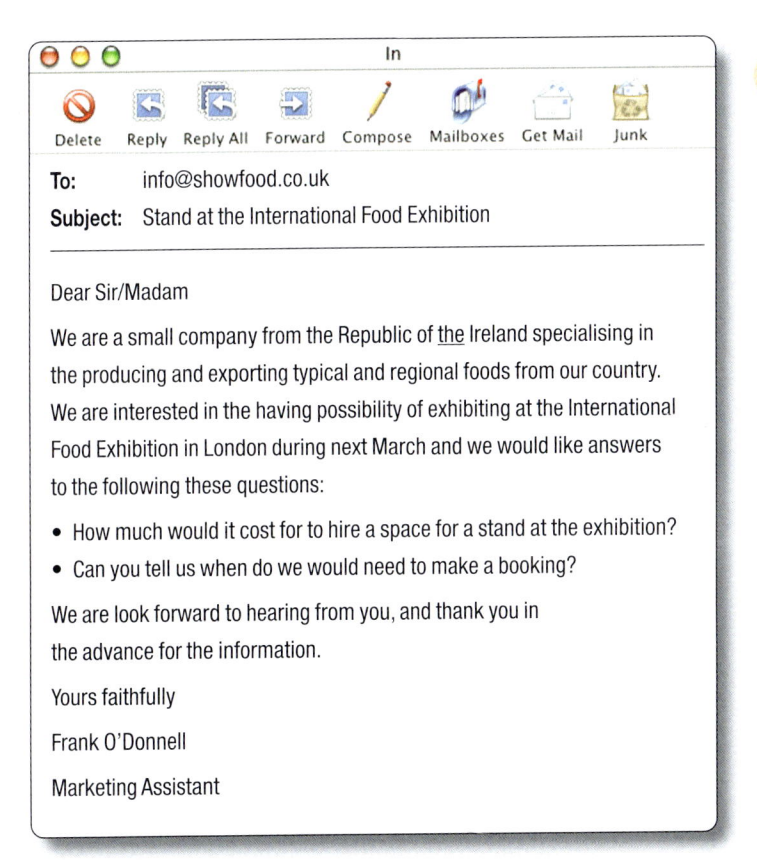

To: info@showfood.co.uk
Subject: Stand at the International Food Exhibition

Dear Sir/Madam

We are a small company from the Republic of the Ireland specialising in the producing and exporting typical and regional foods from our country. We are interested in the having possibility of exhibiting at the International Food Exhibition in London during next March and we would like answers to the following these questions:

- How much would it cost for to hire a space for a stand at the exhibition?
- Can you tell us when do we would need to make a booking?

We are look forward to hearing from you, and thank you in the advance for the information.

Yours faithfully

Frank O'Donnell

Marketing Assistant

---

4 There is one extra word in each line. Find and underline them.

Listening

1 Look at Frank's notes and decide what type of information you need for each gap. Compare your ideas with a partner.

International Food Exhibition

Cost of 1 .... : from £120 to £200 per square metre

Reservations to be made 2 .... by 1 September

Reservation deposit: 50% of total — payable 3 ....

Will send 4 ....

Full amount to be paid one month before exhibition. Otherwise space not 5 ....

2 Showfood Ltd phones Frank with some information. Listen to the conversation between Frank and Mandy (who works for Showfood Ltd) and complete Frank's notes above.

Writing

1 Use the information from Frank's notes to write his email to Bill Cowley, answering the questions in Bill's first email.

2 When you have finished writing, compare your email with your partner's.

Grammar workshop

Forming questions

1 Look at these two ways of asking questions.

A How much would it cost to hire a space for a stand at the exhibition?
B Can you tell us when we would need to make a booking?

2 Form questions by putting the words in the correct order.

1 how cost does a much the exhibition ticket to?
2 me to how a ticket costs you the can much exhibition tell?
3 many could me year how you visitors to came tell exhibition the last?
4 there the exhibitors many were at exhibition how?
5 centre would to is I how the London far the exhibition know like centre from of.

Preparing an exhibition stand

Writing 1

1 Work with a partner. Read Bill's next email to Frank and discuss what information Frank should include in his email.

2 Write Frank's email to the companies which build stands.

Reading

1 Look at these questions and underline the key words.

Which builder:

1 can <u>keep costs down</u> by supplying you with <u>existing equipment</u>?
2 has wide international experience of exhibition stands?
3 promises to provide your stand on time?
4 will be more involved in your promotional activity than just providing the stand?
5 will provide you with a stand you know you can afford?
6 will supply stands which you needn't buy?
7 will try to ensure that as many people come to your stand as possible?

Frank

Thanks for the prices and other details. I think quite a small stand in one of the less expensive parts of the exhibition is possible on our budget. I'm busy in meetings all day, so can you look on the Internet and find some companies which can build a stand for us? Then email them and ask them:

- for an estimate of the price of building a stand for the exhibition
- when they can build it
- when they can visit us to discuss the design of the stand if we like their prices.

Bill

---

2 Read the publicity from three stand builders that Frank found on the Internet and answer the questions in Exercise 1

A

STAND the PACE

Do you want your company to stand out at business exhibitions and trade events? **Stand the Pace** can do this for you by supplying custom-built exhibition stands – for hire or for sale.

We guarantee to meet our clients' needs with our free computer planning service. Our prices are keen and competitive due to our huge stocks of ready-made equipment.

We will take the work out of your hands by liaising with the exhibition organisers, transporting all equipment and associated publicity material to the event, setting up the stand, installing all the equipment and mounting all graphics.

All you have to do is arrive, walk on to the stand and start promoting your products. What could be easier?

For more information, please contact James Steel, our Marketing Director.

B

MAXIM DESIGN & DISPLAY has the creativity, experience, skills and commitment to bring you a solution that will give you an edge over your competition.

Every stand we build is an opportunity for your company to make an impact. We ensure you make the very best of that opportunity by providing you with a solution that meets your brief and matches your budget.

We have delivered customised exhibition solutions worldwide and designed stands for almost every market you can name.

Our computerised designs provide walk-through and fly-over images to give you a 3D view of your design. Our project management skills ensure deadlines are met, costs controlled, workshop and on-site construction monitored.

C

Apex.co.uk

When you exhibit, it's all about customers – you want to impress your current clients and attract potential new ones.

So whatever your exhibition opportunity, **Apex.co.uk** can offer you not just a great-looking stand, but creative designs with a commercial edge. We can provide a complete marketing solution for your project, including pre-event promotions, stand design and show activity. We'll not only design an attractive stand that grabs people's attention, we'll also work with you to maximise your visitor numbers.

You'll get an exhibition stand solution that enhances your products and services, impresses your customers and gives you that all-important marketing advantage. With over 18 years' experience in exhibitions, we know how to win you new business.

A stand at a trade fair

3 Frank contacted James Steel at Stand the Pace to ask for an estimate. Read this fax from James Steel and choose the best word – A, B, C or D – for each gap.

STAND the PACE

Tel.: 4502 39873321
Fax: 4502 39873322
Stand the Pace Ltd

To: Mr Frank O'Donnell   **From:** James Steel
Fax: 392 783929   **Date:** Thursday 24 June
Tel.:   **Page:** 1 of 5
Ref.: OF/243   **CC:**

Dear Mr O'Donnell

I'm **1** .... a number of designs for you to consider for your stand at the International Food Exhibition next March. **2** .... you will see, there are a number of decisions you will have to make **3** .... we can offer you an exact quotation. You should let us know:

- exactly how much floor space your stand will **4** ....
- whether you require the stand to be open or closed
- how many shelves you would like for displaying products
- how many people you wish to accommodate on the stand at any one time, **5** .... both sales personnel and visitors.

6 .... you would be so kind as to supply us with this information, we will send you a draft design **7** .... with an exact quotation.

Kind regards

James Steel

1	A enclosing	B attaching	C joining	D fixing
2	A So	B For	C As	D Like
3	A before	B when	C until	D prior
4	A take	B hold	C employ	D occupy
5	A including	B involving	C adding	D combining
6	A Unless	B Whether	C Please	D If
7	A also	B joined	C together	D connected

4 Find phrases in the fax which mean the following.

1 When you look at the designs you will realise …
2 Please tell us …
3 at the same time
4 Please could you give us this information.

Writing 2

1 Work with a partner. Imagine you are Frank and Bill. Look at the designs and decide which you like best.

2 Decide what answers you should give to James Steel's fax (you can invent them) and write a fax in reply.

Useful language

Replying to queries

Thank you for your .... (of .... [date])
Here are the answers to the questions you raised: …
In answer to your questions …
We would like …
We would prefer …
Looking forward to receiving your design and quotation.

3 When you have finished, compare what you have written with other students' faxes.

4 Now imagine you are Bill. Write a short memo to the sales staff.

- Inform them that the stand is being designed
- Ask them what equipment they will need for the stand
- Suggest they prepare graphics for the stand.

Use the memo on page 36 as a model.

A stand at a trade fair

Unit 8

Establishing relationships and negotiating

Getting started

Work in small groups and discuss these questions.

- How can retailers (people who run shops) find out about new products to sell in their stores?
- How important is it for retailers to have new products in their stores?
- For customers, is the price always the most important factor to consider when buying a product?
- Which of the factors in the box on the right do you think is important for negotiating successfully? Why?

- Establishing a good relationship with your customer/supplier.
- Being ready to reach a compromise, i.e. being flexible.
- Sticking to your demands.
- Preparing in advance, e.g. by making sure you have all the information about the product you are buying/selling.
- Taking a long-term view of your relationship with your customer/supplier.

Establishing a business relationship

Listening

You will hear two buyers from a chain of stores (Jack and Susie) talking to some salespeople (Tessa and Sam) who have invited them to visit their stand at a trade fair. However, business conversations are not always limited to talking about business.

1 Look at this list of topics and decide which would be most likely to be said by a visitor and which by a salesperson at a trade fair. Write V (for visitor) or S (for salesperson) in the first column.

	Who would express it?	Correct order
• Asking about the other person's journey	S	
• Saying they like the stand		1
• Asking the other person where they are staying		
• Saying how busy the fair is		
• Offering refreshment		
• Saying how nice the city is		
• Offering to show their products		
• Thanking the other person for the invitation		

13 2 Listen, and write the order in which they talk about the topics in the second column.

3 Complete the conversation you have just heard by writing one word in each gap.

Jack   Hello. Good morning. Tessa Marcovitz? My name's Jack Lemming, and **1** .... is my colleague, Susie Chen.

Tessa   Hello. Nice to **2** .... you. So you got my letter? That's great.

Jack   Hello.

Susie   Hello. Nice to meet you **3** .... So this is your stand? Very smart, and **4** .... for inviting us, by the way.

Tessa   Well, we've been wanting to **5** .... to you people for some time, and we like to let people know when we've got a stand at a fair. Did you have a good **6** .... ?

Jack   Yes, thanks. Very good.

Susie   Yes, the airport's so convenient for this fair. **7** .... city, isn't it?

Tessa   Yes, lovely. Where are you **8** .... ?

Susie   We're staying at the Ritz, in the city centre.

Tessa   Good. They say it's the best hotel in town. When did you **9** .... in?

Jack   Just last night, but not too late.

Tessa Oh, good. Now, can we show you a few of our products? Take a seat if you like.
Jack Thanks. **10** .... , isn't it?
Tessa Incredibly, and it's been like this all week. This fair is getting more popular every year.
Would **11** .... of you like a cup of coffee or a cup of tea before we get started?
Susie Yes, please. I could really do **12** .... a cup of coffee myself. What about you, Jack?
Jack Tea for me, please.
Tessa Fine. I'll just send one of our people out for it. Sam! Can you bring two cups of tea and one cup of coffee, please?
Sam Sure.

13 **4** Listen again to check your answers.

Role-play

1 Work in pairs. Your teacher will tell you whether you are Pair A or B. Read your role card and discuss your ideas.

Pair A
You are visiting a company in a town or city you have not visited before. Think of two or three pleasant things you can say to start building a relationship with the people in the company you are visiting. You can use the conversation above for ideas.

Pair B
You are working in a company. Think of two or three pleasant things you can say to your visitors to start building a relationship. You can use the conversation above for ideas.

2 Work together in groups of four (Pair A + Pair B); have conversations from the moment Pair A arrive at the office.

Asking questions about a product

Reading

The **Talking Kitchen Scale** helps you weigh food for those special recipes or diets. A wonderful weighing machine for people with low vision.

1 Look at the above product. It is the first thing Tessa shows Susie and Jack. Discuss with a partner what you think they might want to know before buying it for their chain of stores.

2 Complete the questions for these answers.

1 Is it .... clean?
To wash it, you just pop the bowl in the dishwasher, and the rest of the apparatus can be cleaned with a damp cloth.
2 Not very heavy, is it? How much ....?
No, it's very light. Let's see. It weighs less than half a kilo.
3 Great! Now, if we stocked this product, how much .... able to sell it for, Susie?
I think it would retail at around €149.
4 OK, and what price .... supply .... to us at?
At €100, so you've got a 50% mark-up.
5 How quickly .... them to us if they were selling well?
Well, we do carry stock because we sell plenty of these in North America, so we could get them to you pretty quickly. Within the week, if necessary. But obviously if you put in a biggish order, we'll give you an extra discount.
6 One more question about the talking weighing machine. .... supplied with a battery, or do customers have .... extra for that?
No, it comes with the battery included.

14 **3** Listen to Tessa, Susie and Jack discussing it to check your answers.

4 Look at the questions in Exercise 2 again.
1 Which questions refer to characteristics of the product or technical specifications?
2 Which questions refer to terms and conditions?

Establishing relationships and negotiating **41**

5 Match these words from the conversation with their definitions. If necessary, listen again to check your answers.

1. stock (v)
2. gadget
3. damp cloth
4. plug it into the mains
5. retail (v)
6. mark-up (n)
7. carry a lot of stock
8. come supplied with

a. amount by which the price of something is increased before it is sold again
b. connect it to the electricity supply
c. keep a large amount of goods in a (chain of) shop(s)
d. keep a supply of
e. piece of slightly wet material
f. sell in shops
g. sell together with
h. small device or machine with a particular purpose – a small apparatus

Role-play

1 Work in pairs. You will play the roles of buyers and representatives at a trade fair. Each of you should take one of the roles below.

Student A is a salesperson working on a stand. Read and prepare situation 1 on your role card on page 43, then have the conversation.

Student B is a buyer for a chain of stores visiting the stand. Read and prepare situation 1 on your role card below, then have the conversation.

2 Change roles and do situation 2.

Student B

You are visiting a stand at a trade fair. Have similar conversations to the ones you have just studied, i.e. greet each other, introduce yourselves, etc. Then ask questions about the products below which you have seen on the stand and complete the information.

Situation 1

CorkPops™
Bottle Opener!

Insert a long needle through the cork and into the bottle, then press a button … **POP!** Your bottle is opened. It's simply the fastest, easiest way to open a bottle!

One cartridge can open .... bottles.

Wholesale price: ....

Recommended retail price: ....

Available: ....

Situation 2

The Speedy Peel Battery Operated Peeler does all the work, so your hands won't ache.

Good news for arthritis sufferers. Now you can peel vegetables without worrying whether you will have enough hand strength.

Details:

Length: ....

Blade can be cleaned ....

Weighs: ....

Requires .... batteries (not included).

Wholesale price: ....

Retail price: ....

42 Establishing relationships and negotiating

Student A

You are staffing your company's stand at a trade fair. Have similar conversations to the one you have just studied, i.e. greet each other, introduce yourselves, etc. and then answer questions about these products.

Situation 1

CorkPops™
Bottle Opener!

Insert a long needle through the cork and into the bottle, then press a button …
POP! Your bottle is opened. It's simply the fastest, easiest way to open a bottle! (One cartridge can open 60 to 80 bottles.)

Wholesale price: €12
Recommended retail price €19.99
Availability: immediately

Situation 2

The Speedy Peel Battery Operated Peeler does all the work, so your hands won't ache.

Good news for arthritis sufferers. Now you can peel vegetables without worrying whether you will have enough hand strength.

Details:
Length: 21 cm
Blade can be cleaned in the dishwasher.
Weighs: 85 g
Requires 2 AA batteries (not included).
Wholesale price: €6
Retail price: €9.95

Terms and conditions

Vocabulary

1 Say which category (A, B or C) each of these terms and conditions belongs to.

- €19.95 on each item if you place an order now   • at sight
- 5% on bulk orders   • 30 days   • 7.5% on 100 or more
- by courier within two weeks of receiving the order
- $2 if you order within one week   • 90 days
- dispatched immediately

A Discount   B Payment terms   C Delivery date

2 Which of the payment terms is better for the seller, and which is better for the buyer?

Negotiating

Listening

15 1 Listen to Tessa, Susie and Jack negotiating a deal and note down the terms of their final agreement.

15 2 Check your answers by listening to the conversation again and reading the transcript for Track 15.

Grammar workshop: First conditional

1 Look at this sentence from the conversation you have just listened to.

If we buy the scales at €100 each, our mark-up won't allow us to make a decent profit.

Mark other conditional sentences in the transcript for Track 15.

2 Complete these sentences in any way you like.

1 If the products sell like hot cakes, ...
2 I won't place a repeat order unless ....
3 You can have the product on sale or return if ....
4 Unless we can have a 100% mark-up, ...
5 We won't be able to cover our overheads if ....

▶ **page 45** (The first conditional)

Role-play

Work in groups of four. Imagine that you are at a trade fair. Two students should take the part of buyers, and two should take the part of sellers. Your teacher will give you role cards to practise negotiating deals. When you have finished, write an email summarising the deal.

Establishing relationships and negotiating

Grammar workshop 2

Units 5–8

Countable/uncountable nouns

- **Countable nouns**
  - use *a/an* in the singular:
    He's **an employee** at the Ford factory.
  - can be made plural:
    Several of our **employees** have left in the last month.
  - can use *some/any* in the plural:
    Some employees have asked for pay rises.
  - use *few/many*:
    There are too **many employees** on the payroll.
- **Uncountable nouns**
  - are always singular, never use *a/an*:
    She's looking for **work**.
  - can use *some/any* in the singular:
    He doesn't have **any time** for meetings this week.
  - use *little/much*:
    We receive too **much junk mail** every day.
- Some words can be both countable and uncountable, but their meaning changes:
  It's difficult to get a job without **experience**. (in general)
  Working for Henry Ford was **an** unusual **experience**. (one particular experience)

A good learner's dictionary will tell you if a noun is countable or uncountable.

1 Classify the following nouns by writing them in the correct column of the table.

~~advertisement~~   advertising   advice   budget
business   cost   direct mail   euro
experience   information   innovation   job
leaflet   marketing   money   news
office furniture   product   profit   progress
promotion   publicity   qualification   sponsorship
transport   travel   trip   work

Countable	Uncountable	Both
advertisement		

2 Complete these sentences by writing *some*, *any*, *few*, *little*, *many*, *much*, *a* or *an* in the gaps. In some gaps, more than one answer is possible.

1 Our promotional campaign brought in *some* new business, but not enough.
2 In such a competitive environment, it's hard to make .... profit.
3 How .... experience do you have of direct marketing? Our other candidate didn't have .... experience at all.
4 Adding a remote control to the product was .... excellent innovation, but not .... progress has been made since then.
5 Marketing is .... significant cost, and we have .... large budget for it.
6 We needed .... advice about how to carry out .... product promotion, so we went to .... firm of consultants.
7 .... businesses were slow to realise the value of having .... company website.

3 Look at the use of *a/an* in these sentences. Correct the ones which are wrong. If a sentence is already correct, put *correct*.

         an   *a*
1 He put ^ advertisement for ^ new sales director in the paper.

2 Advertising is a very expensive form of publicity.
correct

3 We need higher advertising budget.

4 The best way to reach target customers is through a direct mail.

5 Our office needs new furniture.

6 If you need a work, there is job being advertised at Benton Electronics.

7 I have a qualification in accountancy and an experience in a wholesale business.

8 The key to a business success is innovation.

9 He enjoys business travel. Recently he went on a trip to Kenya.

10 For an information or advice, ring 253977.

44   Grammar workshop 2

-ing forms and infinitives

- Use **infinitives**
  - to express purpose:
    *He borrowed money **to start** his own business.*
  - after adjectives:
    *It's **great to talk** to you.*
  - after *too* and *enough*:
    *He's **too busy to speak** to you at the moment.*
  - after certain verbs such as *agree, appear, arrange, ask, decide, demand, expect, fail, help, hope, intend, manage, offer, plan, promise, refuse, threaten, want*:
    *I've **arranged to meet** the marketing manager at 11 o'clock.*
- Use **-ing** forms
  - after prepositions:
    *How **about running** a new advertising campaign?*
  - as subjects or objects of a verb:
    Borrowing *money can be risky.*
    *He finds **asking** for help difficult.*
  - after certain verbs such as *admit, avoid, consider, delay, deny, enjoy, finish, involve, mind, postpone, risk, suggest*:
    *Running your own business **involves working** 12 hours a day, seven days a week.*
  - after these expressions: *it's no good, it's not worth, it's no use, it's a waste of time*:
    It's not worth spending *a lot of money on new leaflets when we can put all the information on the website.*

Put the verbs in brackets into the correct form (-ing form or infinitive).

1. My company doesn't spend enough money on .training. (train) staff.
2. My job involves .... (deal) with money.
3. I would be happy .... (get) a more responsible job.
4. .... (advertise) on television is too expensive for my company .... (invest) in.
5. It's not worth .... (develop) a new product unless you know who your target customers are likely .... (be).
6. I wouldn't risk .... (leave) my job .... (start) up a business on my own.
7. If a member of my family had a good business idea, I would help them .... (develop) it by .... (lend) them money.
8. .... (study) for a business degree is essential if you want .... (be) successful in business.

The first conditional

- The first conditional is formed by:
  If/Unless + present tense, future tense/modal verb
- You can put the *if* clause before or after the main clause. If it comes before, you must use a comma:
  If *prices rise**,** demand will fall.*
  *Demand will fall **if** prices rise.*
- Instead of *if* or *unless*, you can use *on condition that, provided (that), providing (that)* or *as long as* to be more emphatic:
  Providing that *you deliver the goods on time, we'll pay at sight.*
  *We'll buy the new machine **on condition that** you give us a two-year warranty.*
  *Our soft drinks should sell very well **as long as** the weather remains hot.*
- The first conditional refers to real possibilities. It talks about the present or the future.

Make complete sentences by matching the first part (1–7) with the second part (a–g).

1. If you buy more than 1,000 units,
2. Unless you're late paying,
3. We'll arrange for extra-fast delivery
4. I might place a very large order
5. As long as your products meet international hygiene standards,
6. We'll be happy to pay in euros
7. We'll sell your products on condition that

a. you make us exclusive agents for this region.
b. on condition that you pay the transportation costs involved.
c. provided we can reach agreement on price.
d. unless the exchange rate changes drastically.
e. we could manage a larger discount.
f. we should have no difficulty in selling them.
g. we'll continue supplying you at regular intervals.

Grammar workshop 2 45

UNIT 9

Going it alone

Getting started

Work in pairs. Discuss these questions with your partner.

1 Why start your own business? (Think of as many reasons as you can.)
2 Would you like to run your own business? Why?/Why not?

Why start your own business?

Listening

1 Here are eight reasons for starting a business. Which of them did you mention?

a Because you are bored with your present job.
b Because you are unemployed.
c Because you have a good business idea.
d To achieve your ambition.
e To be your own boss.
f To become rich.
g Because you see a gap in the market.
h To work at what really interests you.

16 2 You are going hear three women being interviewed on a radio programme about people who have started their own businesses. Which of the above reasons does each of them give for starting her business? Write one letter (a–h) for each name.

1 Lisa ☐   2 Naiara ☐   3 Marcelle ☐

Vocabulary

1 Complete the following sentences from the radio programme by writing a word or phrase in the gaps.

Tonight on *Building your Future* we talk to three women who have made a 1 ..go.. of starting their own businesses. We talk to them about the excitements and risks of 2 .... your own business and find out what it takes to be an 3 .... in the 21st century. But first we ask them why they 4 .... up their businesses in the first place.

So, I thought, here's my opportunity – no 5 .... and a really good product – why not open my own 6 .... ?

So with my redundancy money, I bought into this 7 .... , which is actually a travel agent's, and since then, I've never 8 .... back.

Basically, it's your own business, but you buy the right to sell the products of a large franchising organisation – you pay 9 .... and part of your profits and you use their logo and benefit from their 10 ....

Frankly, I want the 11 .... for myself. I know I'm just 12 .... out, but I think I'm good enough to make a lot of money.

16 2 Listen again and check your answers.

3 Discuss the following questions in pairs.

1 Which woman do you think has the best reason for starting up her own business?
2 When starting up a business, what are the advantages and disadvantages of buying into a franchise?

Buying into a franchise

Reading

1 Read the newspaper article on page 47 fairly quickly to find the answers to these questions.

1 Why Toby and Rebecca chose to run a franchise instead of starting their own business.
2 Why they chose Oil and Vinegar.

We're doing it our way

After 13 years of working nine to five, Toby and Rebecca Ruddle have bought a franchise and are becoming independent.

When my wife and I open the doors of our own business, a gourmet gift shop, next month, we will be leaving 13 years in secure office jobs behind. We are finally giving up the safety of a regular income to take the risk, to fly or to crash. **1** *G*

Since we met in 1998, Rebecca and I have had beautiful ideas about escaping office life. We have brainstormed everything from retailing to dot.com start-ups to British-style hotels in the US. We've looked at premises, sourced suppliers and researched markets. But until we discovered franchises, one thing always held us back: fear.

Starting up your own business means taking a massive risk; 70% of all new businesses fail in the first three years. Our survival chances were slim, and that safe regular income that paid the mortgage didn't seem so bad after all. **2** ......

Then we started looking at franchises. I was sceptical. Many didn't seem legitimate, advertising spectacular earnings. They leave you to sell an unsellable product while the franchiser takes your profits. A little research, however, showed that if you were careful, this did not have to be the case. **3** ...... Despite the national or global nature of the company, each shop is a small business. And the failure rate of legitimate franchises is a mere 10%.

There are drawbacks, of course. You have to pay the franchise a start-up fee and a percentage of your profits for the use of their concepts and trademarks, and you have to follow their plan. **4** ......

When we went to the British Franchise Exhibition at Wembley to find a franchise last April, we found the range was incredible. However, after years of working in jobs in which we had little interest, we wanted a business for which we would have a passion. **5** ......

The company was called Oil & Vinegar. The idea, John Blogg, the co-founder, explained, was a gourmet gift shop where the customer buys luxury foods such as truffles, stuffed olives, herbs and spices and kitchenware all beautifully presented and gift-wrapped. **6** ...... The company was now looking at the British market.

John Blogg

So to the future. Rebecca and I have quit our decently paid, safe jobs. When we open in a month's time, it will be the first Oil & Vinegar shop in England. (The first British shop opened in Glasgow in July.) Are we still scared? Very. Are we doing it anyway? Definitely.

Adapted from *The Observer*

2 Choose the best sentence (A–G) to fit each of the gaps in the article. There is one extra sentence.

A However, a 90% success rate encouraged us to start looking more closely.
B I was surprised to learn that some household names are franchises, such as Bodyshop, McDonald's and Thorntons.
C The shops had taken off in their native Holland and were spreading across Belgium and Germany.
D We could have bought into estate agencies, interior designers, coffee shops, car repairers, but nothing caught our imagination until we came to the last stand.
E A friend told us that franchises were extremely expensive and that we would do better to invest in something else.
F We fell into a pattern of becoming discontented with our jobs, looking into going it alone, getting scared and dropping the idea.
G It is terrifying and exciting.

Task tip

Reading activities of this type help you to understand the structure of a text and how the argument develops – a useful skill in work situations.

Vocabulary

Match these words from the text (1–7) with their definitions (a–g).

1 dot.com start-ups (line 8)   a go bankrupt
2 premises (line 10)   b land and buildings used by a company
3 fail (line 14)   c loan to buy a house
4 mortgage (line 16)   d money from sales
5 earnings (line 20)   e money you pay for a service
6 fee (line 27)   f new Internet companies
7 taken off (paragraph C)   g started successfully

Talking point

Work with a partner. Imagine a friend of yours is considering buying into a franchise and she has asked for your advice. What would you tell her? Deal with:

- interest in what she is selling
- estimating costs
- support from the franchising company
- researching the market
- anything else you think she needs to know.

Grammar workshop: Time clauses

> For time clauses beginning with *after, as soon as, before, until, while* and *when*:
>
> A use the same tense as you use in the main clause when talking about the present or past:
> *People **work** extremely long hours when they first **start** a business.*
> *I **was** never satisfied with my job when I **worked** / **was working** for someone else.*
>
> B use a present tense to talk about the future:
> *We'**ll research** the market thoroughly before we **start** our own business.*
>
> C With *since*, use the present perfect in the main clause and a past tense in the time clause:
> *He **hasn't made** a profit **since** he **started** the business.*

1 Look at these sentences from the article and study the rules above. Which rule does each sentence follow?

1 When my wife and I open the doors of our own business, a gourmet gift shop, next month, we will be leaving 13 years in secure office jobs behind.
Rule: ...B...
2 Since we met in 1998, Rebecca and I have had beautiful ideas about escaping office life.
Rule: ....
3 They leave you to sell an unsellable product while the franchiser takes your profits.
Rule: ....
4 When we went to the British Franchise Exhibition at Wembley to find a franchise last April, we found the range was incredible.
Rule: ....
5 ... nothing caught our imagination until we came to the last stand.
Rule: ....
6 When we open in a month's time, it will be the first Oil & Vinegar shop in England.
Rule: ....

2 Complete these sentences by putting the verbs in brackets into the correct tense.

1 Before we ..*opened*.. (open) our first business, we researched the market thoroughly.
2 When we .... (meet) in June, we'll discuss the project.
3 She'll call you as soon as she .... (come) out of the meeting.
4 Our sales increase spectacularly when the Christmas shopping season .... (start).
5 We .... (be) so happy since we .... (decide) to go it alone.
6 I'll phone the suppliers while you .... (deal) with the customers.
7 She always answers the phone as soon as it .... (ring).
8 They didn't change premises until they .... (find) somewhere cheaper.

> page 62 (Tenses in time clauses)

Financial terms

Vocabulary

1 Match these financial terms (1–7) with their definitions (a–g).

1 profit — a debt
2 turnover — b money which is earned after paying the costs of producing and selling goods and services
3 asset c money paid to the government, which is based on your income or profits
4 liability d something valuable belonging to an organisation which can be used for the payment of debts
5 tax e the amount that a bank charges on money that it lends
6 costs f the money you need to spend to keep an organisation functioning
7 interest rate g the total amount of money received from sales of goods and services

48 Going it alone

2 Use the words from Exercise 1 to complete this leaflet.

PLANNING TO START YOUR OWN BUSINESS?

Before you start, there are a few things you should do.

- Research the market before you do anything and make a sales forecast: this way, you will know how much **1** *turnover* to expect.
- Make an estimate of your **2** ...., for example what the rent will be on your premises, how much interest you will have to pay on your loan, your salary bill, etc.
- By subtracting your costs from turnover, you should be able to make a **3** .... forecast. The people who lend you money or invest in your business will want to know this.
- If you are going to borrow money from a bank, check the **4** .... – can you afford to pay back so much? Also, your bank will want some security on the money they lend you, so do you have a house or other **5** .... which you can use as a guarantee?
- Of course, the government will require you to pay **6** .... on your profits.
- Your main **7** .... will probably be your loan from the bank.

A letter to a franchiser

Reading

1 Work with a partner. What questions would you ask a franchiser (a company which sells franchises) before buying a franchise? Use some of the vocabulary in the previous exercise in your questions.

2 A friend of yours has written this letter to a franchiser and has asked you to check that there are no mistakes in the English. Read the letter: in most lines there is one extra word. Find the extra words and write them in gaps on the right. Some lines are correct. Mark them with a tick (✔).

Dear Sirs,

I am a 28-year-old marketing specialist and have worked for a large multinational retail company since I was graduated 5 years ago. When I was last time in London, I saw some of your shops and I am interested in the possibility of taking out a franchise with your organisation in Austria.

I would be the most grateful if you could send me details of your franchises. Could you please supply me with these answers to the following questions?

- What costs are involved in terms of start-up fees and what is percentage of turnover will I have to pay for you?
- How long, on average, do new franchisees have to be in business before they will start making a profit?
- Do you offer credit facilities for to cover the initial costs?
- Will you be able to help me with finding the suitable premises?
- Will you assist to me by supplying marketing and promotional materials until I will achieve profitability, or at least in the early stages?
- What is the typical return on an investment for one of your franchises? Would I make enough money to make a living salary in the first year, or is it so advisable for me to continue with my present job while I establish the business?

I look forward to hearing from you.

Yours faithfully,

Günther Fischer

1 ✔
2 *was*
3 ....
4 ....
5 ....
6 ....
7 ....
8 ....
9 ....
10 ....
11 ....
12 ....
13 ....
14 ....
15 ....
16 ....
17 ....
18 ....

Talking point

Work in pairs and discuss the following questions.

1 Did Günther ask the same questions as you?
2 What sort of franchise would interest you?

Writing

Write a letter of enquiry (about 150 words) to a franchiser which interests you. Include some of the questions you thought of. Use Günther's corrected letter as a model.

UNIT 10

Financing the start-up

Getting started

1 Work with a partner. Match these statements (1–5) with the people below (a–e).

1 Although I'm still quite young, I think I know quite a lot about my field. If I set up in business, it would be a consultancy to help other people publicise and sell their products.
2 If I had the money, I'd buy into a franchise – probably a clothing retail outlet.
3 If I lost my job, I'd start a business doing something completely unconnected with the classroom. I think I'd set up a small hotel in the country.
4 If I started my own company, it would have something to do with producing specialist software for educational purposes.
5 If I was given early retirement, I wouldn't just retire. I'd start up a specialist travel company with my son. I think my knowledge of finance would come in useful there.

a Len Murray, 42, teacher 
b Nesreen Abd al Aziz, 21, student of fashion design 
c Willi Bosch, 33, computer programmer  
d Francesca Santinelli, 24, assistant marketing manager 
e Marcel Lefebre, 48, bank manager

2 Discuss these questions with your partner.
1 If you started your own business, what would it be?
2 What problems would you expect to have if you started your own business?

Useful language
If I started my own business, it would be …
If I set up in business, I would …
I would expect to …

▶ **page 62** (The second conditional)

Start-up opportunities

Vocabulary

A	B
raise	a business plan
borrow	a company
carry out	a loan
launch	finance
cover	market research
write	money
repay	overheads

1 Combine the verbs in Box A with the nouns/noun phrases in Box B to form phrases connected with starting companies. In some cases, more than one answer is possible.

Example: *raise a loan, raise finance, raise money*

2 Use phrases from Exercise 1 to complete these sentences. Remember to put the verb into the correct form.

Before you start a business or 1 .... , it's a good idea to 2 .... to see if anyone will buy your product. If you don't have a lot of personal savings, it may be necessary to 3 .... This may involve taking out a mortgage or some other form of loan from a bank, in which case you will have to 4 .... This will show how you plan to set up and run your business. In your business plan, you will have to forecast sales and profits because the bank will want to be sure that you can 5 .... , as well as 6 .... such as the cost of electricity or social security.

Setting up a food consultancy

Listening

You are going to hear Jane Milton talking about her business.

Company background *not just food*

Jane Milton founded Not Just Food, a food-development consultancy after 16 years working for other companies in product development and food marketing.

1 Before you listen, read these notes and decide what sort of information is needed for each gap.

> Company's activities: writing recipes, preparing food, organising 1 ....
>
> Before launching her company, she did a business 2 ....
>
> Her tutors insisted on a realistic 3 ....
>
> About half of the people she contacted when carrying out market research became 4 ....
>
> She is better at attracting new customers because she is 5 ....
>
> To cover overheads, at first she did a 6 .... job.
>
> Her advice for people starting new companies: Don't borrow more than you can afford to 7 ....

Task tip

The words in the notes are not exactly the same as the words in the recording, but you should write **words you hear** in the gaps.

2 Listen and complete the notes above with one or two words in each gap.

Financing the start-up 51

Raising finance

Reading

1 Look at these ways of raising money to start a company. Discuss these questions in small groups.

- Which are the most popular?
- Which are the safest?
- Which are the easiest to obtain?
- Do you know any other ways of raising finance?

> A bank loan
> A mortgage (a loan normally used to buy a house)
> A government grant
> Venture capital (investment from companies which specialise in high-risk new businesses)
> Personal savings
> Going into partnership
> A loan from family or friends

2 Read these statements and check you understand the vocabulary.

1 As long as you can pay your debts, they are not worried about how profitable your company is.
2 Do not accept their money without signing a formal contract.
3 Share information openly with them in order to get funding from them.
4 They have a reputation for financing technology companies.
5 They will not lend money to people starting a business for the first time.
6 You must have property to guarantee the loan.

3 Read these three paragraphs, which give information on how to obtain finance for business start-ups, and decide which one each statement (1–6) in Exercise 2 refers to.

A | Banks like to use assets such as premises, motor vehicles or equipment as collateral (or security) against loans. Banks don't care whether or not your business has great profit potential. They are only interested in the business's ability to cover the principal and interest payments.

B | If your friends and family express an interest in helping you with your business financing, try to persuade them in a professional way. Make a presentation in exactly the same way as you would to a bank. Don't be embarrassed to show financial statements, tax returns or whatever else they want to see. Do anything to get that money! You should prepare a written agreement about any loans. If you don't, bitter arguments will damage the relationship eventually.

C | Some venture capital firms will consider financing a start-up. However, they will only be interested in entrepreneurs who have experience of successfully starting up businesses. They are best known for financing high-tech firms, but they do finance other types of businesses.

Financing the start-up

Advice about starting a business

Role-play

Work in pairs. Your teacher will tell you whether you are Pair A or Pair B.

Pair A

You are business advisors. You will give advice to a pair of entrepreneurs about how to finance the small printing business they want to start.

Before talking to them, decide what types of finance might be suitable for them: a bank loan, a loan from family or friends, a mortgage or using personal savings.

You will need to ask them:
- about the type of business
- if they have done market research
- about their personal financial circumstances.

Prepare some questions and when you are ready, meet the entrepreneurs, discuss their plans with them and give them your best advice.

Pair B

You are entrepreneurs who are thinking of starting a new business, but you need advice on how to finance it, so you are going to consult some small business advisors.

Type of business: a photocopying and printing firm specialising in leaflets, small brochures, business cards, etc.

Your personal financial circumstances: between you, you have savings of €50,000

Financing requirements: approximately €70,000 if you are ready to use your personal savings. This extra money is for:
- equipment
- preparing your premises
- initial advertising
- materials, etc.

Work together and decide what questions to ask and what advice you need from the advisors.

When you are ready, explain your business idea to the business advisors, and get their advice on how best to finance your business.

Setting up a multimedia company

Listening

1 Read these questions and answers and underline the key words in them.

1. Where did the idea for Espresso come from?
   A It was Lewis's idea.
   B It was suggested to him by someone else.
   C Schools asked him to develop the idea.
2. What market research did Lewis do initially?
   A He didn't do any market research.
   B He asked schools what they needed.
   C He employed a market-research company.
3. How did they first obtain funds to start the business?
   A From investors in London.
   B From a bank.
   C From an international organisation.
4. Why has the business been successful?
   A They followed conventional business advice.
   B They were fortunate.
   C They followed the example of other companies.
5. According to Lewis, how can you reduce the risks of starting a new business?
   A By employing good staff.
   B By renting good premises.
   C By limiting your overheads.

Company background

espresso education

Espresso Ltd delivers multimedia educational resources to schools using satellite technology. It was formed in 1997 by Lewis Bronze and Tony Bowden.

18 2 Listen to Lewis Bronze talking about how he set up Espresso Ltd and choose the best answer for each question.

Task tip

You should not expect to understand every word the speaker says. You should try to understand the general meaning in order to choose the best answers.

Talking point

1 Work in pairs and discuss the following question. While you are talking, take notes.
- What is important when looking for finance to start up a business?

19 2 Listen to Lewis's answer to the same question and note down what he said.

3 Add any of Lewis's ideas which you agree with to your notes.

4 Change partners and take turns to talk for a minute to your new partner about what is important when starting up in business. When your partner is speaking, you should listen without interrupting.

Financing the start-up

UNIT 11

Starting up in a new location

Getting started

1 Work in small groups. Read the following email which Charles Langley, BioBok's CEO, sent to Alicia Flores, BioBok's operations manager in Europe.

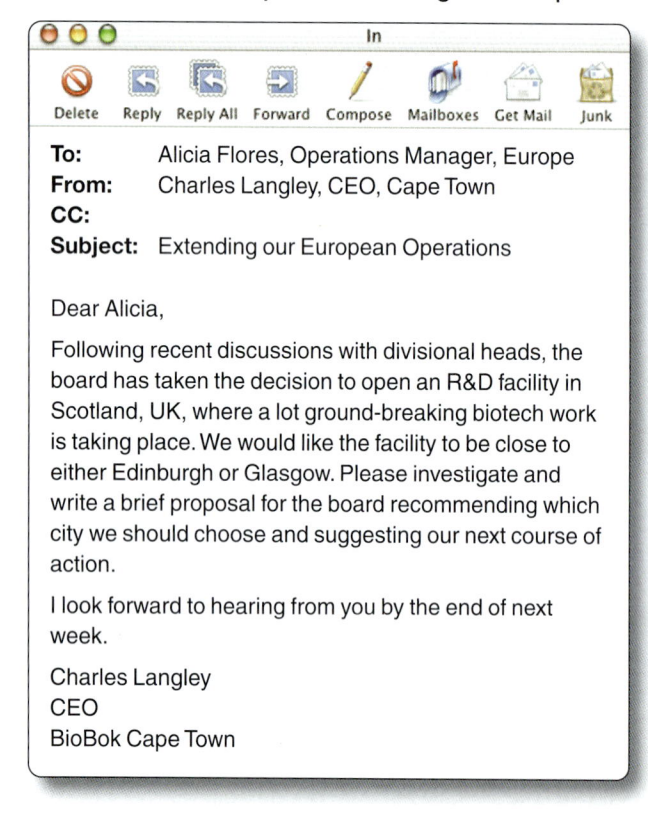

To: Alicia Flores, Operations Manager, Europe
From: Charles Langley, CEO, Cape Town
CC:
Subject: Extending our European Operations

Dear Alicia,

Following recent discussions with divisional heads, the board has taken the decision to open an R&D facility in Scotland, UK, where a lot ground-breaking biotech work is taking place. We would like the facility to be close to either Edinburgh or Glasgow. Please investigate and write a brief proposal for the board recommending which city we should choose and suggesting our next course of action.

I look forward to hearing from you by the end of next week.

Charles Langley
CEO
BioBok Cape Town

---

2 Discuss what extra information Alicia needs about BioBok's plans before she starts investigating.

3 Discuss what factors are important when choosing a location for a new operation. Think about these questions.

- Will you be able to find staff?
- What are communications and infrastructure like?
- How close is it to your markets?
- Are your suppliers within easy reach?
- How will the new location affect your costs?
- How will the new location affect the image of the company?

A new location in Scotland

Listening

1 Discuss with a partner what sort of information you will need to complete these notes.

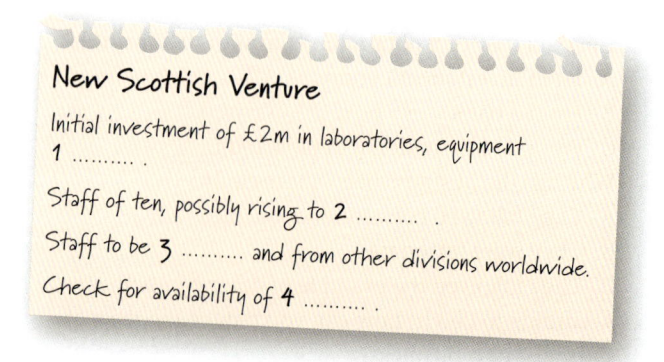

New Scottish Venture

Initial investment of £2m in laboratories, equipment 1 ....

Staff of ten, possibly rising to 2 ....

Staff to be 3 .... and from other divisions worldwide.

Check for availability of 4 ....

---

20 2 Listen to Alicia phoning Charles and complete her notes with one or two words or a number.

54 Starting up in a new location

Reading

1 Look at these notes which Alicia made about Glasgow and Edinburgh.

2 Read the two print-outs from the Scottish Enterprise website. Which city does each of Alicia's notes refer to?

3 Work in small groups. Discuss the situation and decide:
- which information is important when deciding where BioBok should locate its premises
- which city would be more suitable.

1 Can offer excellent scientific facilities.
2 Facilities encourage co-operation with other companies in the sector.
3 Has a high rate of unemployment.
4 Has excellent communications.
5 Has more students than anywhere else in Scotland.
6 Is the biggest city in Scotland.
7 Leads research in biotechnology.
8 Premises would be cheaper.

Why choose Glasgow?

Glasgow is the largest city in Scotland, with a population of nearly 600,000 people. This represents 11.8 per cent of the population of Scotland.

Glasgow's economic growth rate continues to be higher than Scotland and UK averages. For a number of years, the city has been the fastest-growing economy of any area in Scotland.

The total numbers of people in employment broke the 400,000 milestone just a few years ago – with the biggest employment gains of any city outside of London.

Unemployment has reduced significantly in Glasgow, but remains above the Scottish rate. In addition, there are more than 100,000 people 'economically inactive' in the city (this means people available for work or actively seeking employment). The figure excludes students.

Glasgow has three universities, five higher-education institutes and ten further-education colleges.

Glasgow has a student population in excess of 168,000, second only to London.

Glasgow is increasingly seen as the UK's second centre for creative business, and has a long-established reputation for high-quality cultural attractions and activity.

Key industries include financial and business services, communications, software, creative industries, health, retail and tourism.

Jobs in the knowledge industries have grown by 22 per cent in the last five years. The sector now employs more than 70,000 people.

Over the past five years, 62 spin-out businesses have been created from local universities and research institutes.

Glasgow ranks second in Europe in terms of offering value-for-money office space.

Welcome to the Edinburgh Science Triangle

Welcome to the Edinburgh Science Triangle, located within the Edinburgh area.

The triangle has been created to encourage active collaboration, promoting the exchange of ideas and expertise to encourage scientific development and to attract national and international companies to the area.

Edinburgh has an international reputation in several sectors, with world firsts including 'Dolly', the first cloned sheep, at the Roslin Institute.

The range of science and technology covered by the Edinburgh Science Triangle is very wide and includes genomics, bioinformatics, animal health and stem-cell research in the life-sciences sector.

There are four universities in the area.

The City of Edinburgh's high quality of life and standard of living are factors in attracting a young, highly skilled workforce.

The Edinburgh Science Triangle can offer state-of-the-art infrastructure and facilities.

All of the premises are built with science in mind, and there is the possibility of designing and building to your own specifications.

Premises are located in quiet surroundings within close proximity to Edinburgh city centre and international airport.

Edinburgh facts

Edinburgh is a major capital city, with a population of over 450,000.

Edinburgh has more graduates per head of population than any other city in Europe.

Edinburgh has excellent transport links, and Edinburgh International Airport provides regular departures to numerous destinations.

Edinburgh is ranked as one of the very top cities in the United Kingdom for 'quality of life'.

Starting up in a new location 55

A proposal

Reading

1 Read Alicia's proposal and write one word in each gap.

Proposal for location of new facilities in Scotland

INTRODUCTION
The purpose of this proposal is **1** .... compare Edinburgh and Glasgow as possible locations for BioBok's new R&D facility in Scotland and to recommend **2** .... city we should choose.

WORKFORCE
Although Glasgow has **3** .... largest number of students in Scotland, I suggest that we should recruit people who are already employed in the sector, and many of the best scientists are in the Edinburgh region.

PREMISES
Property prices appear to be lower in Glasgow. However, it would be a good idea to try to find suitable premises in the Edinburgh area, **4** .... it contains a 'Science Triangle' with purpose-built laboratories. Also, the Science Triangle encourages the co-operation and knowledge-sharing we need.

LIFESTYLE
Glasgow has a dynamic and exciting lifestyle with many cultural events. On the other hand, Edinburgh is **5** .... of the cities with the highest quality of life in the UK. This will help us to attract staff to live and work there.

RECOMMENDED COURSE OF ACTION
I strongly recommend that we choose Edinburgh **6** .... the reasons given above. Our next steps should be to contact:
- Scottish Enterprise in order to find a suitable building
- a recruitment agency to find the staff we require.

2 Read the proposal again and answer these questions.
1 What do you notice about the layout of the proposal?
2 Does the proposal concentrate on the existing situation or what should be done next?
3 What are the purposes of the first and the last sections?
4 A proposal should usually be written in a formal style. Can you see any phrases or expressions which make this proposal sound formal?

3 Discuss your answers with a partner.

Making recommendations

Writing

Useful language

Making recommendations

I suggest that we should recruit people who are already employed in the sector …

I suggest that we recruit people who are already employed in the sector …

1 Underline phrases in the proposal which introduce recommendations.

2 Write other recommendations using the ideas given below. Use different phrases to introduce them.
1 Find premises close to airport.
2 Design our own building.
3 Contact Edinburgh University.
4 Advertise for staff in science magazines.

Grammar workshop

Contrasting ideas

1 Study these sentences from the proposal.
A **Although** Glasgow has the largest number of students in Scotland, I suggest that we should recruit people who are already employed in the sector …
B Property prices appear to be lower in Glasgow. **However**, it would be a good idea to try to find suitable premises in the Edinburgh area …
C Glasgow has a dynamic and exciting lifestyle with many cultural events. **On the other hand**, Edinburgh is one of the cities with the highest quality of life in the UK.

2 Complete this grammar rule with *although*, *however* and *on the other hand*.

We use **1** .... to join two sentences. **2** .... and **3** .... are used at the beginning of the second sentence to contrast it with the sentence before.

56 Starting up in a new location

3 Complete these sentences in any way you think is suitable.

1 Although our factory is rather old, ...
2 We have a very small training budget. However, ...
3 We do not pay our staff as much as our competitors. On the other hand, ...
4 Our new CEO has made the company very successful, although ....
5 The business was not very profitable last year. However, ...

> **page 63** (Comparing and contrasting ideas)

Agents and distributors

Talking point

1 Companies who want to launch their products in a new market, often in another country, may use *agents* or *distributors*, or set up a *joint venture*. Write one of the three words in each gap below.

1 .... are businesses which are owned by two companies. One is often a foreign company which wants to break into the local market. The other is often a local company with contacts, infrastructure and knowledge of the market.
2 .... buy your products at the best price you can give them, and then sell them again to other customers at the best price they can get. They have local contacts and knowledge of the local market.
3 .... will sell your products on commission. They are usually local people or firms with contacts and knowledge of the local market. They do not buy or own your products before selling them.

2 Discuss in small groups what you think the advantages and disadvantages of each are.

Writing

Your company, which produces electrical components, wants to break into a new market in another country, and is looking for a distributor in that country. The managing director has asked you to write a proposal, saying which distributor you recommend. Using the adverts for two potential distributors below and all your handwritten notes, write your proposal. Use the proposal on page 56 as a model.

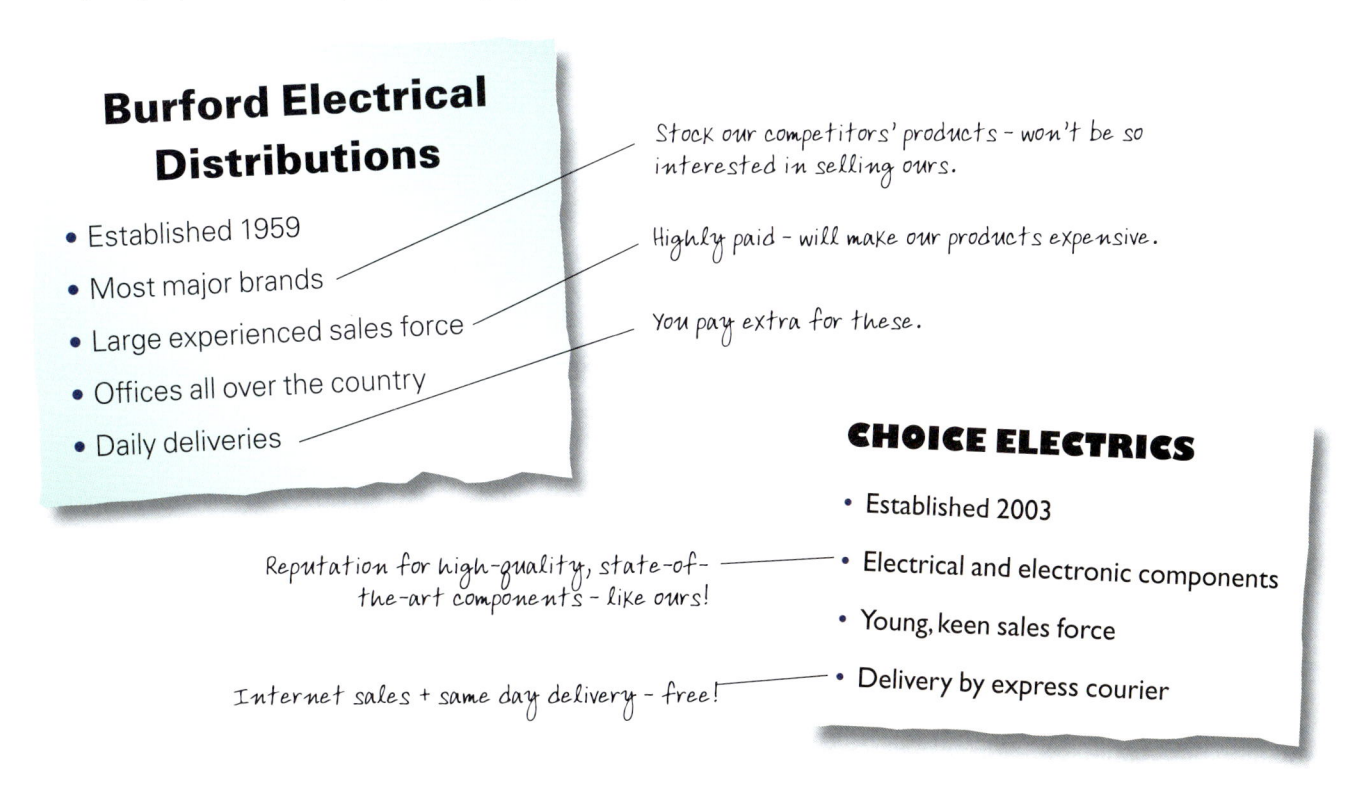

Burford Electrical Distributions

- Established 1959
- Most major brands
- Large experienced sales force
- Offices all over the country
- Daily deliveries

Stock our competitors' products – won't be so interested in selling ours.

Highly paid – will make our products expensive.

You pay extra for these.

CHOICE ELECTRICS

- Established 2003
- Electrical and electronic components
- Young, keen sales force
- Delivery by express courier

Reputation for high-quality, state-of-the-art components – like ours!

Internet sales + same day delivery – free!

UNIT 12

Presenting your business idea

Getting started

1 Discuss the following in pairs.

1 What is happening in the picture?
2 Do you ever have to give presentations? What about?

2 Label the objects with the words from the box.

data projector
flipchart
handouts
laptop
pointer
remote control
samples of product
screen
speakers

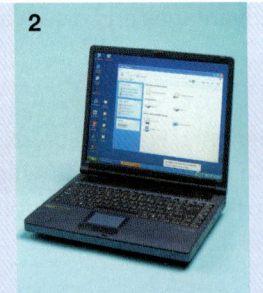

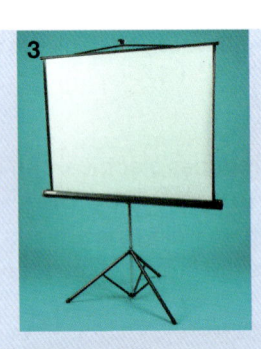

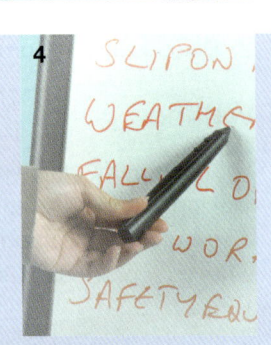

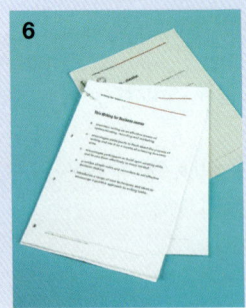

Structuring a presentation

Talking point

When you give a business presentation, it is important that your presentation has a clear structure which your audience can follow easily. It is also important to repeat the important points several times.

In pairs, look at these stages in a typical presentation. Write the correct phrase (a–g) in each box on page 59.

a Conclude and invite questions.
b Give the main part of your talk.
c Greet audience and thank them for coming. ✓
d Introduce your talk.
e Introduce yourself (and your colleague(s)).
f Outline what you are going to say in your talk and suggest people leave their questions to the end.
g Summarise the main points you have made.

58 Presenting your business idea

1 *Greet audience and thank them for coming.*

▼

2

▼

3

▼

4

▼

5

▼

6

▼

7

Signalling the parts of a presentation

Listening

Good presenters make it easy for their audience to know where they are in the presentation. Handouts and slides can help you to do this, but it's also important to use phrases which signal where you are in the presentation.

1 Look at these extracts from a presentation. In which part of the presentation (1–7 above) would you use each of them?

a And I think that just about covers the market research, so now let's deal with the third part of my presentation, which is to explain our financial requirements and plans …

b Good morning and welcome to the Adelphi Hotel.

c In my presentation, I'm hoping to do three things. First, I'll … Then I'll tell you … and finally I'll …

d Now to move on to my second point: market research …

e If you have any questions you'd like to ask, please leave them to the end, when I'll be very happy to answer them.

f Now, if I can just summarise the main points again, they are these: first, …

g So, finally, I'd like to finish off by saying that it's been a pleasure talking to you all and thank you for your patience and interest in listening to me. If you have any questions, please feel free to ask them now.

h So, let me introduce myself: my name's … and this is my partner, …

i Let's start with my first point – our main business idea …

j Thank you all very much for coming; some of you have travelled a long way to hear us today …

k The purpose of this presentation is to explain our business plans to you …

21 2 Listen to Peter Furlong giving a presentation of his business ideas and check your answers.

21 3 Listen again and complete the notes below by writing two words or a number in each gap.

Name of company
Clock Options Express

Business idea
Information and **1** .... display panels.
Will provide information for **2** .... and other travellers.
Information on time, **3** .... , parking and public transport.
Will be placed at **4** .... accesses to the city.
Income from **5** .... space for advertisements.

Market research
Interviewed more than **6** .... motorists and other travellers.
Advertisers will pay **7** .... for space on panels.

Financial requirements
First year: **8** .... pounds.

Presenting your business idea **59**

Talking point

Work with a partner. Choose one of the following topics (A–C) and prepare a brief presentation of about two or three minutes.

- Follow the seven steps of the presentation structure.
- Do not write exactly what you are going to say; make brief notes.
- Finally, change partners and take turns to give your presentations to each other.
- Listen to your new partner's presentation and ask two or three questions at the end.
- Give your partner feedback on what he/she did well and what could be improved.

| A | **Present the company or organisation you work for. You can say:**
• what the company or organisation does
• how it started
• what it will do in the future. | B | **Present a product or service you know well. You can say:**
• what the product is
• what the advantages of buying it are
• how it is marketed. | C | **Present the town you live in to a business person who is thinking of starting a business there. You can say:**
• what industries there are in your town
• what facilities there are for new businesses
• what the advantages of opening a business in your town are. |

Making the most of presentations

Reading

1 Work in pairs. Read the advice about giving presentations (1–8) and decide if each piece of advice is:

a excellent advice
b quite useful advice
c not very useful advice

1 Do a course on presentation skills.
2 Speak at a suitable speed.
3 Improve the way you speak by taping yourself and listening to it.
4 Look directly at your listeners when speaking.
5 Plan your presentation carefully.
6 Practise in order to reduce nervousness.
7 Prepare for possible questions.
8 Use photocopies for anything too long and complex.

2 Read the paragraphs (A–D). Which paragraph does each of the pieces of advice (1–8) refer to?

| A | The fear of speaking is considered by many business people as their number-one fear. They may even avoid speaking opportunities that could advance their career. While there are many effective methods of relaxation that can help reduce the fear of speaking, for most people it is not something they can simply get up and do effectively without having at least some basic training. Rehearsing the presentation will greatly reduce anxiety. The more familiar the material, the more credible the speaker will sound. |

| B | The first step in making a really effective presentation is to prepare. As the saying goes, 'failing to prepare is preparing to fail.' You will need to spend some time thinking about the material you want to cover, brainstorming all the things it might be possible to include, and then ranking them according to which topics you must include, which topics it might be nice to include if time allows, and which things it is worth knowing about in case anybody asks you about it. |

| C | Nothing will improve your presentation more than seeing yourself on screen. You will notice mannerisms that you never noticed before. And you will instantly begin to make changes. Recording and listening to yourself is another tool to use when you rehearse your presentations. You'll immediately know if you are speaking clearly or if some words are difficult to understand. You will hear mistakes in grammar and inappropriate 'ums' and 'ahs'. |

| D | • Enthusiasm is essential. Try to smile, and make eye contact with members of the audience as often as possible.
• Remember to speak slowly and clearly. Pause regularly to allow the audience to digest what you have said.
• Short words and simple sentences will have more impact than long and complicated sentences. Avoid technical language, too.
• If you are worried about drying up, then use notes. These should be prompts only – don't read straight from your notes.
• Convert statistics into charts and graphs wherever possible, and put any lengthy detail into a handout which people can read at their leisure. |

Presenting your business idea

Grammar workshop

Modal verbs

Look at these sentences from the paragraphs you have just read. Phrases containing modal verbs have been highlighted in *italics*. Match each of them with an explanation (1–4).

A You will need to spend some time thinking about the material you want to cover, brainstorming all the things *it might be* possible to include, and then ranking them according to which topics *you must* include …

B If you are worried about drying up, then use notes. *These should be* prompts only …

C Put any lengthy detail into a handout which *people can* read at their leisure.

1 it is advisable, a good idea if these are
2 it is essential, necessary or obligatory for you to
3 it is perhaps
4 people will be able to

> **page 63** (Modal verbs)

Presenting your business idea

Role-play

Work in pairs. You have an idea for a new business start-up, but you need to raise finance in order to make your dream a reality (it might be one of the ideas in the photos). One possibility is to get financial support from a 'business angel' – a private investor who specialises in putting money into new enterprises.

A group of angels are meeting at a hotel in your area to listen to presentations from would-be entrepreneurs like yourselves. Your job is to prepare a presentation, rehearse it and give it to the angels.

Use one of the ideas in the pictures if you want to. Otherwise use your own idea.

Follow these steps:

1 Decide what your business idea is, i.e. what kind of company you want to start up, your product, the size of the company to start with, your location and the premises you need.
2 Imagine you have carried out some market research and invent some results to present to the investors.
3 Decide how much money you need from your investors. Invent a few financial details such as your sales and profit forecasts, your projected return on investment, etc.
4 Prepare the presentation which you are going to give together. Write notes to work from. Decide which of you is going to give each part of the presentation.
5 Rehearse your presentation together.
6 Imagine that the other members of your class are the business angels. Give your presentation to them.
7 While you are listening to other people's presentations, think of one or two questions you would like to ask them at the end.

Grammar workshop 3

Units 9–12

Tenses in time clauses

- When you talk about an action which finishes before the action in the main clause, you can use either simple or perfect tenses in the time clause:
  *I'll go for lunch as soon as my boss **comes back** / **has come back** from lunch.*
  *He only bought the franchise after he **had gone** / **went** to the trade fair.*
- If you are talking about an action in the time clause which takes place over a period of time, you use the perfect tense:
  *He opened his business after he **had done** extensive market research.*
  *I'll come home as soon as I**'ve written** these emails.*
- If the actions take place at the same time, you use the simple tense …
  *Bring him up to the boardroom when he **arrives**.*
  (not: *When he has arrived* …)
  *When he **phoned** the supplier, nobody answered.*
  (not: *When he had phoned* …)
  … although if both happen over a period of time, you can use continuous tenses to emphasise the length of time:
  *While he **was training** to be an accountant, she **was studying** at university.*
- If one action happens at the same time as another, the action which happens for a longer time needs a continuous tense:
  *She often **phones** me when she**'s travelling** to work.*

Put the verbs in brackets into the correct tenses in these sentences. In some cases, more than one answer is correct.

1 When I ..*have written*.. (write) the report, I'll circulate it to the whole department.
2 She was taking notes while you .... (give) the presentation.
3 People asked a lot of interesting questions after she .... (give) the presentation.
4 Send the samples to the research department as soon as you .... (receive) them.
5 I'll ask him for a decision when the meeting .... (finish).
6 When we .... (launch) the MC30, it was a total innovation.
7 When they .... (build) the factory, they had to install the equipment.
8 While I .... (try) to write the letter, people kept interrupting me.
9 He didn't get to the bank until after it .... (close).
10 We'll have a team meeting when everyone .... (come) back from holiday.

See also page 48.

The second conditional

- The second conditional is formed by:
  If/Unless + past simple tense, + *would/could/might* + infinitive
  *If I **lost** my job, I **might start** my own business.*
- The second conditional talks about imaginary, improbable or hypothetical situations (unlike the first conditional (see page 45), which talks about real possibilities). Compare:
  *I hear the company is going to open an office in Thailand. If they **send** me to work in Thailand, I**'ll be** delighted.* (first conditional)
  *If I **was** managing director, I **wouldn't send** you to Thailand!* (second conditional)
- The second conditional is often used to give advice, using the phrase *If I were you* …:
  If I were you, I would ask my family to help me start the business.
- As with the first conditional, the *if*-clause can come first or second in the sentence:
  I might start my own business if I lost my job.

1 Put the verbs in brackets into the correct tense.

1 I would take out a loan if interest rates ..*weren't*.. (not be) so high.
2 I .... (start) up a business if it wasn't so risky.
3 I'd stay in this job if they .... (pay) more.
4 I .... (can/work) in the Paris office if I spoke French.
5 I .... (take) that job if I were you.

62 Grammar workshop 3

2 Complete these sentences in any way you want.

1 If I spoke perfect English, …
2 I wouldn't work so hard if …
3 If they don't give me promotion, …
4 If I started my own business, …
5 If I needed money to start a business, …
6 I'll study another language if …

Comparing and contrasting ideas

- *Although* joins two sentences:
  Although *he left school at 16, he was a millionaire by the age of 30.*
- *However* and *on the other hand* are adverbs and normally start new sentences:
  He was a lazy student. **However,** *he became a hard-working and successful businessman.*
  The risks are very high. **On the other hand**, *the potential profit is enormous.*
- *In spite of* and *despite* are followed by nouns or *-ing* forms:
  In spite of *the risks, they decided to go it alone.*
  Despite *working very hard, their business was never very profitable.*

1 Complete these sentences with *although*, *however*, *on the other hand*, *in spite of* or *despite*.

1 I asked for a loan *although* interest rates were high.
2 .... we met our sales targets, my manager was not satisfied.
3 .... high interest rates, he took out a loan.
4 The world economic situation was bad. .... , the firm decided to expand.
5 He has original ideas. .... , he's bad at putting them into practice.
6 .... the meeting lasted three hours, they were unable to reach a decision.
7 He couldn't convince them to buy the new machine .... he tried very hard.
8 He finds his job very stressful .... doing a stress-management course.
9 .... I tidy my desk every day, it always ends up covered in papers.

2 Complete these sentences about yourself. Then compare your answers with a partner.

1 I am successful despite …
2 I've made progress learning English, although …
3 Although I enjoy some aspects of my work, …
4 In spite of working hard, I …
5 Money is important to me. On the other hand, …
6 I like the town where I live, in spite of …

Modal verbs

To express these meanings, you can use modal verbs.

- **perhaps:** *may/might*
  You should make a back-up copy because the computer **might** *have a virus.*
- **able to:** *can*
  He's a brilliant presenter because he **can** *hold everything he wants to say in his head without looking at notes.*
- **it's obligatory/essential:** *must* or *have to*
  - *must* for an obligation the speaker agrees with:
    You **must** *help me write this report because I can't do it on my own.*
  - *have to* for an obligation from someone else:
    I'm afraid I **have to** *work late at the office tonight – my boss wants the report finished by tomorrow lunchtime.*
- **it's a good idea/advisable:** *should / ought to*
  If you think you've got too much work, you **should** *speak to your boss. He* **ought to** *take on an assistant to help you.*
- **it is generally likely:** *can*
  Speakers who just read from their notes **can** *be very boring.*
- **it is allowed:** *may/can*
  In this company, you **can** *wear jeans and a T-shirt on Fridays.*

Rewrite these sentences about giving presentations using one of the modal verbs above.

1 I advise you to rehearse your presentation before you give it.
  You should rehearse your presentation before you give it.
2 It's a good idea to put complicated details on a handout.
  ....
3 It's essential to speak loudly and clearly so that everyone can hear you.
  ....
4 Giving presentations to senior managers is generally likely to be very frightening.
  ....
5 You are allowed to pause to drink water if your mouth is dry.
  ....
6 Perhaps people will interrupt your presentation with questions.
  ....
7 You are allowed to tell them to save questions till the end.
  ....

Grammar workshop 3   63

UNIT 13
Business hotels and sales conferences

Getting started

Discuss the questions below in small groups. When you have finished, find a partner from another group and report what you decided.

- How is the business traveller different from the ordinary tourist?
- If you were choosing a hotel for a business trip, which of these amenities would you consider more important and which less important?
    - guest rooms
    - general decor
    - lobby and other public areas
    - meeting rooms
    - business centre
    - restaurants and bars
    - room service
    - gym/health club
    - hotel staff
    - high-speed Internet access
    - wi-fi Internet access
    - other
- Do you have a favourite hotel?
- How important do you think the hotel's cost is when business people make their travel plans?
    - very important
    - quite important
    - not important

The results of a survey

Writing

1 Look at the graph (top right), which shows the results of a survey of American business travellers, and complete the paragraph below it by writing one word in each gap.

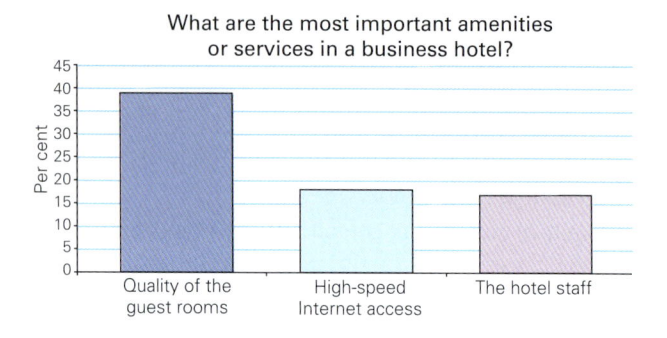

What are the most important amenities or services in a business hotel?

In our survey of 1,200 business travellers, **1** .... found that 39% considered the quality of the guest rooms **2** .... the most important amenity, whereas 18% rated high-speed Internet access **3** .... the most important, and 17% valued the hotel staff **4** .... highly.

2 Write similar paragraphs for these two graphs. When you have finished, compare your paragraphs with a partner.

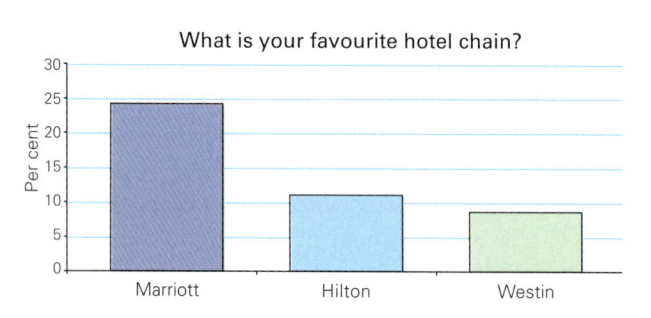

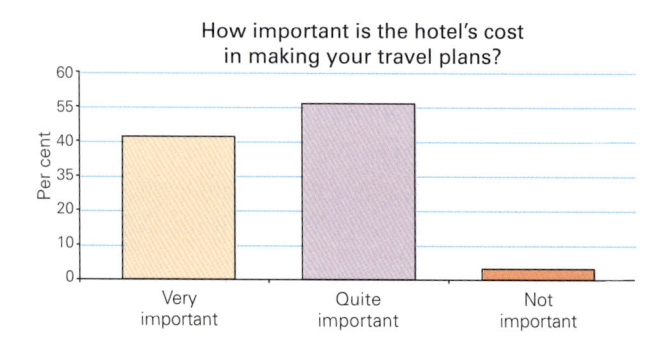

What is your favourite hotel chain?

How important is the hotel's cost in making your travel plans?

64 Business hotels and sales conferences

Useful language

Contrasting ideas

While/Whereas 25% of respondents valued room service, only 10% rated the quality of the beds. *However*, just 3% considered the business centre to be an important service.

> **page 80** (*While* and *whereas*)

Business accommodation

Reading

1 Read the article below about business hotels. In each paragraph, underline the key phrase(s) which give the main idea of the paragraph. This will help you to see the clear line of argument which runs through the text.

2 Choose the best sentence (A–H) from the list below to fill each of the gaps. Make sure the sentence fits with the main idea of the paragraph where you want to put it.

Home Sweet Hotel

BY CHRISTOPHER PALMIERI

We turned to the smartest business folks we know – our readers – and asked them to name the best places for the business traveler to stay. Nearly 1,200 subscribers participated in this, our first hotel survey. They logged on to BusinessWeek.com and told us where they like to stay – and why. The results were revealing.

It was virtually impossible to find the single best hotel. We asked readers to name their favorite property and got almost 1,200 different answers. **1** ..*E*.. The hotel staff and health club were also high on the list, but the real surprise was high-speed Internet access, which came a strong second.

We had no problem identifying the top chain. Marriott International, with 24%, was the winner by a wide margin. True, Marriott is the largest hotelier in the world, and its range of locations gives it an advantage. **2** ...... "They never provide an unpleasant surprise," said one reader. "In every Marriott throughout the world, the staff is always caring," gushed another. One person recalled how a Marriott staffer in Wichita made some sandwiches at no cost after the kitchen was closed.

Such attentive service is no accident. "We spend well over $100 million a year on training," says J.W. Marriott Jr., chairman and CEO. "**3** ...... I tell our people: 'We don't manufacture anything. We provide experiences.'"

Consistency and number of locations were also reasons 12% of the respondents picked Hilton Hotels – the No. 2 finisher in the survey. **4** ...... This allows members to earn points for each stay in both an airline frequent-flier program and the Hilton plan. The number of brands under the Hilton umbrella was also a plus. "I can stay at a Hampton Inn and earn points toward Hilton stays," one subscriber noted.

No. 3 on the best-chain list was Westin, something of a surprise since, with just 120 hotels worldwide, it's much smaller than many of its rivals. Readers cited Westin's exclusive Heavenly Bed – a custom-designed bed – and its Heavenly Shower.

Readers' picks of their favorite loyalty programs came up much like their favorite chains, with Marriott first and Hilton second. Here again, readers chose these programs for the number of locations and variety of brands under one plan. Last summer, Marriott tweaked its program to allow frequent guests to earn free stays 30% faster than many of its rivals. **5** ......

Some 85% of respondents said their company didn't require them to stay at specific hotels or chains. About 60% said the hotel's cost was only somewhat or not important in making their plans.

Adapted from Business Week

A "For customers, the bottom line is how soon they can take their families on a free vacation," says the CEO.

B Although business people do not appreciate having to mix with ordinary tourists.

C As a result, profits are up by nearly 30% this year.

D But respondents almost universally praised the company for its consistency.

E But they did center on what really counts (after price and location, of course): 39% said the quality of the guest rooms was the most important thing.

F Every day, there is a 15-minute exercise on things like how to greet a guest, how to handle a complaint.

G Good hotels need to be able to provide good meals as well.

H They often singled out the company's loyalty program.

3 When you have finished, compare your answers with a partner. If you don't agree, explain why you chose your answers.

Business hotels and sales conferences

Vocabulary

Find words or phrases in the text which mean the following.

1. people who buy a service or a magazine on a regular basis (paragraph 1)
2. visited a website (paragraph 1)
3. a company with many different branches (paragraph 3)
4. member of staff (paragraph 3)
5. paying a lot of attention to customers (paragraph 4)
6. always being the same quality (paragraph 5)
7. mentioned specially (paragraph 5)
8. competitors (paragraph 6)
9. changed slightly (paragraph 7)
10. the most important factor (in a decision) (paragraph 7)

Presenting your opinions

Talking point

1. Work in groups of about three. Your company is considering changing its policy about business travel, and you have been invited to a meeting to discuss this. You have been asked to make a short presentation.

   Each of you should choose one of these questions to talk about. Spend one minute preparing what you are going to say.

   > What is important when choosing a business hotel to stay at?
   > Think about location, amenities, etc.

   > What is important when preparing a foreign business trip?
   > Think about local customs, local working hours, etc.

   > What is important when choosing an airline to fly with?
   > Think about prices, schedules, etc.

2. Make your presentation to your group. You should speak for about one minute. When you have finished, your colleagues should say if there is anything they disagree with, and why.

Conference problems

Listening

1. Read this list of things (A–I) which could go wrong at a conference and discuss what the problem could be in each case.

   A the access
   B the accommodation
   C the dates
   D the keynote speaker
   E the location
   F the conference rooms
   G the programme
   H the staff
   I the technology

2. You will hear five colleagues in a meeting complaining about things which went wrong in different conferences they attended. Listen and choose what each speaker is complaining about.

   1 Candice: .....E.....
   2 Igor: ....
   3 Paola: ....
   4 Harry: ....
   5 Susan: ....

3. Complete these sentences from the conversation you have just heard.

   1 They .... us to South America or the Far East or something.
   2 She had a PowerPoint presentation prepared, but she couldn't make it work. She really .... a bit beforehand.
   3 They .... one of those purpose-built conference centres.

4. Which speaker said which sentence?

5. Check your answers by listening to the recording again.

6. Discuss in small groups what the organisers could/should have done to avoid the problems mentioned.

   ▶ **page 80** (Modal verbs: perfect forms)

66 Business hotels and sales conferences

Planning a lively sales conference

Reading

Read the article below about how to plan a sales conference and choose the best word to fill each gap.

Company background

Kimberly L. McCall is the president of McCall Media & Marketing Inc. (www.marketingangel.com), a business communications company in Durham, Maine, USA.

Bye-bye BORING

By Kimberly L. McCall

You can plan a lively sales conference without breaking the bank.

For a sales representative, there are few things more boring than being asked to endure three days of sales meetings. But because sales conferences are an excellent **1** ..C.. for reps to discuss a new product launch or get new ideas, there are many powerful **2** ...... to plan a gathering.

Would you like to pull together a lively sales conference that will **3** ...... your reps to sell better, bond and share their most **4** ...... selling practices? Here are a few great ways to plan a conference.

Create a mix of fun and focus. Schedule a keynote speech from a speaker the sales staff respect. And when **5** ...... activities, remember: one salesperson's idea of a fun experience may be another's waste of **6** ...... time.

Planners should create a menu of entertaining activities and let people decide. While some may choose golf, **7** ...... may go for a massage and a manicure. A well-planned meeting should be a mixture of 25 per cent fun and 75 per cent education.

Book well and **8** ...... money. Rio during Carnival may make you bankrupt, so **9** ...... booking a great resort in the off-season. Think Maine in March or Dallas in June. You'll get wonderful facilities at **10** ...... prices – and probably a lot more attention from the hotel staff.

If you are on a tight **11** ......, you should be especially careful at the development stage. Plan and get competitive bids from **12** ...... providers. Analyse the costs **13** ...... to your goals, and organise the meeting so that it will be as cost-effective as possible.

Engage your **14** .... Motivate reps before the conference by giving them an assignment, such as reading industry articles they should be **15** ...... to discuss, or sharing the finest proposals they have ever written.

© Kimberly McCall

	A	B	C	D
1	position	point	place	area
2	reasons	intentions	needs	advantages
3	force	inspire	move	involve
4	capable	effective	certain	able
5	doing	thinking	making	arranging
6	costly	pricey	worthy	valuable
7	one	another	others	any
8	save	keep	spend	pay
9	think	plan	consider	arrange
10	lowest	exclusive	falling	bargain
11	estimate	budget	quote	spending
12	few	varied	distinct	various
13	next	similar	relative	near
14	attendees	attendants	assistants	attention
15	pleased	supposed	ordered	prepared

Planning a conference

Talking point

Work in pairs or groups of about three. Your company has decided to hold a two-day conference for people from your company and you have been asked to help plan the conference.

Discuss the situation together, and decide:

- what kinds of activities should be organised for the main part of the conference
- what entertainment could also be provided
- where the conference should be held.

Business hotels and sales conferences

UNIT 14

Business conferences

Getting started

Work in pairs. Say briefly what is happening in each of the pictures then answer these questions.

1 Which of these things do business people find interesting or useful, and which things do they find a waste of time or not so enjoyable?
2 Do you travel for business? What do you enjoy or dislike about it?

Arranging conference facilities

Listening

Sally McBride is organising a conference for the South Pacific Tourism Organisation (SPTO). You are going to hear two telephone conversations.

1 Read both sets of notes carefully and try to guess what type of information you will need to complete them.

2 Listen and write one or two words or a number in the spaces in the notes.

Conversation 1
Sally phones Martin Forbes, who works for the SPTO.

South Pacific Tourism Organisation
Annual Conference

Number of delegates: 550 plus 1 ....
(numbers to be emailed)

Also: eight 2 ....

3 .... : Maori poi dance

Umukai Polynesian feast: fireworks sponsored by Air New Zealand with 4 ....

Conversation 2
Sally calls the centre where the conference will be held.

South Pacific Tourism Organisation
Annual Conference

Equipment available:
- In main conference room: screen, projector and 5 ....
- Guest speakers should bring 6 ....
- In smaller meeting rooms: flipcharts; screens and projectors 7 ....
- Stands for exhibitors in the 8 ....
- 9 .... available at all times.

68 Business conferences

A conference programme

Reading

Read the conference programme below and answer these questions..

Which speaker will talk about …?

1. his own job *Dr Bowden-Kerby*
2. how businesses may be influenced by changing circumstances
3. how his/her country is marketed to tourists
4. how the industry in which he/she works is changing
5. how the key to success is the way tourists are treated
6. how tourists are now given a different view of local people
7. the beneficial effects of tourism
8. the winning combination for tourist businesses in the region

South Pacific Islands Tourism Organisation
CONFERENCE PROGRAMME
Tuesday, 21 October

9.00–10.00 am OPENING CEREMONY

SESSION A
10.00–10.45 am
Branding: The South Pacific Brand: What is it? What does it have to compete against? How can it survive?

Wally Stone, Chairman of Tourism New Zealand will cover the recent success story of Tourism New Zealand's '100% Pure Brand' and its relationship with other sectors, and the relationship of member country's brands with the South Pacific brand of 'Discover Paradise'. Mr Stone is also a director of a number of private and non-profit-making organizations. He says the formula for success is a business based on a powerful mix of indigenous people, culture, heritage and environment.

10.45 am–12.00 pm JASONS TRAVEL MEDIA NETWORKING BREAK
12.00–1.30 pm ISLAND HOPPER VACATIONS LUNCHEON

SESSION B
1.30–2.30 pm
Marketing

Mike Tamaki, Managing Director of award-winning Tamaki Tours Ltd, Rotorua and Director NZ Tourism Board will address local entrepreneurship, marketing cultural and eco-tourism products, emerging markets, and event tourism.
Mr Tamaki has been an inspiration to New Zealand Maori in reinventing the way in which Maori culture is presented to the tourism market.

SESSION C
2.30–3.30 pm
Aviation trends

Roger Poulton, Vice President for New Zealand, Pacific Islands and Inbound Tourism for Air New Zealand will address the latest air-travel indicators and trends, including the changing face of aviation, airline alliances and the growing cost of operations. This will be your chance to gain more insight into the challenges facing international air travel and how they will affect your business.

3.30–4.00 pm THE FLAMETREE NETWORKING BREAK
6.00–8.00 pm AIR RAROTONGA COCKTAIL PARTY AT TRADER JACKS

Wednesday, 22 October

SESSION D
10.10–11.05 am
Sustainable development of coastal tourism destinations

Dr Bowden-Kerby will talk about practical examples from work he has done on protecting, enhancing and restoring the beach and marine environment. He will demonstrate that tourism can be a 'good neighbour', especially in terms of its impact on the fragile coastal environment.

11.05–11.45 am THE RAROTONGA ACCOMMODATION COUNCIL NETWORKING BREAK

SESSION E
11.45–12.45 pm
Tools for destination competitiveness: 'Good service is good business'

Catherine DeVrye (Msc, CSP), best-selling author of *Good Service is Good Business* and winner of the Australian Executive Woman of the Year Award, is an outstanding communicator with proven international management experience in the private and public sectors.

1.00–2.30 pm AIR TAHITI NUI LUNCHEON
3.15–4.00 pm **CONFERENCE SUMMARY/CLOSURE**
7.00–10.00 pm UMUKAI AT THE RAROTONGA BEACH RESORT & SPA

Vocabulary

Match the words from the text (1–8) with their definitions (a–h).

1. formula
2. networking
3. emerging markets
4. reinventing
5. insight
6. enhancing
7. outstanding
8. implementation

a building and maintaining informal business relationships
b changing radically
c combination of things which will produce the result you want
d excellent
e improving
f new or developing markets
g putting something into action
h understanding

Talking point

Discuss the following in pairs.

- Which sessions at the conference would interest you?
- Which parts of a conference do you think are most useful: the sessions or the opportunities for networking?
- How important is the social programme and entertainment at a conference?

Networking at a conference

Listening

1 Match each of the phrases (1–8) with one of the functions (a–h).

1. He's a great manager, isn't he? Really gets things moving. [g]
2. How about having lunch together the next time you're in Zurich?
3. I thought it was very persuasive. I wish we'd had the same idea ourselves.
4. It's unfortunate. You see, what happened was this …
5. Look, if you like, I could drop her an email and …
6. No, we'd be really happy if you people did it for us. Would it interest you?
7. Well, actually I've heard about you from various friends, so this really is a stroke of luck.
8. You know, if I were you I'd try B&H. They're really the best people for this sort of thing.

> a Arranging to meet after the conference
> b Congratulating someone on a promotional campaign
> c Explaining a problem
> d Offering a contract
> e Offering to contact someone
> f Recommending a consultancy
> g Talking about someone they both know
> h Talking to someone he/she wanted to meet

2 You are going to hear five short conversations in which people are networking during a break at a conference. Listen and, for each conversation, decide what the main speaker is doing. Choose from alternatives (a–h) above. (Note: the speakers will not use exactly the same phrases as those in Exercise 1.)

Speaker 1 .... Speaker 2 .... Speaker 3 .... Speaker 4 .... Speaker 5 ....

3 Look at the transcript for Track 24 and underline the phrases which gave you the answers.

70 Business conferences

Role-play

Work in pairs. You are at a conference. You have never met before, but you have a mutual business friend, Frank Parker. Before you start speaking to each other, study your role and think about some of the things you can say.

Student A
- Introduce yourself.
- Say how you know Frank Parker (you used to work together).
- Ask Student B how he/she knows Frank.
- Tell Student B you are interested in talking to someone who can find places for your company to advertise on the Internet.
- Respond to Student B's suggestions.

Student B
- When Student A introduces him/herself, say you've heard about him/her from Frank Parker.
- Say how you know Frank Parker (one of your best customers)
- Ask if Student A is enjoying the conference.
- You have a lot of contacts in the advertising industry, and one of your specialities is web-based advertising.
- Suggest a meeting somewhere else at another time to organise the advertising.

A destination management company (DMC)

Listening

25 You are going to hear Charlotte Weston talking about her company, Pacific World, and about incentive events. Incentive events are conferences and other events which companies use for thanking customers, rewarding their staff and motivating their personnel. For each question, choose the correct answer, A, B or C.

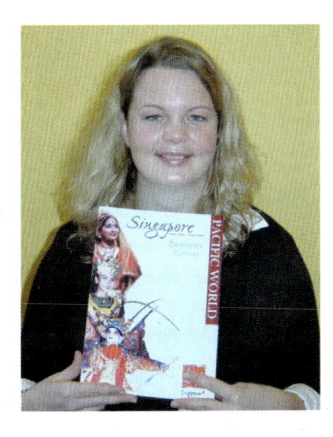

1. Pacific World is a company which …
    A sells package holidays.
    B organises conferences.
    C makes arrangements for travellers.
2. Who are the main clients of destination management companies?
    A Tourists
    B Business travellers
    C Event-management agencies
3. How many people will be attending the conference Charlotte is organising at the moment?
    A 150
    B 1,500
    C 15,000
4. Why are DMCs essential for organising conferences in China?
    A The phone service is unreliable.
    B Business is based on personal contacts.
    C It is necessary to have someone who speaks the language.
5. Why is Shanghai suitable for such a large conference?
    A It is easy to reach.
    B It is less expensive than other destinations.
    C It has plenty of large buildings.
6. Why did the finance company choose Shanghai for their staff conference?
    A They will be motivated by their surroundings.
    B They will make business contacts while there.
    C It is more interesting than Hong Kong.

Talking point

1 Discuss the following question with a partner.

What factors are important when choosing a conference destination?

You can consider:
- the conference centre
- hotels
- the atmosphere of the destination
- accessibility

etc.

2 When you have finished, compare your ideas with another pair of students.

Business conferences 71

UNIT 15

Reports

Getting started

Work in pairs. Look at these three charts which refer to the Forest Conference Centre. Discuss what each chart shows and means.

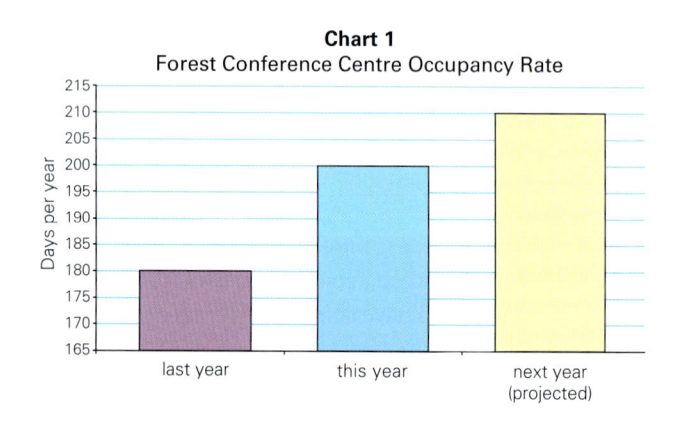

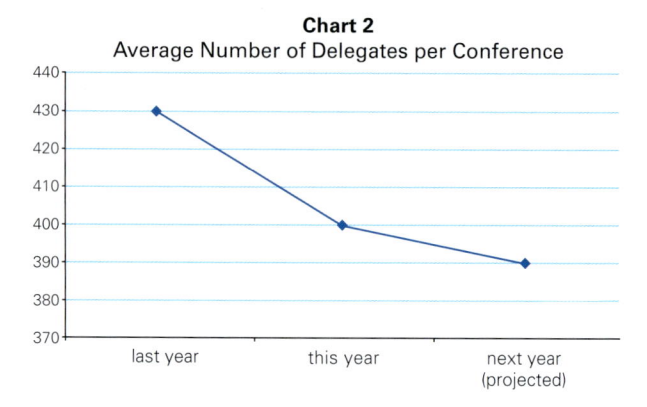

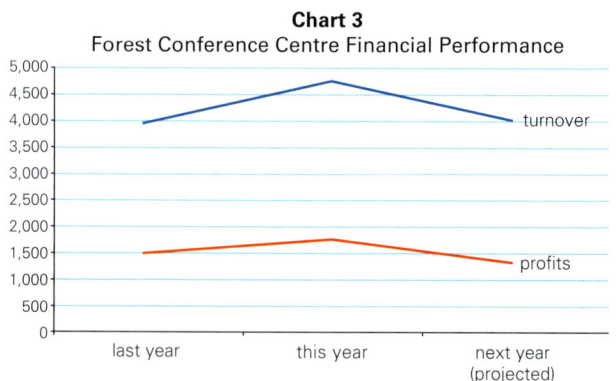

Chart 1 Forest Conference Centre Occupancy Rate

Chart 2 Average Number of Delegates per Conference

Chart 3 Forest Conference Centre Financial Performance

The Forest Conference Centre

Reading

1 One of your colleagues wrote this report for the Board of Directors. It reflects the information in the three charts above. He has asked you to check that the English is correct. In most of the lines (but not in the section headings) there is one extra word. Write the extra word in the column on the right. Some lines, however, are correct; put a tick (✔) where a line is correct.

Report on the performance of Forest Conference Centre

INTRODUCTION
The purpose of this report is to show off the performance of the Forest Conference Centre in the last two years and its projected performance of next year.

USE OF CONFERENCE CENTRE
The number of days that the conference centre is used has increased by a 10% this year from 180 to 200, and so this trend is expected to continue next year, with a projected occupancy rate of 210 days.
However, the number of delegates per conference has been falling down: last year there was on an average of 430 delegates per conference, whereas the average was reached 400 this year. It is predicted that delegates per conference will decrease to just 390 next year.

FINANCIAL PERFORMANCE
Turnover rose from just under £4m last year near to £4.5m this year. However, this figure will probably not drop to approximately £4m next year. Profits also went up slightly this year. They were increased by about £200,000 from £1.5m to £1.7m, although this figure is forecasted to fall to about £1.25m next year.

CONCLUSION
While our now level of activity is rising, our financial performance is suffering due to increased in costs and falling revenue.

1 _off_
2 ....
3 ....
4 ....
5 ....
6 ....
7 ....
8 ....
9 ....
10 ....
11 ....
12 ....
13 ....
14 ....
15 ....

72 Reports

2 Read the report again and answer these questions.
1 What do you notice about the layout of a report?
2 Which is it most similar to: a letter or a proposal? (You can see an example of a proposal on page 56.)
3 How is a report different from a proposal?
4 Which piece of information in the report is *not* included in the three charts?
5 Is the style of the report formal or informal? Give reasons for your answer. (For the difference between formal and informal styles, please see Useful language on page 21.)

3 When you have finished, discuss your answers with a partner.

Grammar workshop

Using the passive

> The passive is formed by the verb *to be* + the past participle.
> **Active**
> *The number of days* **people use the conference centre** *each year has increased by 10% …*
> **Passive**
> *The number of days* **the conference centre is used** *each year has increased by 10% …*
> The passive is more impersonal and more formal. It is often used when you want to talk about the effect of an action, but it is not necessary to mention who did the action.

1 Read the report again and find other examples of the passive.

2 Complete this section from a report by putting the verbs in brackets into the correct passive form.

This hotel has several disadvantages: it **1** *is not equipped* (not equip) to function as a conference centre. It **2** .... (see) by the management as a means of filling empty rooms. Adequate technical equipment **3** .... (not provide), and some of the rooms can **4** .... (use) only when they **5** .... (vacate) by guests at 11 o'clock. They then serve as meeting rooms, but first the rooms must **6** .... (clean) and the beds have to **7** .... (remove).

3 Look at this sentence from the Forest Conference Centre report.

*This trend **is expected** to continue next year…*

This can also be expressed like this:

***It is expected that** this trend will continue…*

Find two other passives like these in the report.

4 Change these sentences in the same way.
1 Profits are believed to be rising at the moment.
It is *believed that profits are rising* at the moment.
2 This figure is forecasted to fall to about £1.25m next year.
It is .... to about £1.25m next year.
3 It is predicted that delegates per conference will decrease to just 390 next year.
Delegates per conference are .... to just 390 next year.
4 It is expected that turnover will increase by 2.5% next quarter.
Turnover .... by 2.5% next quarter.
5 Visitor numbers are predicted to fall over the next five years.
It is .... over the next five years.

> pages 80–81 (Passives 1 and 2)

Vocabulary and speaking

1 How many other words can you find in the report which mean the following?
1 rose   2 fell

Milton Manor Hotel

Reports 73

2 Draw a chart below like Chart 3 on page 72 to show turnover and profits for a company for last year, this year and next year (projected).

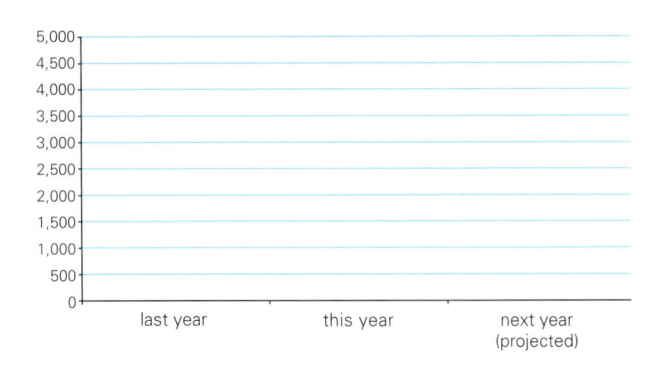

3 Take turns to describe your chart to your partner without letting him/her see it.
Draw your partner's chart below.

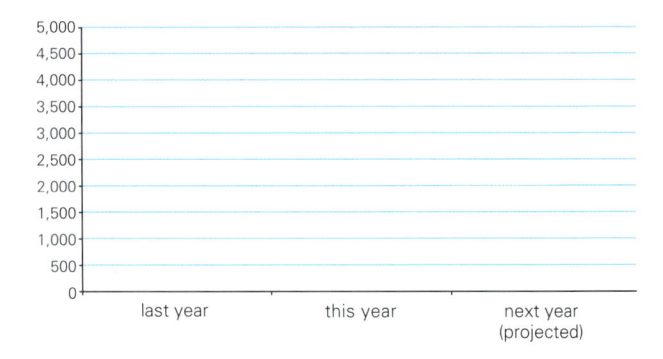

A report on the use of private company jets

Talking point

Discuss the following in pairs.

What do you think the advantages of using a private company jet for business trips instead of a normal commercial flight might be? List as many advantages as you can.

Listening

1 Compare the list you made with the list (A–G) below. Did you think of the same reasons? Did you think of other reasons which are not given on this list?

A Gets more work done
B Can discuss business matters during trip
C Impresses potential customers
D Saves on journey time
E Can deal with customer problems quickly
F More comfortable than commercial aircraft
G Has more flexibility

2 You will hear three executives from Florentino International being interviewed about why they prefer using the company jet instead of a normal commercial flight. Listen and, for each person, decide what their main reason is. Choose from the list A–G in Exercise 1.

1 Mariano Merano: ....
2 Pascuala Fernández: ....
3 Nicole Lefranc: ....

74 Reports

Talking point

Work in pairs. Look at the two charts. Discuss what each one shows.

Chart 1
Average number of flights by departmental directors and above Florentino International

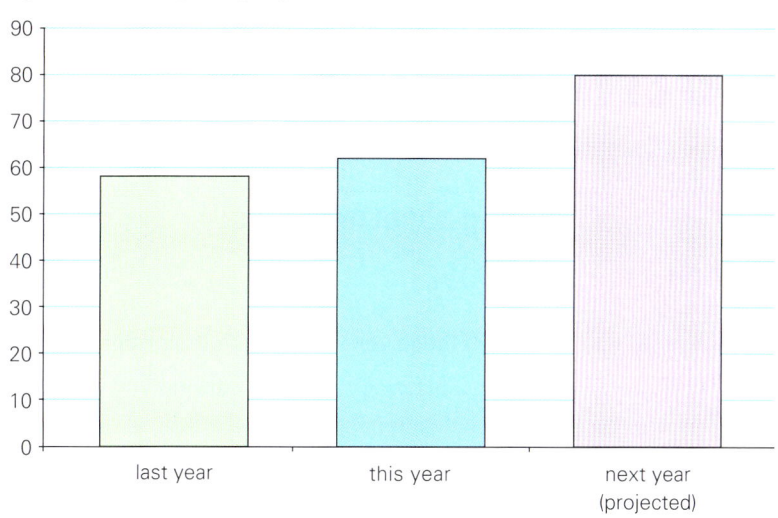

Chart 2
Reasons for flights
Florentino International

Writing

1 Work in small groups. Look at this writing task and discuss the questions which follow.

You work for Florentino International.
- The CEO has asked you to write a report on how the company aircraft are used by departmental directors.
- Look at the graphs above and use the information to write your report for the CEO.
- Write about 150 words.

1 What title could you give the report?
2 What section headings could the report have?
3 Should the style be formal or informal? Why?

2 Write the report. Use the report on page 72 as a model.

Reports 75

Unit 16

Business meetings

Getting started

1 Work with a partner and match the words from the first column with words from the second column to make reasons for holding different types of business meeting. (Although different combinations may be possible, you should use each letter only once.)

Meetings can be held in order to …

1	produce action	a	creativity
2	exchange or pass on	b	decisions
3	build	c	ideas
4	motivate	d	information
5	solve	e	plans
6	brainstorm	f	problems
7	stimulate	g	sales staff
8	take	h	teams

2 Discuss these questions with a partner.

- Do you attend any of these types of meeting?
- Which do you think are the most enjoyable? And which the least?

3 Read the following statements and decide whether you agree or disagree with them. Then compare your opinions in small groups.

1. Every meeting should have an agenda.
2. The agenda should be circulated in advance.
3. The chairperson is responsible for the success of a meeting.
4. In every meeting, there should be someone taking the minutes.
5. At the end of meetings, the participants should agree a list of action points.
6. All meetings should be for a fixed length of time.
7. If people are going to attend meetings, they should always prepare beforehand.
8. Everyone should have a chance to speak at meetings.

Talking about meetings

Listening

1 Match these verbs (1–7) with their definitions (a–g).

1	set up a meeting	a	cancel
2	chair a meeting	b	disturb
3	call off a meeting	c	lead or supervise
4	put off a meeting	d	not attend
5	adjourn a meeting	e	organise
6	skip a meeting	f	postpone
7	interrupt a meeting	g	stop temporarily

27 2 You will hear four people talking about meetings. Listen and decide which of the above things each of them had to do. Write one number by the name of each speaker.

1. Jenny: ....
2. Darron: ....
3. Shirley: ....
4. Paul: ....

76 Business meetings

A survey of meetings

Talking point

1 A recent survey in the United States revealed the information shown in these charts. Work in groups of about three and study them.

Chart 1
Percentage of managers who think their meetings are productive

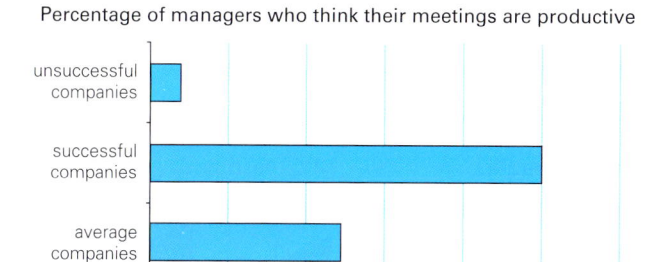

Chart 2
Division of time for senior and middle managers
- doing other things 22%
- in meetings 78%

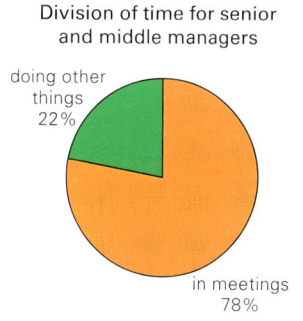

Chart 3
Number of business meetings per day in the US

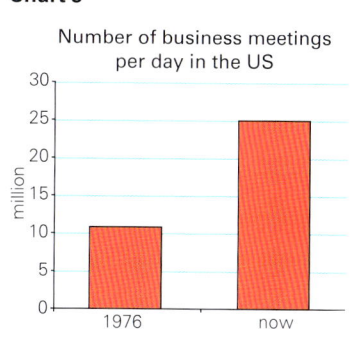

2 Prepare to present the information in the charts to someone from another group. Work with a partner from another group and take turns to present the information.

3 Discuss what might be the problem with meetings.

Think before you meet

Reading

Read the four paragraphs (A–D) and decide which one each statement below (1–8) refers to.

1 Encourage positive feedback.
2 In large organisations, meetings are essential.
3 Informal meetings tend to be more successful than formal meetings.
4 It is a good idea to check what people have understood at the meeting.
5 Large meetings often fail due to poor preparation.
6 Meetings tend to be more useful in successful companies.
7 Producing ideas should be accompanied by ways of implementing them.
8 Well-formulated questions will save a lot of time at meetings.

A Too many meetings are a waste of time

What do corporate leaders do all day? Much of their time is spent in meetings. Meetings are the cornerstone of teams, which in turn are the basis of corporate existence. But meetings, like teams, do not necessarily achieve what they set out to do. One recent study in America by Synectics, a consultancy, found that senior and middle managers spent more than three-quarters of their time in meetings. On average, only 12% of managers thought their meetings were productive. In high-performing companies, that figure rose to 25%, and in the unsuccessful ones it dropped to 2%.

B Running meetings well is clearly an art. Lots of meetings, of course, happen in the corridor or around the coffee machine, and those are probably the most efficient sort, because they tend to be spontaneous, small and quick. Bigger meetings are usually more problematic. Often, not enough thought goes into the agenda, the location, the people asked to attend and the outcome. That allows unimportant ideas to be given too much time or tedious individuals to speak too much.

C Meetings tend to be held either to share information or to solve problems. For the first sort, Roger Neill of Synectics advocates asking everyone to say at the end what they think they have heard, and correcting their accounts if they are wrong. With problem-solving, the aim should be not just brainstorming but paying proper attention to putting solutions into practice. He also thinks it is wise to ask people what they liked about the things they heard; criticism usually comes unasked. Pessimism, scepticism and challenge all cause trouble.

D David Bradford, who specialises in studying teams, argues that meetings often waste huge amounts of time. The way to get a good decision is to frame the question carefully. If you want to invest in China, do not announce that you are planning to do this, or ask the meeting whether you should. Instead, enlist your colleagues' help by saying: 'We want to be in the Chinese market: how do we get there?'

Adapted from *The Economist*

Business meetings

Vocabulary

1 Find words or phrases in the text which mean the following.

1. essential, extremely important thing (paragraph A)
2. what they want to do when they start (paragraph A)
3. unplanned (paragraph B)
4. result (paragraph B)
5. boring (paragraph B)
6. is in favour of (paragraph C)
7. doubt, not believing (paragraph C)
8. very large, enormous (paragraph D)
9. formulate, phrase (paragraph D)
10. ask for (paragraph D)

2 Complete the following sentences with a preposition. Then check your answers in the text.

1. Managers should pay more attention .... the agendas of meetings.
2. After thinking of solutions, it's important to see how these solutions can be put .... practice.
3. Martin Smith specialises .... training managers to run meetings.
4. We've decided to invest .... some new video-conferencing equipment.
5. Many meetings do not achieve what they set .... to do.

Grammar workshop: *Too* or *enough*?

1 Which of these ideas are expressed in the article?

1. Managers spend too much time in meetings.
2. Meetings aren't productive enough.
3. Most people are too busy to go to meetings.
4. Some meetings don't work because too many people have been invited.
5. People don't spend enough time preparing meetings.
6. Boring people often speak too much at meetings.
7. People aren't positive enough at meetings.

2 Complete these sentences with *too* or *enough*.

1. Most meetings go on .... long.
2. People find meetings stressful because they have .... much other work to do.
3. Not .... meetings have positive outcomes.
4. Many meetings are not organised well .... to produce outcomes.
5. Often managers are not given .... training in how to run meetings.
6. In reality, there are .... many meetings, and managers don't use .... imagination to find other ways of communicating.

➔ page 81 (*Too* and *enough*)

A business meeting

Listening

1 The following phrases (1–10) are typically said at meetings. Classify them as:

a agreeing   c asking someone's opinion
b disagreeing   d introducing your own opinion

1 ... don't you think?   6 Personally, I feel that ...
2 Frankly, I think that ...   7 That's true.
3 I'm not sure.   8 What do you think?
4 That's right.   9 Yes, and ...
5 Well, I think ...   10 Yes, but ...

28 2 You are going to hear part of a business meeting at a company which produces watches and clocks. The export manager, Barry, is discussing with colleagues how to break into the Chinese market. Listen and tick the phrases in Exercise 1 as you hear them.

28 3 Listen again, this time looking at the transcript for Track 28. Check that your answers to Exercise 1 were correct and underline any other useful phrases you hear.

Writing

Imagine you are Sandra or Mark. Write an email to Barry (40–50 words) in which you:

- agree to go to China to investigate distributors and suggesting dates
- say what promotional literature and samples you will need
- request details of expenses the company is prepared to pay for your trip.

If you need examples of how to write emails, look back at Unit 7 on pages 36–37.

> **Useful language**
>
> **Agreeing and requesting**
> I would be happy to ...
> By the way, could you please tell me ...

78 Business meetings

A meeting

Role-play

Work in groups of four. Study the background and instructions below. Each student should take one of the roles. Study your role for a few minutes and decide what you will say at the meeting. Hold a meeting to discuss the problem.

Background

You work for a large company which specialises in manufacturing and supplying high-technology medical equipment to hospitals and patients in a number of countries in your region.

Last year, the sales department's budget for travel (for example, for sales personnel to visit hospitals, health authorities, etc.) was $2m. The finance department has asked whether it would be possible to save money on this, and an initial meeting has been called to discuss the problem.

In this meeting, you will have to exchange ideas and opinions, but you needn't reach a firm decision.

A Finance Director

You think:
- significant savings could be made by using email and video conferencing to talk with customers, especially for routine visits by sales staff to existing customers.
- you would like sales staff to use economy class and low-cost airlines where possible. This could reduce travelling costs by up to 50%.
- when visiting different cities, you would prefer sales staff to go for one day only instead of staying in a hotel overnight.

B Sales Director

You think:
- face-to-face meetings are essential, both to meet potential new customers and to show existing customers new products and innovations.
- it is difficult to get high-quality sales staff who know the very specialised products which you sell, and it is important to treat them well, for example, by allowing them to fly business class.
- your staff try, as far as possible, to make several visits to different customers when they are in a different city, and this may involve a stay of several days.

C Marketing Director

You think:
- new technology (video conferencing, etc.) could replace some visits by sales staff – there are many routine visits which do not result in increased sales.
- it should be possible to reach agreements with certain airlines and hotels to arrange discounts for sales staff who use them.
- sales staff should state the objectives of each visit before they make them, so that managers can decide whether the visit is worth the cost.

D Senior Sales Manager

You think:
- your clients (doctors, hospital managers, etc.) are very busy people, and unless you actually visit them, they don't have time to look at your products.
- you spend a lot of time travelling – at least 150 days a year – and it's important to do so in comfort.
- you work in a very competitive sector where you know sales people from other companies visit your clients regularly.
- the products you sell are highly technical and very expensive. Sales staff have to make high-quality presentations and answer detailed technical questions, so face-to-face meetings are essential.

Grammar workshop 4

Units 13–16

While and whereas for contrasting ideas

- *While* and *whereas* can be used to join two sentences which have contrasting meanings:
  While/Whereas Rhône Poulenc produces chemicals, Nestlé produces food products.
- This can also be expressed:
  Rhône Poulenc produces chemicals while/whereas Nestlé produces food products.

Use these prompts to write sentences using *while* or *whereas*.

1. Marriott Hotel / situated / city centre / Hyatt Hotel / located / near airport
   While the Marriott Hotel is situated in the city centre, the Hyatt Hotel is located near the airport.
2. Expo Hotel / caters / business people / Bali Hotel / looks / tourists
3. British Airways / offers / business class and tourist class / EasyJet / has / only one class
4. Forty per cent of business travellers / choose airlines / price / 35% of business travellers choose them / schedules
5. Hilton Hotel / excellent conference facilities / Paradise Hotel / quiet / small / family-run

Modal verbs: perfect forms

- When you want to criticise people for past mistakes, you can use *should have* or *ought to have* + past participle:
  *They **should have planned** the conference better. It **ought to have been** held in a more interesting place.*
- When you want to say that something was possible, but it didn't happen, you can use *could have* + past participle:
  *They **could have held** the conference in Shanghai, but they didn't because it was too expensive.*
- When you want to say that perhaps something happened in the past, you can use *may have*, *might have* or *could have* + past participle:
  *The accident **may have happened** because the workers didn't follow safety procedures. They **might have been** smoking in a non-smoking area.*

Complete this paragraph with *should have*, *could have* or *might have* with the correct form of the verb in brackets.

My boss really irritates me. For example, he **1** *should have asked* (ask) me which was the best hotel to stay at, but he didn't because he doesn't like asking for advice. So we found ourselves staying at a noisy, ugly hotel by the motorway when we **2** .... (stay) at the luxurious lakeside hotel where all top managers go. If we had stayed there, we **3** .... (rest) between meetings, but as it was, the noise was so great that we couldn't relax at all. I don't know why he chose that hotel. It **4** .... (be) because he has already spent all the travel budget when he went to that conference in Singapore. Or he **5** .... (make) a mistake – after all, they're next to each other in the telephone book. He **6** .... (just dial) the wrong number. Still, he **7** .... (tell) me to make the booking. After all, I am his PA, and that's what I'm paid to do!

Passives 1

You use the passive when:
- you want to emphasise what happened to something, not who did it. Compare:
  Renault launched the Megane in 1997. (active: you are emphasising Renault, who did it)
  *The Megane **was launched** in 1997.* (passive: you are emphasising what happened to the Megane)
- the agent (the person/thing doing the action) is not important, or you don't want to mention who did it, or you don't know who did it:
  *The consignment **was sent** last week.* (I don't know who sent it, or it's not important.)
  *€2m of goods **were stolen** from our warehouse last weekend.* (We don't know who did it.)
- you want to use a more formal style. Compare:
  We pay salaries on the 28th of each month.
  *Salaries **are paid** on the 28th of each month.*

Make the following statements more formal by using the passive.

1. We've sent your application to head office.
   Your application *has been sent to head office.*
2. The Minister for Trade and Industry will open the conference.
   The conference ....

3 You must submit your application by 19 March.
   Your application ....
4 The Board of Directors has taken a number of important decisions this morning.
   A number of important decisions ....
5 They're interviewing candidates for the job at the moment.
   Candidates ....
6 In our manufacturing process, we reject 9% of finished articles as substandard.
   In our manufacturing process, 9% ....

3 According to the announcement, profits have reached record levels.
   It has ....
4 It is reported that Sunshine Cruises Ltd is losing money.
   Sunshine Cruises Ltd is ....
5 Most people think he is an excellent personnel director.
   He is ....
6 We expect the project will meet its deadlines.
   The project is ....

Passives 2

Here are two common passive structures:
- X is/was   believed   + infinitive with *to*
              reported
              said
              considered
              expected
              thought

  *His personal fortune **is believed to exceed** €500 million.*

- It is/was/has been   agreed   + *that* + clause
                       announced
                       believed
                       considered
                       decided
                       expected
                       explained
                       hoped
                       reported
                       said
                       suggested
                       thought

  *It **was agreed that** we should implement the new measures at the end of the financial year.*

- These are excellent structures to use when
  - you want to use a more formal style
  - you don't know, or don't want to say who thinks or said the thing.

Complete the second sentence of each pair so that it means the same as the first.

1 We expect that turnover will fall next year due to increased competition.
   Turnover is *expected to fall next year due to increased competition.*
2 We expect prices of raw materials will rise by 50% in the next six months.
   Prices of raw materials ....

Too/enough

Too and *enough* are used in the following ways:
- *too* + adjective/adverb
  *Business class is **too expensive**. Perhaps we should fly economy class.*
- *too* + *much/many* + noun
  *This project has **too many costs** – it'll never make a profit.*
- adjective/adverb + *enough*
  *She isn't **qualified enough** for this job.*
- *enough* + (adjective) + noun
  *We don't have **enough vans** to deliver all our orders.*
  *Our town has **enough comfortable hotels** for us to be able to host large conferences.*

Typical constructions are:
- *too* + *for* + noun/pronoun + infinitive with *to*
  *She spoke **too quickly for me to understand** what she was saying.*
- *enough* + plural/uncountable noun + infinitive with *to*
  *We haven't **enough resources to finish** the project on time.*

1 **Write *too*, *too many*, *too much* or *enough* in the gaps in the following sentences.**

1 Top executives of big corporations get salaries which are ...*too*... high.
2 There are not .... jobs for recently qualified graduates.
3 University courses are not focused .... on the needs of industry.
4 Most people spend .... time in the same job. They should change jobs more often.
5 There are .... men in the top jobs in industry. Women aren't given .... opportunities.
6 When travelling on business, I don't have .... time to do much sightseeing.

2 **Discuss with a partner which of the sentences you agree with and which you disagree with.**

UNIT 17

New technologies and change

Getting started

1 Work in pairs. Match these recent technologies (1–7) with the pictures (a–g).

1 video conferencing
2 laptops
3 BlackBerries
4 the Internet
5 mobile phones
6 robots
7 PDAs (Personal Digital Assistants)

2 Discuss with your partner which of these inventions you think has made the biggest difference to the way people work.

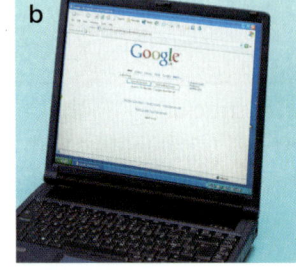

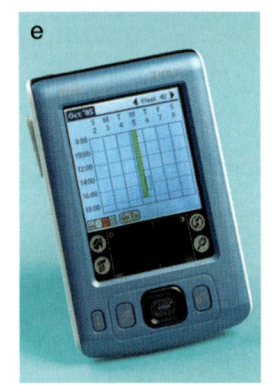

New technology

Grammar workshop

Used to

Study this sentence and answer the question which follows.

In the past, people used to work together in the same geographical area, but nowadays this is no longer necessary because you can collaborate in real time with people in different parts of the world.

What does the verb *used to* express?

A something that happened often in the past, but has now changed
B something that happened once in the past, but doesn't happen now
C something that happened often in the past and still happens now

▸ page 98 (*Used to*)

Talking point

1 Work with a partner. Choose and discuss one of these questions.

1 How have new technologies changed relationships between work colleagues?
2 How have new technologies changed relationships between businesses and customers?
3 What problems have new technologies caused in our working lives?

2 When you have finished, form groups with people who discussed other questions. Tell the others about your conclusions.

82 New technologies and change

Grammar workshop

The definite article

Read extract A. In each gap, write *the* or leave the gap blank (–).

A

Salesforce.com

Mr Benioff, **1** *the* president of Salesforce.com, wants to liberate **2** ...... firms from current practice in **3** ...... software industry. Traditionally, firms used to pay for **4** ...... new software with **5** ...... large licence fees, and then spend more money and time trying to install **6** ...... new applications on their computers and training **7** ...... employees.

With Salesforce.com's service, by contrast, **8** ...... companies rent software—for $65 per user per month. They do not need to invest in new hardware or install software on existing computers, as all **9** ...... computing takes place on Salesforce.com's machines. Users (mostly salespeople) access **10** ...... service through a web browser. Training usually takes hours rather than weeks.

> page 98 (Articles)

The Internet and change

Reading

1 Study these statements about businesses and the Internet (1–8), then read the four extracts (A–D). Which extract does each statement refer to?

1. E-commerce companies which simplify the buying process have an advantage. ☐ *C*
2. For companies, e-commerce reduces labour costs. ☐
3. Many people use the web to obtain information rather than to buy. ☐
4. Customers no longer need to speak to staff to buy a company's services. ☐
5. People visit this website to read its advertisements. ☐
6. Software purchases are not necessary for this business-to-business solution. ☐
7. The company's revenue comes from recruitment. ☐
8. Employees learn to use the applications more quickly. ☐

B

Self-service

Millions of people now manage their finances, refinance their home loans, track packages and buy cinema and theatre tickets while sitting in front of their computers. And they do all of this with no human employees in sight.

Self-service appeals to companies for an obvious reason: it saves money. The customer does the work once done by an employee, and does not expect to be paid. So to work well, self-service requires the marriage of customers with machines and software. That union is now significantly cutting costs.

C

Online travel

The majority of all travel purchases are expected to take place online within a decade. Travel websites already represent roughly 45% of all online sales in America. Yet the industry's record could be even more impressive, except for two stumbling blocks. Many people research travel options in cyberspace and then book their trip through a retail travel agent. Second, many use a number of different sites to purchase different elements of their trip. That places a premium on sites that are able to offer one-stop shopping with the lowest prices.

D

Craigslist.org

There are San Franciscans who have found their spouse, job, house and pet on Craigslist.org. The top two categories among its three million classified ads in any given month are for job vacancies (23%) and accommodation (21%).

With a billion page views a month, this is the sort of success that most dotcoms can only dream about. All the money still comes exclusively from employers advertising job vacancies; they represent less than 0.1% of all users. For everyone else, Craigslist is free. This generates a genuine sense of community.

Adapted from *The Economist*

2 Discuss the following in small groups.

- What changes in business do these extracts reflect?
- Have you bought anything online? What are the advantages and disadvantages of buying online?
- If you work for a company or organisation, does it use any of the innovations mentioned in the texts?

Vocabulary

Find words or phrases in the extracts which mean the following.

1. amount of money paid for the right to use some software (extract A)
2. computer programs/software (extract A)
3. computer equipment (extract A)
4. program which allows you to explore the web (extract A)
5. mortgages (extract B)
6. check the movements of parcels and documents (extract B)
7. ten years (extract C)
8. approximately (extract C)
9. problems (extract C)
10. puts a high value on (extract C)
11. husband or wife (extract D)
12. feeling that you are part of a group or society (extract D)

Changes at work

Listening

29 1 You are going to hear Christina Bunt, Jane Milton and Lewis Bronze talking about changes in the way people work. Which topic (A–F) does each speaker talk about?

A Company organisation   D Technology
B Offices   E Training
C Relationships   F Work location

1 Christina Bunt ....
2 Jane Milton ....
3 Lewis Bronze ....

29 2 Listen to the three speakers again. Which of these opportunities or difficulties (A–F) does each speaker mention?

A Increased opportunity for promotion
B The ability to work at any time of day
C The difficulty of meeting customers
D The difficulty of supervising staff
E The opportunity to sell more products
F The speed at which people have to work

1 Christina Bunt ....
2 Jane Milton ....
3 Lewis Bronze ....

Company background

Founded in 1982, Adobe today is one of the world's largest software companies, with an annual turnover of more than US$1.2 billion and more than 3,700 employees. Adobe has its headquarters in San Jose, California.

Change at Adobe Systems

Reading

1 Work in pairs. Briefly predict the answers to these two questions.

1 What are Adobe's main products?
2 What do you think is the main motivation for working for a company like Adobe?

2 Scan the article on page 85 to see if you were correct.

3 Read the article again and choose the best answer for questions 1–5 below it.

4 Discuss the following in small groups.

1 What changes did Adobe make in order to be successful?
2 Describe how your company, or a company you know well has changed in recent times.
3 What is important when making changes in a company?

Talking point

Work in pairs and do the following task.

Your company is planning to introduce some new computer technology to improve the way the company looks after its customers. You have been asked to plan its introduction.

Discuss the situation together and decide:
- how computer technology can improve services to customers (e.g. by keeping more complete databases, by allowing the company to target individual customers)
- how employees can be prepared for these changes.

84 New technologies and change

Ability to change is essential in the new business environment, as we found out when we talked to Bruce Chizen of Adobe Systems

Adobe Systems is a software company which survived the dot-com crash of the late 90s. As Bruce Chizen, its CEO, recalls, 'By that time, we had already refocused our business. Our strategy had several elements. First, we said we were going to focus our key markets. In other words, we were going to concentrate on creative professionals and people who really cared about the *quality* of the information they communicated.' They also decided to focus on documents and to streamline the company.

'Our mission hasn't changed,' he adds, 'It's always been about developing, designing, marketing, selling software to help people to communicate better. But being able to stay with what we do well – and then growing the number of our constituents (people who use our programmes) – was a major transformation for the company.

'The biggest growth opportunity for Adobe is around documents. On the desktop, our approach has been to use Acrobat. To date, we've only sold about 14 million new units of Acrobat. According to Microsoft, there are at least 200 million knowledge workers who have Microsoft Office. We believe at least 60 million of them want to send reliable documents – either through email, or on the web, or through networks. We think Acrobat is a great solution for that.'

The company has gone through various transformations. One involved changing the way they did business. The second involved focusing on new products. And the third involved moving toward new customer bases, especially business clients.

But, as Chizen recognises, the key to successful change is the people working for the company. 'Employment was easy and attractive, so someone who left Adobe could get a job somewhere else with relatively little risk and a great deal of upside. In fact, back then, 20% of the people in the company were leaving on an annual basis, which is a lot. So the people who chose to stay really saw the potential in this company. And because we had committed employees, the motivation to change was there.

'It was important that the employees felt proud about what they were doing; that they believed what they were doing was having an impact on the world. For example, the type you see is probably an Adobe font. The image you see on the web was probably touched by Adobe Photoshop. The title effect you see in a movie was probably enhanced by Adobe After Effects. And just about any important document you see on the web is communicated with PDF and Acrobat.

'The fact that we have had *that* kind of impact on society – and the belief that we could continue to have that impact on society – is, I believe, what has motivated our employees more than anything else. It certainly wasn't the money, because they could have gone to a lot of other places to get rich. It was the *potential* that we had as an organisation, the richness of technology and innovation, and our ability to direct that against real customer solutions.'

Adapted from www.knowledge@warton.com

---

1 How did Adobe survive the dot-com crash?
   A They changed before it happened.
   B They changed their markets.
   C They took on new staff.
   D They reduced the size of the company.

2 According to paragraph 2, what is Adobe's main objective?
   A To become the world's largest software company.
   B To become a telecommunications company.
   C To make products which improve how people exchange information.
   D To diversify their product range.

3 What represents Adobe's main business opportunity?
   A A new operating system.
   B A word-processing program.
   C A program for producing web pages.
   D A program for transmitting documents.

4 Why did employees stay with Adobe?
   A They were afraid of being unemployed.
   B They thought the company had a good future.
   C They enjoyed working for Adobe.
   D They did not want to change their lifestyles.

5 What, according to Chizen, has motivated Adobe's employees?
   A They are paid more than in other companies.
   B The variety of products they make.
   C The belief that all businesses use Adobe's products.
   D The way Adobe's products are changing the world.

New technologies and change

UNIT 18

Using the Internet

Getting started

1 Discuss the following in small groups.

- Which are your favourite websites?
- Why do you visit them, and how often do you visit them?
- Which of these are the most important characteristics of a good website?
  - good graphics
  - easy navigation
  - interesting information
  - fun to visit
  - useful links
  - helpful with your work or studies
  - other

2 Match these words (1–9) with their definitions (a–i).

1	to click	a	connected to the Internet
2	user-friendly	b	easy to operate
3	to download	c	to press the mouse button
4	cyberspace	d	to search the Internet
5	to browse	e	the imaginary place where Internet data exists
6	search engine	f	to transfer information from the Internet to a computer
7	portal	g	website which helps you to find other websites
8	online	h	first/front page of a website
9	home page	i	website which provides information and links to other websites

E-shopping at Tesco.com

Listening

1 Look at the sentences on the right and decide what sort of word (noun, verb, etc.) will fit each gap, and what sort of information is needed in the context.

2 Listen to Christina Bunt talking about the Internet and Tesco supermarkets. For each gap, write one or two words or a number.

Online shopping at Tesco involves an employee from your
1 .... doing your shopping for you.
In Cornwall, the number of online stores has increased from two to 2 ....
The main advantage of having a website is that it provides
3 .... between the company and its customers.
A good website is one where everything can be found on the 4 ....
She uses Tesco.com because if she does her own shopping, she will be 5 .... as an employee.

Talking point

Discuss the following with your partner.

Which of these is important when buying over the Internet? Put them in order of importance:

- Good description of product or service
- The product or service is not available in shops
- The product or service is cheaper or easier to buy on the Internet
- Quick delivery
- Secure method of payment
- Other

Vocabulary

1 Label this screenshot of a web page using the words in the box.

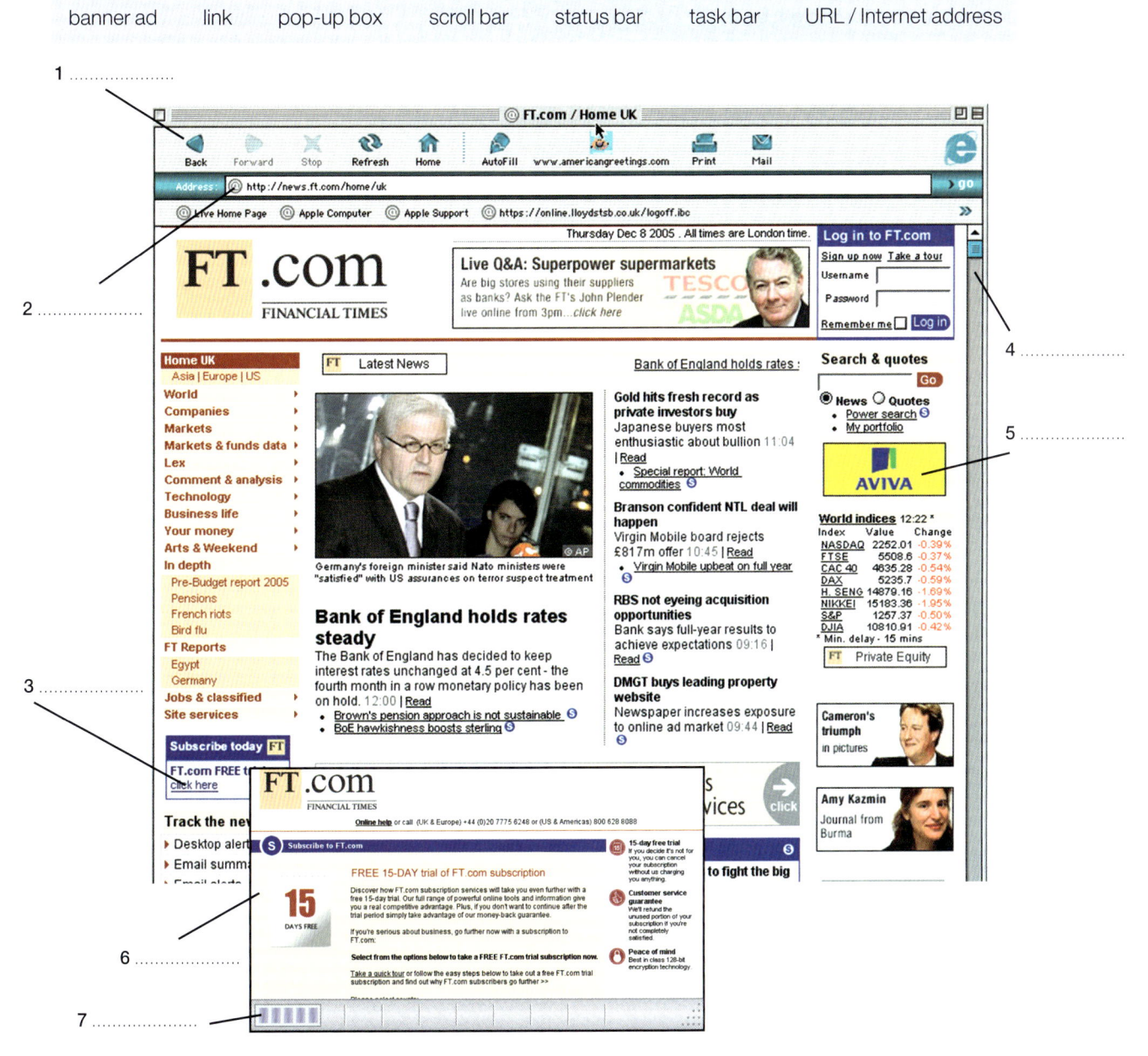

banner ad   link   pop-up box   scroll bar   status bar   task bar   URL / Internet address

1 ....

2 ....

3 ....

4 ....

5 ....

6 ....

7 ....

Adapted from http://news.ft.com/home/uk

2 Now complete these sentences with one of the words or phrases from the box above.

1 If you want to go to another part of the website or to a different website, you can click on a .... on this web page.
2 To get the website you want, you need to type in the ....
3 There are all sorts of useful icons on the ...., such as *Favourites* and *History*.
4 Look at the .... to see whether you have downloaded all the elements of a website.
5 You can click on the .... if you want to move a web page up or down.
6 Sometimes if you click on a link, another part of the website will appear in a ....

Talking point

Work in pairs. Imagine your partner is new to using the Internet. Take turns to explain how to reach one of your favourite websites and how to print out a page from it. Use some of the vocabulary from the exercise above.

Using the Internet   **87**

Website design

Reading

1 In pairs, discuss what you think might be the answers to questions 1–8 about website design. If you have no idea, move on to the next question.

1 How can you make your site easy to navigate?
2 How long do people look at a web page before deciding if it's useful or interesting?
3 Why is it difficult to create a website which is simple?
4 What should be the main purpose of a company's website?
5 When is text more important than graphics?
6 When should you use good graphics on a website?
7 Why is it important to avoid advertising language?
8 Why is it important to update your site regularly?

2 Read either Text A or Text B and find answers to the questions above. You will not find answers to all of them because some may be in the other text.

Text A

Some rules of website design

Understand your site's purpose
The visual appearance of a website depends entirely on the objectives you want it to achieve. For information-rich sites, the emphasis should be on straightforward navigation rather than fancy graphics. Think of how Yahoo! and other portals present their material. If, however, your main objective is to consolidate your brand identity, it may be more appropriate to limit the amount of text on the site and concentrate on the graphics. A website is the starting point for your relationship with a target audience.

Keep it human
There is no set way of designing a website. Designers use images, formats and links to each other to create pages. According to the *New York Times'* David Weinberger, 'this makes the web unpredictable, creative and always the result of human hands'.

Be imperfect
The aim should be to start a two-way conversation with your target audience, not to tell them that this is the only way things can be done.

Avoid the language of advertising
Most people now appreciate that having your page turn up in the top search engine finds is far more effective than web advertising. If the role of advertising is to present the best possible face of a company, this is made redundant by the nature of the web, where criticism will always be there: just ask Nike or McDonalds. The speed of 'word of mouth' online is restricted only by how fast people can type, so it is worth remembering that when designing a website, honesty is always the best policy.

Keep it simple
This is perhaps the most important rule of website design, yet it takes a lot of time and effort to keep things straightforward. Stephen Freeman, creative brain for Retail.co.uk, draws attention to this. 'Simple isn't easy,' he says. 'Sites that are confusing and filled with flashing gizmos that perform clever tricks without reason are the ones which were created in an afternoon.' Take a look at Epic Heroes (www.epicheroes.com) and The Organic Shop (www.theorganicshop.com) for inspiration.

Adapted from *The Guardian*

Text B

Some rules of website design

Use straightforward navigation
There are a number of ways you can make it easy for people to find their way around your site. One way is to make sure no page of your website is further than three clicks away from any other. Another is to tell people where they are. You can do this by providing a site map or by changing the colour of the current section in the navigation area.

Satisfy itchy fingers
Goldfish are said to have an attention span of five seconds, which is approximately two seconds longer than a visitor to your website. If they are visiting your site via a search engine, they may have up to ten other sites they want to visit before they log off. The trick is to make your design stimulating while keeping it user-friendly. Slow download times, repetitive text and lengthy e-commerce processes must therefore be avoided.

Less is more
As web software has developed over the years, many web designers have felt the urge to demonstrate all these advances simultaneously on one web page. Multiple animated images, blinking text, Javascript status-bar messages, rainbow-coloured divider bars and pop-up windows may signify hard work on the part of the designer, but will also result in hard work on the part of the user.

Update your site
A week is a long time in cyberspace. Internet time is believed to move at seven times the velocity of normal time. Many people who browse the Internet return to the same sites every day. Information needs to be updated at regular intervals to keep a website fresh.

Adapted from *The Guardian*

3 Discuss your answers with your partner.

4 Change partners. Work with someone who read the other text and exchange your information so that you have answers to all the questions.

Vocabulary

Find words in the two texts which mean the following.

1. simple, uncomplicated (Text A, paragraph 1)
2. strengthen (Text A, paragraph 1)
3. the people who you want to visit your website (Text A, paragraph 1)
4. unnecessary (Text A, paragraph 4)
5. things which are more complicated than necessary (Text A, paragraph 5)
6. restless, wanting to move (Text B, paragraph 2)
7. speed (Text B, paragraph 4)
8. brought up to date (Text B, paragraph 4)

Websites and business

Listening

1 Read the following questions and underline the key words in each one so that when you listen, you are sure what you are listening for.

2 Listen to Jane Milton talking about the Internet and her company's website. Answer the questions by choosing the correct option.

1. What disadvantage of email does Jane mention?
   A She receives too many emails.
   B Most emails are just publicity.
   C Her email breaks down frequently.
2. What was the advantage of using the web to find American-style lunch boxes?
   A It was quicker.
   B It was cheaper.
   C It was the only way to find them.
3. According to Jane, what is the main advantage of using the Internet for research?
   A You can easily build a database of information.
   B You can build up a good list of contacts.
   C You can do the research more quickly.
4. What does Jane say is the problem with many websites?
   A They are only for consumers.
   B They are only for people in the trade.
   C They are not directed at a definite target audience.
5. What is the purpose of Jane's website?
   A To encourage people to get in touch with her.
   B To entertain people.
   C To explain her company's services.

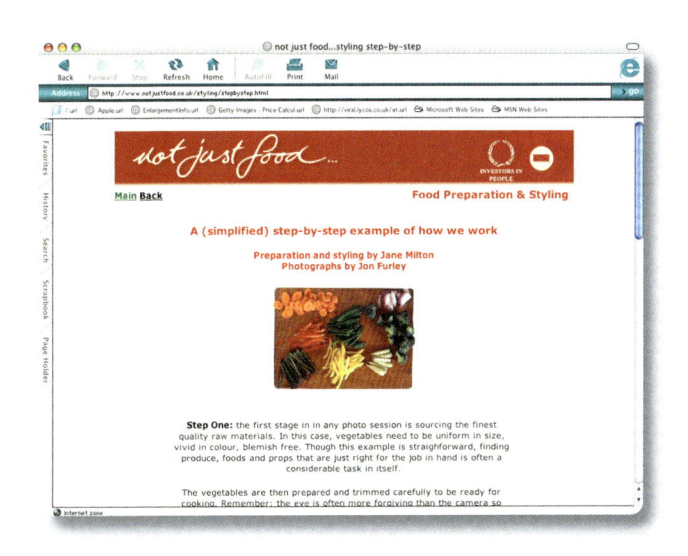

6. How does she think technology will change things in the future?
   A People will work more from home.
   B People will do more shopping from home.
   C She finds it hard to predict the future.

3 Discuss the following in small groups.

- How do you think new technologies will change the way we work in the future?
- How do you think they will change the way we shop?

Upgrading a website

Writing

1 Work in pairs. Read the following writing task.

Your manager has asked you to contact a web-design company in order to upgrade the company website. Write an email to Olga Strauss at High Performance Web Design:

- giving your company's web address
- saying why the website needs upgrading
- saying how you think it should be changed
- asking for an estimate of how much it will cost.

Write about 50 words.

2 Discuss what information and ideas you should include in the email.

3 Work alone and write the email.

4 When you have finished, compare your email with those of other students.

UNIT 19

A staff survey

Getting started

1 You work for the human resources department of a company which produces machine tools. Recently you have been considering changes in working practices. Before implementing the changes, you carried out a staff survey to get employees' reactions. Study the results.

RESULTS OF STAFF SURVEY

	Would be interested	Not interested	No opinion
Flexible working hours	76%	13%	11%
Career breaks	29%	37%	34%
Optional part-time working	17%	48%	65%

Additional staff request:
Nursery facilities for small children

2 Work in small groups and discuss the following.
1 Which change would involve staff choosing:
   a to work a shorter week?
   b to take time away from work, e.g. to travel or study?
   c when to start and stop work?
2 What would be the benefits of the changes?

A working party

Listening

Your assistant invited staff members to form a working party to discuss possible changes. You are going to hear part of what they said when they met.

1 Before you listen, check that you know what each of the following jobs, benefits and problems means.

Jobs

A Production manager
B Human resources director
C Managing director's PA
D Accounts manager
E Shopfloor worker
F Maintenance engineer
G Team leader
H Delivery driver

Benefits or problems

I Higher productivity
J Better work-life balance
K Lower staff turnover
L Lower costs
M An opportunity to do other things
N Less stress
O More motivated staff
P Lower absenteeism

2 Listen to five extracts from the interviews and decide which job each person does. Write a letter A–H in the table below.

	Job	Benefit/ problem
1 Linda		
2 Brian		
3 Olga		
4 Dan		
5 Martin		

3 Listen again and decide which benefit or problem (I–P) each person mentions and write it in the second column of the table.

90   A staff survey

Reading a report

Reading

1 Read the report based on the survey. For each gap, choose the best word.

Task tip

Read the sentence carefully before choosing the word.
- Which word has the right meaning?
- Is there a dependent preposition?
- Is it part of a collocation (words often found together)?

REPORT ON STAFF SURVEY

Introduction

The aim of this report is to summarise points which have **1** ..A.. from our recent staff survey about changes in working practices.

Reasons for changes

Staff **2** ...... represents a major cost in our company. It involves **3** ...... recruitment processes and staff training. We hope that by introducing these changes we will increase staff retention, motivation and efficiency.

Opinions of staff

A large **4** ...... of our staff (three-quarters) said that they would be interested in flexible working. Several people stated that they **5** ...... travelling to work at **6** ...... times stressful and time-consuming.

A significant number of our employees (29%) thought that career breaks would be attractive. One **7** ...... of staff told me that he had always wanted to travel round the world, and that he would like to return to his job **8** ....

A smaller percentage expressed interest in optional part-time working. These were generally people with young children. Several employees asked me if we could provide on-site nursery care for pre-school children.

Recommendations

I believe we should go **9** ...... with these changes because staff reactions have been generally positive and because employees can choose whether to take **10** ...... of the changes or not.

1	A arisen	B raised	C rose	D risen
2	A outcome	B turnover	C changeover	D downturn
3	A pricey	B valuable	C extravagant	D costly
4	A variety	B quantity	C majority	D range
5	A suffered	B experienced	C found	D discovered
6	A top	B high	C key	D peak
7	A worker	B member	C colleague	D partner
8	A next	B after	C following	D afterwards
9	A on	B up	C ahead	D into
10	A for granted	B advantage	C note	D hold

2 Read the report again and answer these questions.

1 Why is the report divided into sections with headings?
2 Does the report contain all the figures from the results table on page 90? Why?/Why not?
3 Does the report contain all the opinions from the table on page 90?
4 What action does the writer say should be taken? Where is this in the report?
5 Does the writer give reasons for his/her opinions? Where?

Expressing numbers

Vocabulary

1 Look at these phrases from the report:

*a large majority   a significant number
a smaller percentage*

Which means:

1 less than the number already mentioned?
2 most people?
3 not a majority, but a number which is worth taking into consideration?

2 Match these phrases (1–7) with their meanings (a–g).

1 a tiny minority of staff
2 growing numbers of staff
3 a substantial majority of staff
4 a limited number of staff
5 around half the staff
6 just over half the staff
7 the vast majority of staff

a approximately 50% of staff
b slightly more than 50% of staff
c not many staff
d nearly all staff
e much more than 50% of staff
f an increasing number of staff
g a very small number of staff

Grammar workshop

Reported speech

1 Look at the way this staff opinion was reported.

A large majority of our staff (three-quarters) said that they would be interested in flexible working.
The speakers' original words were '*We would be interested in flexible working.*'

▶ **page 99** (Reported speech)

Tense changes in reported speech
These are some of the changes you make when putting direct speech into reported speech:

- Present simple → past simple:
  '*I **work** for Ford.*' → She said (that) she **worked** for Ford.
- Present continuous → past continuous:
  '*I'm doing the accounts.*' → He said (that) he **was doing** the accounts.
- Present perfect → past perfect:
  '*I've written the report.*' → She said (that) she **had written** the report.
- Past simple → past perfect:
  '*I **missed** the meeting.*' → He told me (that) he **had missed** the meeting.
- Will → would: '*Profits **will** rise.*' → She predicted (that) profits **would** rise.
- These modal verbs also change:
  – can → could:
  '*I **can** see you at ten o'clock.*' → She said (that) she **could** see me at ten o'clock.
  – may → might:
  '*Costs **may** fluctuate.*' → He stated (that) costs **might** fluctuate.
- *Would* and *must* do not normally change:
  '*I **would** prefer to work in London.*' → She said (that) she **would** prefer to work in London.

---

2 Look at these things which people said when they were interviewed for a staff survey. Put them into reported speech.

1 'I find travelling to work at peak times stressful and time-consuming.'
One worker told me that she *found travelling to work at peak times stressful and time-consuming*.
2 'If the new scheme is introduced, I hope I'll be able to take a career break.'
The accountant told me that if …
3 'I have always wanted to travel round the world.'
One employee said that she …
4 'Can you provide on-site nursery care for pre-school children?'
Several members of staff asked me if we …
5 'In my last job, we used flexitime, and it was very successful.'
One person told me that in her last job, they …
6 'If you introduce these changes, I may decide to work part-time.'
One of the secretaries said that if …

Grammar workshop: Reporting verbs

- Some reporting verbs must take an indirect object (in reported speech, the indirect object is the person or people the speaker is addressing):
  He **told me** the meeting was cancelled.
- Some reporting verbs cannot take an indirect object:
  She **said** that the price was too high. NOT *She said me that the price was too high.*
- Other verbs can work both ways:
  He **asked me** how much the work would cost.
  He **asked** how much the work would cost.

1 Find these reporting verbs in the report (in the past tense) and say which have to take an indirect object and which can't. Write them in the table below.

ask   say   state   tell   think

Must have indirect object	Can't have indirect object	Both
tell	say	ask

92 A staff survey

2 Read the following sentences and decide whether each of the reporting verbs needs an indirect object and add them to the table in Exercise 1.

1 She predicted that prices would rise by 5%.
   'Prices will rise by 5%.'
2 My boss has ordered me to carry out a security check.
3 I informed them that there would be budget cutbacks in the next financial year.
4 He requested her to book the flights.
5 Several customers are demanding that we return their money.
6 Mrs Jones enquired how much the flights cost.
7 She promised me that she would meet the deadline.
8 He promised to look into the problem as soon as possible.
9 The CEO answered that they had no plans to close the factory at present.

3 Write the actual words which the speaker used for each sentence in Exercise 2.

A survey report

Writing

1 Your company's offices were built 30 years ago and they are urgently in need of modernisation. There have been several proposals for what changes should be made to the offices. You were asked to carry out a staff survey to get staff feedback on the proposed changes and then write a report for the Board of Directors. Look at the charts below which reflect staff opinions.

2 Work in pairs and:
- discuss what the charts show
- decide what section headings the report should have
- discuss which phrases from the vocabulary exercise expressing numbers would be useful.

3 Work alone and write your report.

Chart 1: How should we change our offices?
- 27% New offices in city centre
- 4% No opinion
- 23% Modernise existing offices
- 46% New offices in same area

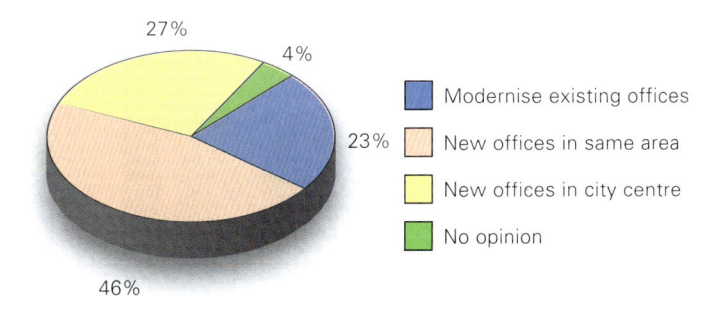

Chart 2: What do you think is the best layout for the offices?
- 15% Individual offices for managers, the rest open plan
- 13% No opinion
- 20% Individual offices
- 52% Open-plan offices

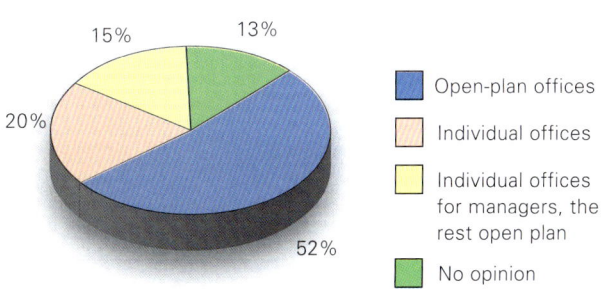

Chart 3: Do you mind working in artificial light?
- 90% All workstations with natural light
- 10% No opinion

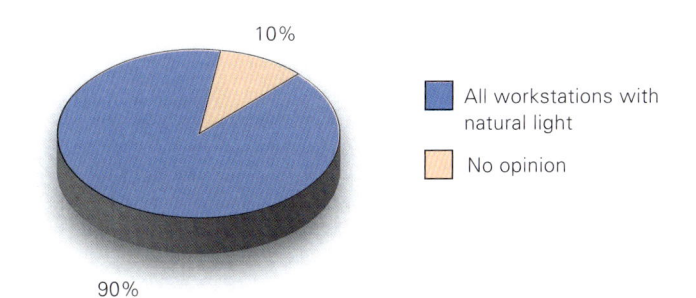

Additional staff request:
Informal rest areas and meeting areas.

UNIT 20

Offshoring and outsourcing

Getting started

Offshoring is when a company moves part of its activities to another country, perhaps because costs are lower or to be closer to their markets. For example, a car manufacturer in Japan might move a factory to Britain. It may include outsourcing the activity to a company in another country.

Outsourcing involves employing a different company to do part of the work your company needs. For example, instead of having an accountant working for your company, you pay a specialised accountancy firm to do the accounts for you.

Can outsourcing work for small businesses?

Reading

Discuss the following in small groups.

1 What do you think are the advantages of offshoring for:
- the company?
- the receiving country?
- the customers?

2 What are the disadvantages?

You can talk about:
- costs and prices
- flexibility
- employment
- efficiency
- customer services

Company background
Hoyt Corporation is a family-owned company based in Westport, Massachusetts USA, which produces dry-cleaning equipment for ships.

1 Skim the following article to find the answer to the question in the title.

Can outsourcing work for small businesses?

John Olinger has no plans to offshore customer-service tasks from his 40-person manufacturing firm to an overseas location. Wages may be cheaper for workers in Asia, but he is sticking with his staff of three customer-service representatives. That's partly because Olinger, president of Hoyt Corporation, doubts he could find overseas staff with the right expertise for his business, which makes dry-cleaning equipment for military submarines and ships. 'It's pretty difficult to find customer-service reps for our industry,' he said. 'It's pretty specialised.'

On the other hand, Olinger has outsourced his payroll operations to a domestic firm called ADP for roughly three years. To Olinger, outsourcing payroll tasks is an obvious solution for a small business like his. He says ADP saves him from having to hire an extra employee to manage the payroll – for less than half the cost of an employee. At the same time, he says, ADP provides better service than an employee of his own could. 'It's absolutely crazy to keep payroll in-house these days,' he says.

Hoyt is like a lot of other small US businesses when it comes to outsourcing decisions. Small family businesses and other small organisations are quite comfortable contracting with other companies or independent professionals for tasks such as tax advice, graphic design work or computer systems help.

But small companies in the United States appear to limit outsourcing activity to their own country. Large companies have been employing overseas firms for services such as call centres. Yet the offshore outsourcing phenomenon is not reaching down to the level of small companies, and probably won't for the foreseeable future, says Debashish Sinha, an analyst with market-research firm Gartner.

According to Sinha, offshoring generally involves setting up an office or other facility abroad. That only makes sense when the company wants to transfer a significant amount of work offshore. You need a minimum amount of work in order for this model to be cost effective. For example, Sinha says, it wouldn't be wise to offshore customer-care contact centre operations unless the contact centre is going to employ 50 people or more.

Adapted from knowledge@warton.com

2 Read the article again more carefully and choose the best answer for these questions.

1 What reason does John Olinger give for not outsourcing customer service work?
   A He believes it will cost more.
   B His main customers are in the United States.
   C He would not find staff who knew enough about his products.
   D His firm is not big enough.
2 What reason does he give for outsourcing payroll operations?
   A It costs him less.
   B An employee would not do the work well enough.
   C The job requires little intelligence.
   D He cannot afford to employ someone in-house for this.
3 According to Debashish Sinha, why do smaller companies not outsource offshore?
   A They do not have the technology to manage it.
   B Their volume of work does not justify it.
   C Overseas companies are not interested in small businesses.
   D There are enough good professionals available locally.

Vocabulary

Find words or phrases in the passage which mean the following.

1 not changing (paragraph 1)
2 knowledge (paragraph 1)
3 management of salary payments to employees (paragraph 2)
4 employ (paragraph 2)
5 places which deal with telephone enquiries for large organisations (paragraph 4)
6 future which can be predicted (paragraph 4)

What should we offshore?

Listening

1 You will hear two senior managers discussing which parts of the company to move offshore. Predict the problem they will mention for each of these departments.

Department	Problem
Information systems	Management may take more time
Administrative work	Training
Customer services	Keeping company secrets

2 Listen and check whether you were correct.

3 Write each of these words and phrases in the table below.

Don't you think so?
Maybe.
Possibly, but …
Sorry, could you explain that again?
That's true, but …
True.
We could consider …

I suppose so.
What do you mean by that?
What do you think?
What else could we outsource?
What else?
Yes, but …
You could be right.

Asking for clarification	Asking someone else's opinion	Agreeing	Disagreeing	Asking for more suggestions	Making suggestions	Being non-committal
	Don't you think so?					

Offshoring and outsourcing **95**

4 Complete the dialogue.

Margaret Things really are getting expensive in this country, and there's no doubt that we could do things more cheaply if we offshored some of our activities.

Jeremy What 1 *do you mean* by that? Moving parts of the business abroad, or outsourcing parts of the business to overseas companies?

Margaret I'm not sure, really. Perhaps outsourcing to companies abroad would be easier and more logical. What do 2 ....?

Jeremy You 3 .... right. But which parts of the business should we outsource?

Margaret Well, we could outsource the IT department. Lots of companies do that.

Jeremy 4 .... , but the problem with that is confidentiality.

Margaret But there are ways of dealing with that, just like we have to protect confidentiality inside our company.

Jeremy I suppose so. 5 .... could we outsource?

Margaret Perhaps some of the back-office administrative work – for example, the salaries and other parts of the accounting.

Jeremy Maybe. Nowadays it's easy to keep in contact – with intranets and email – although it may be a bit more time-consuming giving instructions or sorting out mistakes.

Margaret Possibly. But you just have to pick up the telephone and call them.

Jeremy That's 6 .... Anyway, it's worth looking into.

Margaret I think so. What 7 ....?

Jeremy We could consider outsourcing the customer service department. You know, they do all their work by telephone anyway, so nowadays with cheap telecommunications and so on, it should be possible to get someone abroad to do the same thing much more cheaply.

Margaret That's true. But they'd have to be given courses …

Jeremy Including pronunciation courses.

Margaret 8 .... There's just something that worries me, though.

Jeremy What's that?

Margaret How are we going to break the news to the staff?

Jeremy Yes, that could be a problem.

Margaret A major problem, I reckon.

4 5 Listen again to check your answers.

Role-play

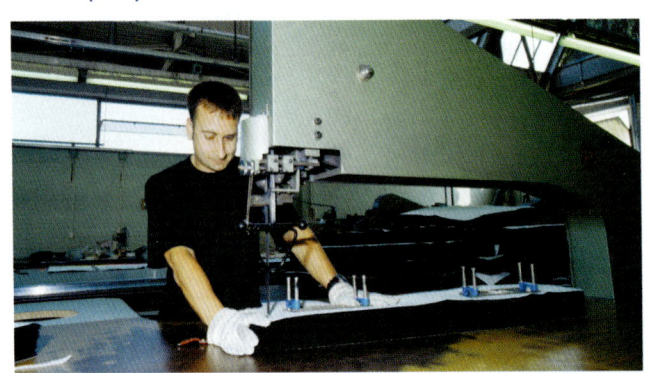

1 Work in pairs or groups of three. You work for a clothing manufacturer with about 1,500 employees based in Western Europe. Your company is considering moving some of its activities offshore. You have been asked to think about how the company could be restructured.
Study the figures in the table below. Then discuss the situation together and decide:

- which of the company's activities could be offshored (some of the options are: the factory, administration, customer service, accounts)
- how your existing staff should be informed of these changes.

	Home	Offshore
Wages	€25,000	€15,000
Production costs (average per item of clothing)	€5	€3
Offshoring costs spread over 10 years*		€10m
Training costs spread over 10 years**		€1m

* including management travel, communications, setting up offshore facilities
** including job-training and language training

96 Offshoring and outsourcing

2 You have been asked to present your ideas on offshoring to the Board of Directors. Prepare two short presentations together, answering the questions below.

1 What is important when considering moving company activities offshore?
2 Which of your company's activities should be moved offshore and why?

3 Each of you should give one of the presentations to the Board (your class), who should decide on a plan of action.

Offshoring from Britain

Listening

1 Match the words and phrases (1–10) with their definitions (a–j).

1	to make redundant	a	to stop employing someone, usually because there is not enough work for them
2	assurance	b	a person who owns shares in a company
3	shareholder	c	a promise
4	prime	d	a reduction in a country's or a business's economic activity
5	to generate profits	e	at risk
6	downturn	f	to keep their customers
7	exposed	g	main or most important
8	insecure	h	not safe or not protected
9	back office	i	part of the office which clients and the public do not see, which deals with the internal administration of the company
10	to maintain their client base	j	to produce profits

2 A British company has just announced that it is offshoring some of its activities to India. Listen to part of a radio news report where people connected with the company express their opinions. Look at the list (A–E) below and decide what connection each person has with the company.

1 Molly: ....
2 Arthur: ....
3 Karen: ....

A employee
B shareholder
C customer
D manager
E supplier

3 Listen again and complete the reporter's notes with one or two words in each gap.

Molly Tyler
Main disadvantage:
• staff will be 1 ....
Advantages:
• savings in 2 ....
• offshoring IT systems will make company 3 ....

Arthur Brown
Disadvantages:
• will move 4 .... overseas
• will stop buying their 5 ....

Karen Weinberg
Advantage:
• lower 6 ....
Disadvantage:
• lower 7 ....

Outsourcing and offshoring – the pros and cons

Role-play

Work in pairs or groups of three.

You work for a large company which manufactures household electrical appliances. The company produces many of the components for the appliances; it manufactures and markets the tools; it has its own transport and distribution department; it owns several warehouses in different countries to aid storage and distribution of its products; and it has a large customer service department, including after-sales service.

With competition from abroad becoming increasingly fierce, your Board of Directors has decided that your company is too exposed to risk.

You have been asked to prepare a report about the situation and to suggest ways of reducing the company's exposure to risk. Discuss the situation together, and decide:

• what risks your company faces
• how outsourcing could reduce those risks
• which parts of your company could be outsourced.

Offshoring and outsourcing **97**

Grammar workshop 5

Units 17–20
Used to

> - Form:
>   Positive: *used to* + infinitive
>   Negative: *didn't use to* + infinitive
>   Questions: *Did … use to* + infinitive ?
> - You use *used to* to describe:
>   - states in the past:
>   *Air travel **used to be** more expensive, in real terms, than it is now.*
>   - repeated actions in the past:
>   *I **used to do** much of my work by telephone, but now I communicate by email.*
> - *Used to* describes things which are not true now. It makes a comparison between past situations or behaviour and the present. *Used to* can only be used in the past. If you want to talk about states or repeated actions in the present, you can say:
>   *He is usually in his office on Monday mornings. He usually spends his first hour planning his week.*

1 Choose the correct forms in these sentences.

1 Our staff *used to complain / were complaining* about the new technology we had installed until we *used to give / gave* them a training course.
2 When I was the finance director, I *was watching / used to watch* the marketing budget very closely.
3 Until the new accounting software *was / used to be* installed, *hadn't you found / didn't you use to find* it very time-consuming making tax returns?
4 Staff *used to use / have used* email for private correspondence, but now we *have installed / used to install* the new monitoring software, they *didn't use to do / don't do* it.
5 I *used to dictate / was dictating* them to a tape recorder called a Dictaphone, and then a typist *used to type / had typed* them up.

2 Complete these sentences in any way you like.

1 When I was at school, we used to …
2 Before the invention of mobile phones, people didn't use to …
3 Before the Internet, we never used to …
4 Software didn't use to …

Articles

> **The definite article**
> - You use *the*:
>   - with things you have mentioned before or it's clear who/what you are referring to:
>   *Sonia bought a laptop from a department store. **The** store assistant told her **the** laptop had a three-year guarantee.*
>   - with things which are unique:
>   ***the** Internet, **the** world*
>   - when the noun is followed by *of*:
>   ***the** introduction of new technology*
>   - when the noun is followed by a defining relative clause:
>   ***The** programme we find most useful is Excel.*
>   - with adjectives to express groups:
>   ***the** unemployed, **the** rich*
>   - with superlatives:
>   ***the** best, **the** longest*
> - You do not use *the*:
>   - when talking in general:
>   ***Business people** prefer **luxury hotels**.*
>   - when using abstract nouns:
>   ***Technology** has changed the way we do **business**.*
>
> **The indefinite article**
> - You use *a* or *an* with singular, countable nouns:
>   ***a** computer, **an** interesting meeting*
> - You do not use *a* or *an* with plural or uncountable nouns:
>   *Companies try to make profits.*
>   *Money is the basis of business.*
> - Notes:
>   - You use *an* before vowels, e.g. *an email,* but not when *u* produces the sound of a consonant, e.g. *a useful suggestion, a united management team*.
>   - When *h* is silent, you use *an*, e.g. *an hour, an honest man*.

1 Write *a*, *an* or – in the gaps in this memo.

To: All staff
From: Office manager

Following **1** ...an... inspection by the health and safety officer from **2** .... headquarters, which was carried out **3** .... month ago, I have been asked to hold **4** .... fire practice sometime during the next fortnight.

Please ensure that **5** .... furniture and other things are not blocking **6** .... safety exits. During the inspection, **7** .... empty box was found on the fire escape. In the event of **8** .... emergency, this could have caused **9** .... unpleasant accident.

10 .... copy of the emergency procedures is posted on the noticeboard next to the photocopier.

2 Write *a*, *an*, *the* or – in the gaps in the following article. In some cases, more than one answer is possible.

Lisa Hook, **1** .... executive at AOL, one of **2** .... biggest providers of **3** .... traditional Internet access, has learned amazing things by listening in on **4** .... calls to AOL's help desk. Usually, **5** .... problem is that **6** .... users cannot get online. **7** .... help desk's first question is: 'Do you have **8** .... computer?' Surprisingly often **9** .... answer is no, and **10** .... customer was trying to put **11** .... installation CD into **12** .... TV set.

Genevieve Bell, **13** .... anthropologist who works for Intel, **14** .... world's biggest semiconductor-maker, has been travelling around Asia to observe how **15** .... Asians use **16** .... technology. She was especially struck by **17** .... differences in how **18** .... westerners and Asians view their homes. Americans tended to furnish them as **19** .... playground, says Ms Bell. **20** .... Asians were more likely to tell her that 'my home is **21** .... place of **22** .... harmony and **23** .... simplicity'. These Asians recoiled from **24** .... gadgets that made **25** .... noises or looked showy or intrusive.

Reported speech

- You usually make the following changes:
  - *you* → *he/she/they*:
    'Could you come into my office?' → He asked her to come into his office.
  - *your* → *his/her/their*; *our* → *their*:
    'Where are your headquarters?' → He asked where their headquarters were.
  - *this/that* (pronouns) → *it*:
    'Could you give this to Joan?' → She asked him to give it to Joan.
  - *this/that* work (etc.) → *the work*; *these/those* documents (etc.) → *the documents*:
    'This work is very good.' → She told him the work was very good.
  - *today / this week/month/year* → *that day/week/month/year*
  - *tomorrow / next month / next year* → **the** *next/following day/month/year*
  - *yesterday / last week/month/year* → *the day before / the previous day/week/month/year / the week/month/year before*
  - *here* → *there*
- For tense changes in reported speech, see page 92.

Put these sentences into reported speech. Begin with the words given.

1 'This computer system was installed last week.'
Sven said *the computer system had been installed the week before.*

2 'I hope to have all this technology up and running next week.'
Sven said …

3 'Our investment in these new systems will reduce staff costs.'
Gabriella informed them that …

4 'We've been working on this new project since last year.'
Rajiv told us …

5 'They can't afford my prices.'
Marionella admitted that …

6 'The work you've been doing may be outsourced to India next year.'
Arnaldo told the staff that …

7 'You sent us the wrong invoice yesterday.'
Max complained that Martin …

8 'When you've finished writing this, print it out.'
My boss told me to print it out when …

Grammar workshop 5   **99**

UNIT 21

Customer loyalty

Getting started

Discuss in small groups which of these statements is true for you.

- If I like the people in a business, I'm willing to pay more for their products.
- If I've had a good experience as a customer, I'll recommend the company to my friends.
- I like the companies where I'm a customer to keep in touch with me and tell me about new products.
- If I don't like the people in a company, I won't buy their products or services, however good they are.
- For me, price is not so important as quality.
- I hate it when a salesperson can't take a decision and has to ask a superior.

Vocabulary

Match the words (1–11) with their definitions (a–k).

1 bond
2 revenue
3 vendor
4 outcome
5 bottom line
6 repurchase
7 return on investment
8 best practices
9 highly engaged
10 competitive advantage
11 empowerment

a being better than your competitors
b best ways of working
c continue buying
d final profit
e allowing people to take their own decisions
f income from doing business
g profit made from something you have bought
h relationship
i result
j seller
k very committed, very interested in the job

From satisfaction to loyalty

Company background — HayGroup people before strategy

Hay Group is a global organisational and human resources consulting firm operating in 43 countries.

Reading

1 Taking into account what you said in the initial discussion, work in small groups and make a list of the factors which make customers loyal to a company.

2 Scan the article on page 101 and check which factors on your list were mentioned. Does the article contain any factors which aren't on your list?

100 Customer loyalty

From satisfaction to loyalty

Just how do you take your customers from satisfaction to loyalty? Those were the questions Dr Jodi Simco and Dr Mark Royal of Hay Group, a human resources consulting firm, answered at LOMA's recent Customer Service Conference. Simco and Royal talked about the link they've found between business culture, employee loyalty, customer loyalty and revenue growth.

'First, it's important to ask ourselves just what our definition of customer loyalty is,' Simco said. 'And based on our research, we've found that it's when your customers have a strong bond to you and come back to you time and time again. They view you as the provider of choice. So they're not just looking for the lowest-cost vendor. They're going to come back to your company and not only use your current products and services, but maybe start using some new ones and recommending them to others.'

Simco identified two factors that decide whether satisfied customers will become loyal ones: the outcome that customers experience and the process by which they receive it. 'We've all bought cars, and the car might be the most wonderful car, so the outcome was positive,' Simco said. 'But we might decide not to go back to the car dealership because they were annoying to work with. In this case, the process was negative.' People, in the form of employees, are part of that process, she explained, and 'people are your key competitive advantage. It's your people who developed those relationships with your customers, and you really need to focus on them.'

Furthermore, when it comes to convincing people in your organisation of the impact that customer loyalty can have on your bottom line, the business case for building loyalty is quite simple. 'None of us is surprised that loyal customers are going to repurchase at two to four times the rate of just purely satisfied customers,' she said. 'And they're going to enthusiastically recommend your company to others. So they can serve as your best marketer. Loyal customers are also willing to pay more for your services.'

Hay Group has identified a few primary factors about a company that can make the difference between customer satisfaction and customer loyalty. 'The top factor is value: "Is this company's product or service having a positive impact on my business? Do I have a strong return on investment?" Ease of doing business is a big thing, too,' Simco continued. 'Are you easy to do business with, or are you problematic? Finally, your people are important, in terms of whether they show responsiveness, integrity, trust and professionalism.'

'In today's marketplace, where most organisations are facing global competitors and a rapid flow of information, it's hard to be different from your rivals because best practices spread across an industry very rapidly,' Royal said. 'But it's much harder for your competitors to duplicate a successful organisation that consists of a lot of highly motivated, highly engaged people who are focused on the customer, and this provides real opportunities for competitive advantage.'

For employees to deliver excellent customer service, Royal said, there are three key ingredients. 'First, there needs to be a strong focus on teamwork. We find that in organisations where employees perceive strong levels of teamwork, there tends to be a much higher level of customer satisfaction. The second ingredient is training: If we want people to drive high levels of customer satisfaction, we have to make sure they have the skills to deliver them. And the third ingredient is empowerment, which means that organisations need to empower employees to make decisions and take risks in carrying out their job roles.'

Adapted from *Resource* © LOMA

3 Read the article again and choose the best answer for these questions.

1 What produces customer loyalty, according to Simco in paragraph 2?
   A The price of the product
   B The quality of the product
   C The relationship with the supplier
   D The recommendation of friends

2 What, according to Simco in paragraph 3, is the key factor in making a company better than its rivals?
   A A superior product
   B Good quality staff
   C Good value for money
   D Good procedures for dealing with customers

3 In paragraph 4, what is given as the main benefit of having loyal customers?
   A It improves the company's image.
   B It increases profits.
   C It is easier than finding new ones.
   D They will accept higher prices.

4 What, according to Hay Group, is the main factor which changes customer satisfaction to customer loyalty?
   A Your customer does not have problems doing business with you.
   B Your customer gets what he asks for.
   C Your customer has confidence in you.
   D Your customer's own business becomes more profitable.

5 Why does Royal believe it is difficult for companies to be different from their competitors?
   A Their competitors can quickly imitate them.
   B Their competitors are spread all over the world.
   C Employees in different companies are equally hard-working.
   D Most companies nowadays are customer-centred.

6 Which of these does Royal say is an essential characteristic of a good employee?
   A They enjoy working alone.
   B They are naturally good at dealing with customers.
   C They consult their superiors before taking decisions.
   D They take responsibility for their actions.

Grammar workshop

Relative pronouns

1 Look at these sentences from the article and complete them with *who*, *which*, *where* or *that*, or leave the gap blank if you think no relative pronoun is needed.

1 Those were the questions .... Dr Jodi Simco and Dr Mark Royal of Hay Group answered.
2 Simco and Royal talked about the link .... they've found between business culture, employee loyalty, customer loyalty and revenue growth.
3 Simco identified two factors .... determine whether satisfied customers will become loyal ones: the outcome that customers experience and the process by .... they receive it.
4 It's your people .... developed those relationships with your customers.
5 ... the impact .... customer loyalty can have on your bottom line.
6 Hay Group has identified a few primary factors about a company .... can make the difference between customer satisfaction and customer loyalty.
7 In today's marketplace, ... most organisations are facing global competitors and a rapid flow of information, competitive differentiation is hard to maintain.

2 When you have finished, check your answers in the article and check other possible answers in the answer key.

> **page 116** (Relative pronouns)

Talking point

Discuss in small groups.

1 Simco and Royal think the quality of a company's employees is what makes the difference when dealing with customers. Do you agree? Why?/Why not?
2 Which do you think they would value most highly in a customer-service employee: efficiency or ability to form a friendly relationship? Which do you think is more important?
3 To what extent do you think technology can replace people in the relationship with customers?

A supermarket and customer loyalty

Listening

1 Listen to Christina Bunt talking about Tesco's relations with its customers. Complete these notes with one or two words in each gap.

Customer complaints
- Usually solved by staff on customer – 1 ....
- More serious complaints put on customer 2 ....

Building relationships with customers
- Tesco Clubcard: a 3 .... with vouchers.
- Visits to 4 .... and other groups.
- Free transport to store from 5 ....
- Vouchers for schools to obtain 6 ....

Measuring customer satisfaction
- 'Mystery Shopper' does a 7 .... every four weeks + report from Head Office
- Accompany customers in store – note down comments about their 8 ....

2 Work with a partner. Talk about a supermarket you know well. How do they go about building customer relationships?

A staff meeting

Role-play

You work in a medium-sized company. You have just received the following memo.

Memo

To: All staff
From: Customer Services Director
Subject: Customer Loyalty

Recent independent customer research has shown a high level of customer satisfaction with our products and services. However, we would like to increase customer loyalty in order to give us better competitive advantage. There will therefore be a meeting of all staff on Friday afternoon at 2 pm where we would welcome ideas from staff on any of the following questions:

- What do customers want in terms of service?
- What is important when serving customers?
- What is important when organising staff to provide better service?

There will be a prize of dinner for two at the Brasserie for the best suggestions.

Please attend the meeting punctually.

Simone

You have decided to give your ideas at the meeting.

1 Choose one of the questions and take two or three minutes to prepare what you are going to say. Prepare to speak on your subject for about one minute.

2 Hold the meeting and listen to everyone's ideas.

3 Discuss whose ideas were the best (and therefore should get the dinner for two).

Customer loyalty 103

UNIT 22

Communication with customers

Getting started

1 Work in small groups. Look at these different ways of communicating with customers. Label each picture with a word or phrase from the box.

| advertisement | company newsletter | email bulletin | leaflet |
| operator at call centre | visiting sales rep | website |

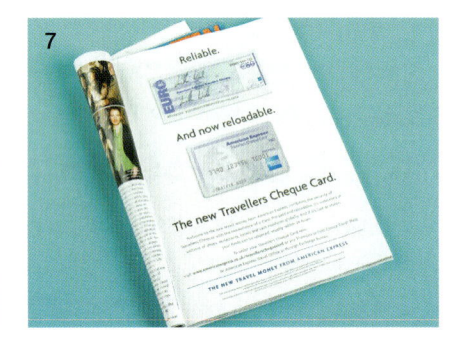

2 Which of the above ways do you think would be the most useful or effective means of communication with customers for each of the following?

- a new product or service
- a price increase
- a survey of customers' opinions
- a change of address
- dealing with an individual customer's problem
- giving general information about a range of products or services

3 Why is it important to get customers' views on your products and services?

104 Communication with customers

Communicating with customers at Espresso

Listening

1 Look at these notes and predict:
- what kind of word(s) you will need for each gap (nouns, adjectives, etc.)
- which words they might be.

2 You are going to hear Lewis Bronze from Espresso talking about how his company communicates with customers. Listen and complete the notes with one or two words.

Espresso – customer relations
- Customer enquiries: customer relations team and 1 ....
- New product information: sent in weekly 2 ....
- Technical support available from 3 ....
- Finding new customers is the job of 4 .... managers.
- Customer satisfaction: dissatisfied customers do not renew 5 ....
- Telephone and email used to encourage 6 .... and to collect ideas for 7 ....

Turning complaints to your advantage

Reading

1 Discuss the following in pairs.
- How should businesses deal with complaints from customers?
- What procedures do companies have for dealing with complaints?
- What are the most common complaints which customers make?

2 Your boss has written an article for a management magazine about customer care. Read it quickly and find out why he thinks you should welcome complaints from customers.

3 Before sending it, he has asked you to check the English. However, there is one extra word in most lines. Find the extra words and write them in the gaps provided. Some lines are correct. Mark them with a tick (✔).

Whenever a customer hands to you a complaint, he's also offering you an opportunity to create a stronger and more profitable relationship with him. That's because of complaints that are handled properly can be converted into the increased loyalty, extra business and recommendations. Although several of my customers have had complaints, initially my organisation wasn't ready to hear the feedback yet. But over the years, listening to customers has helped me to shape our services so they're easier, better and faster. Here's how to encourage them to communicate their comments, feedback and complaints are directly to you: firstly, at the point of purchase, provide with comment forms and an email link or phone number to you personally. Secondly, answer to each and every complaint or suggestion. Also, put your personal signature on each response. Finally, create a customer-user group and pay for attention to what they tell you. The golden rule it is this: when customers give you valuable feedback, make sure they're rewarded in some special way. You should to send them a handwritten thank-you note, a free gift or a unique discount. Be sure to tell them that their input is valuable.

1 *to*
2 ......
3 ......
4 ......
5 ......
6 ......
7 ......
8 ......
9 ......
10 ......
11 ......
12 ......
13 ......
14 ......
15 ......

Talking point

Discuss the following in pairs.

1 As a customer, have you ever complained?
2 What advice would you give about the best ways for customers to complain in order to get what they want? For example:

- Is it better to write a letter or complain in person?
- Should you insist on seeing the manager?
- Should you show you are angry or should you keep calm?
- When should you use a lawyer?

Customer communication at Not Just Food

Listening

1 Read these questions and underline the key words.

2 Listen to Jane Milton from Not Just Food talking about her customers, then choose the best answer for the questions.

1 How does Jane normally approach potential clients?
  A By calling them first.
  B By sending company literature and then calling.
  C By visiting the client.
2 What was the original purpose of her website?
  A To attract new clients.
  B To show potential clients the type of work they do.
  C To help existing clients to keep in contact.
3 How does her company demonstrate its commitment to clients?
  A By always quoting the correct price for a job.
  B By doing more work than her clients expect.
  C By reducing the price if the work doesn't take as long as she quoted.
4 Why does her company take trouble with small clients?
  A They often grow into bigger clients.
  B They are easy to deal with.
  C They improve the reputation of the company.
5 How has Jane avoided having dissatisfied customers?
  A By always exceeding customers' expectations.
  B By working from written instructions.
  C By continually speaking with the client while the job is being done.

3 Discuss the following with a partner.
1 How does Jane Milton exceed customers' expectations?
2 What does she do to build long-term relationships with clients?
3 Do you think staff can be trained to treat customers well, or is it just a natural ability

Vocabulary

Match these collocations (1–9) with their definitions (a–i).

1 customer helpline
2 customer services manager
3 customer care
4 customer profile
5 target customer
6 customer help desk
7 customer dissatisfaction
8 loyal customers
9 after-sales service

a a place customers can visit or phone when they have problems
b a telephone service for when customers have problems
c a typical customer
d customers who always buy from the same company or organisation
e the way customers are treated
f person responsible for before- and after-sales service
g services which are provided for customers after they have bought a product
h the person or organisation you would like to have as a customer
i when customers are unhappy with the product or service

Training in customer communication skills

Reading

1 You have been asked to investigate how to train staff in your organisation in customer care. Discuss with a partner what you would expect to learn on a customer care course.

2 You have found four courses on the Internet. Which course on page 107 does each statement on the right refer to?

1 Organisations are changing the way they do business. [D]
2 This course suggests that having a good reputation is the best way for a company to attract customers. ☐
3 You will study writing skills. ☐
4 You will become surer of your abilities in the job. ☐
5 You will learn how gestures, facial expressions and body language are understood by clients. ☐
6 You will learn how to deal with difficult customers. ☐
7 You will learn how to give a better service than the customer imagined. ☐
8 You have to understand how your customers think in order to give them what they need. ☐

106 Communication with customers

A

Communicating with your customers

You will learn how to build rapport with your customers and how non-verbal communication is interpreted by customers. In addition, you will be trained in telephone skills, including how to project professionalism and how to provide quality customer service over the telephone. Finally, you will learn how email can be used for effective communication with your customers.

B

A first-class service

Providing a first-class customer service and creating the right impression first time is a must for front-line staff. To be successful at customer care requires an understanding of customer expectations and the skills to exceed that expectation. This practical and interactive course provides the personal and professional skills for staff that are often the first point of contact for customers. Throughout the course delegates will have the opportunity to practise customer-handling skills with role-play and in discussion groups, enabling a confident return to the workplace.

C

Customer care

Word of mouth is the cheapest and most effective way of marketing your business and extending your customer base. Treat your customers badly, and you could be paying a heavy price for what are essentially simple people skills. This course is designed for anyone who wants to know how to make a positive impression to retain customers, eliminate customer dissatisfaction and learn how to handle awkward customers appropriately.

To address your customers' needs you must be able to think like them, respond to whatever they throw at you and still show you're pleased to be able to help them.

D

Telephone skills and customer-care training course

More and more companies are setting up customer helplines as the quickest and most convenient way of establishing customer contacts. Call centres and mail order are the fastest-growing operational departments for UK organisations. It is essential that all employees represent their organisation in a professional and friendly way. Clear and effective communication is essential to ensure that the business is not lost. If your staff are not trained properly on telephone skills, how much business are they losing your company?

Vocabulary

Find words or phrases in each paragraph with these meanings.

1. a good understanding of someone and an ability to communicate well with them (course A)
2. communication without using words (course A)
3. give an impression of (course A)
4. essential (course B)
5. staff who deal with customers (course B)
6. place where people do their jobs (course B)
7. people telling each other about your product or business (course C)
8. ability to deal with people (course C)
9. keep clients (course C)
10. deal with difficult clients (course C)

Talking point

Work in pairs or groups of three. The company you work for has been losing important customers to your competitors. You have been asked by your manager to find out why this has been happening and prepare a proposal to say how you can win these customers back. Discuss the situation together, and decide:

- why, in general, companies lose customers
- how you will find out why customers are leaving your company
- what actions you might be able to take to win back the lost customers.

Useful language

Expressing causes

These phrases can be used in spoken and written English:
The reason why companies lose customers is often poor service.
Poor service often **causes** companies to lose customers.
Poor service often **leads to / results in** companies losing customers.
In written English, we can use these phrases:
Companies lose customers **due to / owing to / because of / as a result of** poor service.

> page 117 (Expressing causes)

UNIT 23
Corresponding with customers

Getting started

1 Work in pairs. Look at the two leaflets and discuss the following.

- What services do companies like these offer?
- If they were going to extend their services, what new services could they offer?
- What sort of things can go wrong with services like these and cause customers to complain?

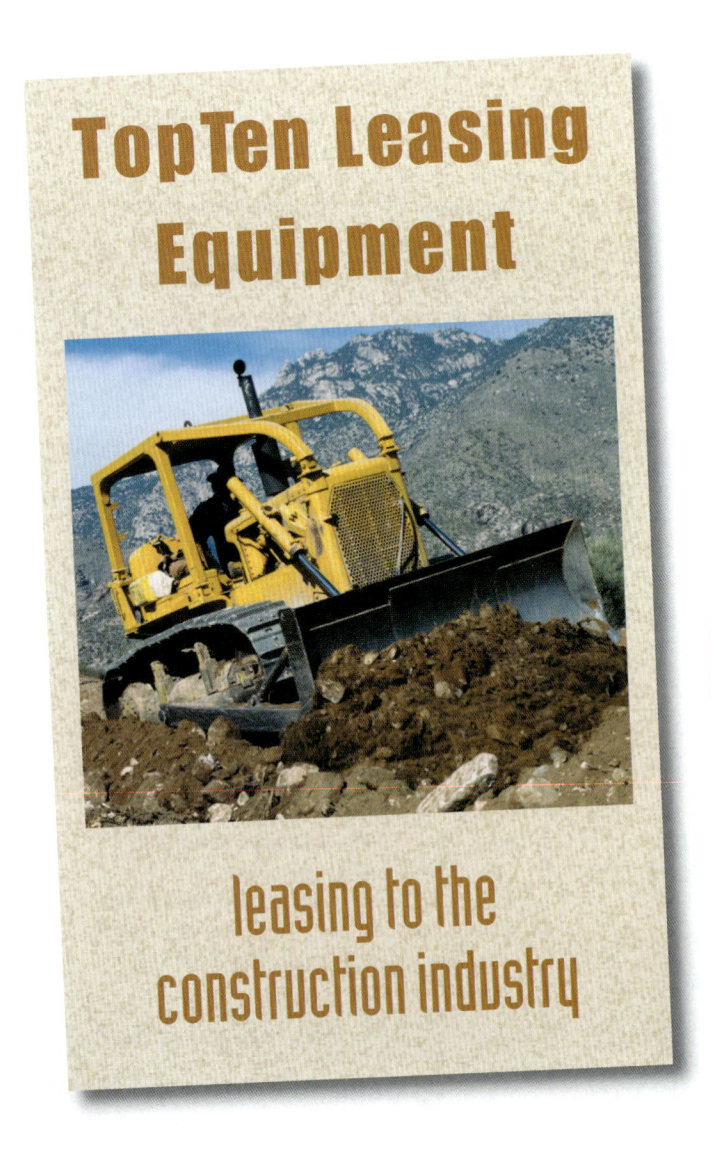

TopTen Leasing Equipment

leasing to the construction industry

BDD Couriers

express courier delivery

anywhere in UK within 24 hours

2 Discuss these questions in small groups.
- When your company launches a new product or service, who would you send information to first: existing customers or potential new customers? Why?
- Why is it important to keep existing customers happy, even when they give you problems?
- Why are dissatisfied customers dangerous for a business? How much should you do to make them happy?

A letter about a new service

Reading

1 Read this letter telling an existing customer about a new service and choose the best answer for each gap.

1	A permanent	B long-standing	C long-term	D lengthy
2	A extending	B sending	C amplifying	D spreading
3	A supposes	B involves	C means	D suggests
4	A height	B amount	C quantity	D level
5	A door-to-door	B house-to-house	C face-to-face	D hand-to-hand
6	A somewhere	B anywhere	C wherever	D elsewhere
7	A asked	B demanded	C required	D charged
8	A fix	B enclose	C insert	D join
9	A do	B perform	C make	D carry
10	A wait	B deliberate	C stop	D hesitate

Dear Mr Sloane,

New services from BDD

As a valued 1 ..B.. client of BDD Ltd, I am sure you will be interested to know that from 1 April of this year, we are 2 ...... our Budget Document Delivery services to the whole of Europe. This 3 ...... we shall be offering the same 4 ...... of service that you have come to expect from our UK operations:

- 24-hour 5 ...... pick-up and delivery service
- documents delivered within 12 hours 6 ...... in Europe
- prices on average less than 30% of prices 7 ...... by our main competitors
- confidentiality and reliability

I 8 ...... a leaflet detailing our new service.

If you would like to know more about this service, or if there is any other way in which we can help you to 9 ...... trouble-free business with maximum efficiency, please do not 10 ...... to contact me personally.

Yours sincerely,

Mohamed Sarawi

Mohamed Sarawi
Managing Director
Enc.

---

2 Read the letter again, and answer these questions with a partner.
1 How can Mr Sloane immediately know the subject of the letter?
2 Which word suggests that Mr Sloane is an important client to BDD?
3 Which phrase implies that BDD's services are high quality?
4 Which words suggest that by using BDD's services, Mr Sloane will avoid problems?
5 Which phrase shows that Mr Sloane will be given personalised treatment?

Writing

You work in the customer relations department of TopTen Leasing Ltd, a company which leases equipment to the construction industry. Your boss has asked you to write a letter to one of your most important clients, Mr Castle of Castle Constructions, to tell him about some new services which your company is offering.

1 Look at the leaflet below, on which your boss has written some notes, and write a plan for the letter. Divide your plan into paragraphs.

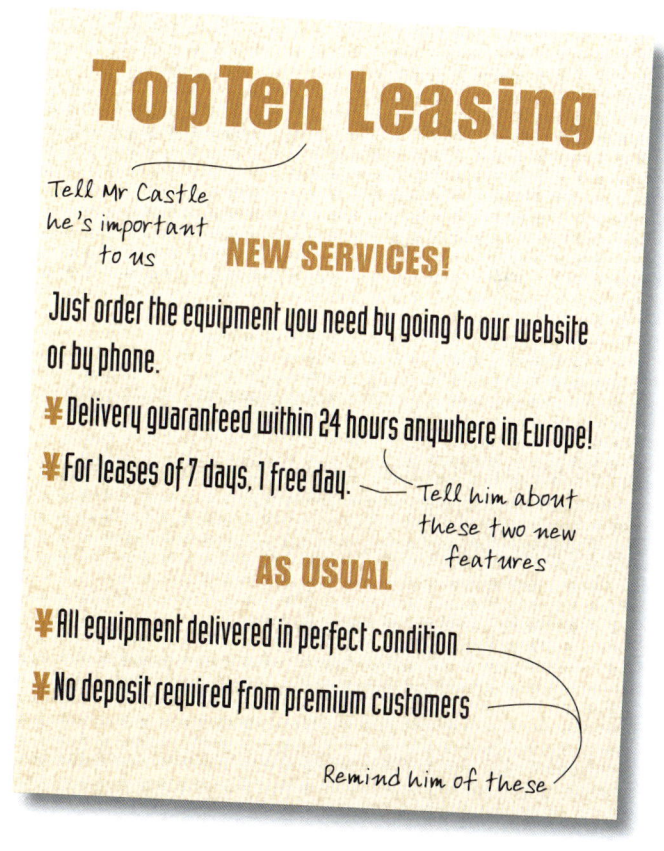

TopTen Leasing

Tell Mr Castle he's important to us

NEW SERVICES!

Just order the equipment you need by going to our website or by phone.

¥ Delivery guaranteed within 24 hours anywhere in Europe!
¥ For leases of 7 days, 1 free day. — *Tell him about these two new features*

AS USUAL

¥ All equipment delivered in perfect condition
¥ No deposit required from premium customers

Remind him of these

2 Write the letter. Use the letter on this page as a model.

3 When you have finished, compare your letter with a partner's.

23 A letter from a dissatisfied customer

Reading

1 Mr Castle dictated this letter over the telephone to his PA. However she had difficulty hearing, and in most lines there is an incorrect word. Read the letter carefully. Cross out the wrong words and write the correct words in the gaps provided. Put a tick (✓) beside lines that are correct. (There are 15 wrong words, including the example.)

Ms M. Morrison
Customer Services Manager
TopTen Leasing
44 Tollgate Road
Carlisle

Castle CONSTRUCTION

Dear Ms Morrison,

Incorrect and late delivery of equipment

~~Referring~~ our telephone conversation last Wednesday, I would like to express my dissatisfaction of your company's recent service in writing.

Past Monday, I ordered the delivery of two Yamaha Mark 5 building hoists who were urgently needed for construction work we are carrying out in the Berlin area. According of your recent letter, we understood we would have an equipment within 24 hours, and so we organised our work schedules to take this into account. Although, the equipment did not arrive until late on Wednesday, nearly 48 hours after putting the order, and instead of sending Mark 5 hoists, your company delivered Mark 2s why do not meet our requirements.

As a consequence of it, we were forced to entirely reorganise our construction teams and our building programmes until the correct equipment arrived. This meant a considerable amount of more work and loss of time on projects where our costs have being calculated very exactly.

We have, in the years, been very happy with your service and we have recommended you to another companies working in the sector. A repetition of last week's incident would result in our having to look for other leasers, it is something we would prefer to avoid.

Yours sincerely,

Angela Hernández
pp.   Bob Castle
       CEO

---

1 *Following*
2 ....
3 ....
4 ....
5 ....
6 ....
7 ....
8 ....
9 ....
10 ....
11 ....
12 ....
13 ....
14 ....
15 ....
16 ....
17 ....
18 ....

---

2 Discuss with a partner which of the following a letter of complaint should contain.

1 Details of the problem which occurred
2 An explanation of the consequences of this problem
3 What action you want them to take
4 An explanation of why you chose their product or service in the first place
5 A threat about what you will do if they do not correct the problem
6 An explanation of how happy you have been with them in the past
7 A comparison of their product or service with their competitors' products or services.

3 Which of these things are in Bob Castle's letter, and in which paragraphs?

Corresponding with customers

Grammar workshop

Expressing results

Study these ways of expressing results (in *italics*). Three of them come from the letter you have just read. Then complete the following sentences in any way you want.

A *As a consequence of this*, we were forced to entirely reorganise our construction teams and our building programmes …
B *This meant* a considerable amount of extra work and loss of time …
C A repetition of last week's incident *would result in* our having to look for other leasers …
D *As a result*, we had to reschedule the shipment.
E *Consequently*, we lost about 250 man hours.
F Your late delivery *meant that* the production line had to stop for one hour.

1 You delivered the wrong model. As a consequence of this, *we had to send it back.*
2 Some of the goods were damaged. As a consequence of this ....
3 You were late sending the information. This meant ....
4 There were several mistakes in the invoice. As a result ....
5 You sent the components to the wrong factory. This meant ....
6 Two of the pieces were broken. Consequently ....

> page 117 (Expressing results)

Preparing a letter of complaint

9 Listening

Your company recently used BDD to deliver some vital documents to a major client in Budapest. Unfortunately, they arrived late. Listen to John Sloane talking to his assistant, Jolan, and complete the handwritten notes with one or two words.

1 .... of this!

It took 2 .... Tell him what 3 .... of this were.

We'll only continue if deliveries are 4 ....

Dear Mr Sloane,

New services from BDD

As a valued long-standing client of BDD Ltd, I am sure you will be interested to know that from 1 April of this year, we are extending our Budget Document Delivery services to the whole of Europe. This means we shall be offering the same level of service that you have come to expect from our UK operations:

- 24-hour door-to-door pick-up and delivery service
- documents delivered within 12 hours anywhere in Europe
- prices on average less than 30% of prices charged by our main competitors
- confidentiality and reliability.

I enclose a leaflet detailing our new service.

If you would like to know more about this service, or if there is any other way in which we can help you to do trouble-free business with maximum efficiency, please do not hesitate to contact me personally.

Yours sincerely,

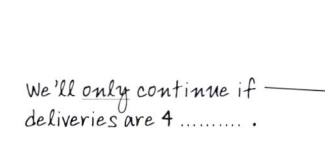

Writing

1 Write a plan of the letter to BDD complaining about their service.
  Use the handwritten notes you made on BDD's original letter (in the listening exercise).

2 Write your letter. Use the letter on page 110 as a model.

UNIT 24

A business seminar

Getting started

Discuss the following in small groups.

- In business, which of these can you learn from other people's experience, and what can you only learn from your own experience?
  - How to build relationships with new customers
  - How to do market research
  - How to handle difficult colleagues
  - How to forecast sales
  - How to interview candidates for jobs
- When you start a new job or project, what ways can you use to get other people to help you by sharing their knowledge and experience?
- What things can sometimes be difficult when trying to learn from other people?

Speakers at a business seminar

Listening

10 1 Listen to these extracts from talks given by five speakers at a business seminar. For each extract, decide what topic (A–H) the speaker is talking about.

Speaker 1 ....
Speaker 2 ....
Speaker 3 ....
Speaker 4 ....
Speaker 5 ....

A Breaking into a new market
B Exhibiting at a trade fair
C Introducing new technology
D Managing change
E Outsourcing operations
F Relocating their headquarters
G Travelling on business
H Trying to attract a new customer

2 Which speaker used each of the following phrases or expressions? Write the number of the speaker beside each phrase. If necessary, listen again to check.

a And another thing … ☐
b Firstly … ☐
c His next point is … ☐
d In actual fact … ☐
e In my experience … ☐
f In retrospect … ☐
g It's no good … ☐
h Just to give you one instance … ☐
i The first is this … ☐
j Then next … ☐
k You really must … ☐
l You've got to … ☐
m It's not worth … ☐

3 Match each of the phrases or expressions from Exercise 2 with one of these categories.

1 Sequencing *And another thing …*
2 Introducing a surprising fact
3 Introducing your own experiences
4 Introducing an example
5 Advising
6 Saying something is not useful

4 Work in pairs and think of other phrases to add to the lists. Compare your ideas with the rest of the class.

112 A business seminar

A short talk

Listening

1 Listen to a man giving a short talk at a business seminar about customer relations. Tick (✔) the phrases or expressions in Exercise 2 on page 112 which you hear.

2 Listen again, and complete the notes below by writing one or two words in each gap.

Company manufactures 1 .... for electronics industry.
Uses 2 .... for day-to-day communication.
Meetings at 3 .... for structuring projects.
Apart from work meetings, managers 4 .... with clients.

Grammar workshop

It's not worth, it's no good, etc.

1 Look at these sentences from the talk you have just listened to.

It's no good relying on reports from junior staff.
It's not worth taking on staff just for a job like that.
It just wasn't worth the money.

1 Which verb form follows *It's no good ...* and *It's not worth ...*?
2 What other type of word can follow *It's not worth ...*?

> These other expressions are followed by *-ing* forms:
> - *It's no use ...*
>   *It's no use writing* to him – he never answers any letters.
> - *It's a waste of time ...*
>   *It's a waste of time advertising* the job in that magazine – not enough people read it.
> - *There's no point (in) ...*
>   *There's no point in changing* the computer system – this one works perfectly well.

2 Complete these sentences by writing a verb or phrase in each gap.

1 I decided it was no good .... the bank for a loan when interest rates were so high.
2 It's just not worth .... for a job when there are 500 other candidates.
3 It's no use .... meetings when no one has prepared for them.
4 It's a waste of time .... a PowerPoint presentation if the data projector doesn't work.
5 There's no point in .... new computers if the ones we've got are perfectly adequate.

Advertisement for a business seminar

Reading

Read this advertisement for a business seminar. Choose the best word for each gap.

BUSINESS SEMINAR
Sharing knowledge for success

Business activities which have brought success is the subject of a morning seminar to be **1** ..D.. at the Benchmark Institute for Good Business Practice on 19 March at our Cambridge headquarters. The seminar will **2** ...... speakers from a range of backgrounds and business sectors. They will bring their business knowledge and experience to share ideas which will **3** ...... your business more effective.

Key areas for discussion will **4** ...... :
- The impact of new technology
- Customer relations
- Marketing
- Recruitment

For further information, contact Nesreen Mahmoud on 0219 493219.

Attendance at the seminar is free of **5** ...... , though places must be booked in **6** ....

1	A celebrated	B convened	C arranged	D held
2	A show	B feature	C star	D present
3	A make	B do	C result	D ensure
4	A involve	B contain	C include	D consist
5	A cost	B charge	C fee	D payment
6	A advance	B ahead	C prior	D beforehand

A business seminar 113

Speaking at a business seminar

Talking point

1 Imagine you are attending the business seminar. You have been asked to give your opinions or talk about your experience on one of the questions on the agenda below. Work in pairs and choose the question you want to answer. (If you are working, you can choose any of the questions. If you are a student, you can choose from the last four questions, which are more theoretical.)

Business Seminar
AGENDA

1 How has new technology affected your company?
(How it has affected communications, how it has affected working practices, what staff reactions have been to it)

2 How does your company manage relationships with customers?
(Your company's customer profile, which staff have contact with customers, how your company communicates with customers)

3 How does your company keep abreast of changes in the market?
(What market research your company does, how it gets feedback from existing customers, how you stay up to date with what the competition is doing)

4 How does your company go about recruiting the staff it needs?
(Does it advertise, go to job fairs, visit universities? Do candidates have to do tests? Interviews?)

5 What is important when introducing new technology?
(Cost, training staff, potential benefits)

6 What is important when dealing with customers?
(Knowing about the products and service, communication skills, problem solving)

7 What is important when keeping abreast of the competition?
(Market research, innovation, customer service)

8 What's important when interviewing job applicants?
(Types of question, number of interviewers, length of interview)

2 Each of you will have to give a short talk of about one minute on your chosen topic to a separate group. Follow these steps to prepare your talk.

1 Brainstorm ideas.
2 Select three of them.
3 Organise them in a logical order.
4 Think of examples to support your ideas.
5 Make brief notes.

3 Work in groups of three or four with students who have chosen a different topic from yours. Hold a seminar, in which each of you speaks for about one minute. Follow these guidelines.

1 Introduce your talk: *I'm going to talk about ...*
2 Speak quite slowly and clearly.
3 Look at the people you are speaking to.
4 Refer to your notes, but don't read from them.
5 Try to use some of the phrases and expressions you studied in this unit.
6 While other students are speaking, listen carefully and:
   - prepare one or two questions to ask them
   - decide whether you have any ideas to add
   - decide if you agree or disagree with the points they make.
7 When each person has spoken, discuss what they have said together and then invite the next person to give their talk.

4 Work in pairs with someone who listened to your talk. Give feedback to each other on the things which you did well and the things you could improve. Use the checklist below to help you.

Performance checklist		
The speaker:	Yes	No
• had well-prepared material.	☐	☐
• introduced the talk clearly.	☐	☐
• spoke clearly.	☐	☐
• maintained eye contact with audience.	☐	☐
• had a clear structure to the talk.	☐	☐
• used good examples.	☐	☐
• looked confident.	☐	☐
• had plenty to say.	☐	☐

Useful language

Adding ideas

I would just like to add that ...
There's something else that I'd like to add, and that's ...

5 Discuss these questions in small groups.

1 Which of these elements do you think makes a talk more effective? Why?
2 Which would be appropriate in a talk of about one minute?
- Giving examples
- Telling jokes
- Telling anecdotes
- Giving a theoretical background
- Expressing your personal opinions
- Using business vocabulary
- Having a confident command of the subject

6 As a final activity, each of you has been asked to give a one-minute talk to all the attendees at the business seminar. Choose the subject of the talk from the list below. If possible, each student should choose a different subject. If you haven't worked in business yet, you should choose a subject starting with *What is important when …?*

1 Talk about how your company trains staff. Say:
- what skills staff in your company need to learn
- how training courses are organised
- how effective staff training is.

2 What is important when deciding how to recruit staff?
- Where to advertise
- Recruitment consultants
- Job fairs

3 Talk about how your company promotes itself and its products. Say:
- what types of promotion it uses
- which types are most effective
- how staff are involved in promotions.

4 What is important when organising a stand at a trade fair?
- Location
- Design
- Staffing

5 Talk about a trade fair you have visited. Say:
- where it was
- why you visited it
- how successful your visit was.

6 What is important when asking a bank for a business loan?
- Terms and conditions
- Business plan
- Guarantees

7 Talk about a presentation you have made. Say:
- what the presentation was about
- what equipment you used
- how successful the presentation was.

8 What is important when breaking into an overseas market?
- Agent/distributor
- Market research
- Advertising

9 Talk about a business conference you have attended. Say:
- what the conference was about
- where it was
- what was interesting or useful about it.

10 What is important when planning a business trip?
- Local customs
- Schedule
- Hotels

11 Talk about a meeting with foreign customers or suppliers. Say:
- why the meeting took place
- where the meeting happened
- how successful the meeting was.

12 What is important when preparing staff for changes in working practices?
- Consultation with staff
- Negotiation
- Information

13 Talk about how your working life is organised. Say:
- what hours you work
- when you have time off
- how much flexibility you have in your work.

14 What is important when dealing with customer complaints?
- Communication skills
- Solutions
- Building the relationship

15 What does your company do to encourage customer loyalty? Say:
- what your company's customer profile is
- how your company tries to keep customers
- how effective your company is at keeping customers.

16 What is important when holding a business seminar?
- Organisation
- Attendees
- Topic(s)

Grammar workshop 6

Units 21–24

Relative pronouns

> - You use *who* or *that* for people:
>   *The customer **who/that** phoned is in the showroom now.*
> - You use *which* or *that* for things:
>   *The machine **that/which** broke down is being repaired at the moment.*
>   Note that you do not use *that* after prepositions:
>   *The company **for which** she works has offices in Edinburgh.* NOT *for that she works*
> - You use *whose* (possessive) for people, countries, towns and companies:
>   *I'm the customer **whose** invoice was wrong.*
>   *He works for Benchmark Ltd, **whose** chairman is Adam Smith.*
>   *Countries **whose** main industry is tourism are very vulnerable to changes in fashion.*
> - You use *when* for times (*in the year **when** I joined the company*), *where* for places (*in the office **where** she works*) and *why* for reasons (*the reason **why** I'm calling you*).
> - You use *what* to mean 'the thing which':
>   ***What** takes the time is answering telephone calls.* /
>   *Answering telephone calls is **what** takes the time.*

1 Join these sentences using a relative pronoun. (You may have to change the word order in some sentences.)

1 He joined the firm 15 years ago. Mr Patel was the managing director.

   He joined the firm 15 years ago when Mr Patel was the managing director.

2 The report has not arrived. It was sent by express courier two days ago.
3 I've visited the website. You advertise your products there.
4 I started working for the company in 1998. It only had 15 employees then.
5 She works at your main office. Your central administration is located there.
6 Garsons Ltd has just announced record profits. Their parent company is Garfield International.
7 He's the new recruit. His CV impressed us so much.
8 Do you remember the customer? He called last week. He wanted a replacement.
9 He called to say you sent a replacement. The replacement was faulty.

2 Complete this letter by writing a relative pronoun in each gap.

Dear Tom,

Thank you for the letter **1** *which* arrived this morning, and in **2** .... you remind me of the need for a solution to the problem of pollution at the factory **3** .... we produce aluminium mouldings.

The most immediate problem **4** .... we have is an inspection by the environmental health officer **5** .... will take place next week. (You will remember her because she is the woman **6** .... report gave us so many problems two years ago.)

We have to present her with a solution **7** .... will convince her that we are serious about solving the problem. Our technical staff have also been working on it since last January **8** .... the new legislation came into force, and they have come up with a number of ideas. The proposal **9** .... is most attractive is a purifying plant **10** .... will allow clean waste water into the river **11** .... flows past the factory site

Our bank manager, **12** .... is very accommodating, is ready to finance any project **13** .... viability we can prove. I enclose costings for the proposal **14** .... you might like to study before I send it to him.

15 .... would be most helpful would be an email with your thoughts as soon as possible, suggesting a date **16** .... work can begin.

Regards

Vanessa

Expressing causes

- *due to / owing to / because of / as a result of* + noun/*-ing* form
  *Companies often fail **due to / owing to / because of / as a result of** bad management.*
  *Many products fail **due to / owing to / because of / as a result of** companies not carrying out market research.*
- *The reason why* + relative clause + clause
  ***The reason why** products fail is often poor market research.*
- noun/*-ing* form + *the reason why* + relative clause
  *Bad management is **the reason why** many companies fail.*
- *cause* + object + infinitive
  *Bad managers often **cause** companies to fail.*
- *lead to / result in* + noun/*-ing* form
  *Late payment often **leads to / results in** cashflow problems.*
  *Poor teamwork **led to / resulted in** them missing their deadlines.*

1 Complete this letter by using a word or phrase from the box above.

Dear Tanya,

Thank you for your letter of 10 March.

1 *The reason why* I haven't been in touch recently is that I have been off sick. However, I have investigated the circumstances which **2** .... our customers to complain.

What happened was failure of our quality control system and this **3** .... a number of defective products leaving the factory. The failure in quality control was **4** .... poor training of new quality control staff, which is something we are trying to put right.

I hope the training **5** .... fewer defective products in the future.

Yours

Mike

2 Write sentences to express causes using the ideas and the words or phrases given.

1 New technology → Companies can keep large databases about customers. (as a result)
  As a result of new technology, companies can keep large databases about customers.

2 Their ability to exploit large databases → Companies are theoretically able to target individual customers. (owing to)
3 Companies have the ability to target individual customers. → Companies think they can give customers personalised treatment. (the reason why)
4 The introduction of new technology → Customers expect personalised treatment. (has led to)
5 Companies have more information than they can manage on their databases. → They are unable to give personalised treatment to customers. (causes)
6 The inability of companies to meet customers' expectations. → Customer dissatisfaction. (results in)

Expressing results

- *As a consequence of this / As a result / Consequently* + sentence
  *It snowed heavily last week. **As a consequence of this / As a result / Consequently**, all our shipments were delayed.*
- *mean / result in* + noun/*-ing* form
  *Your failure to deliver the goods on time **meant** the loss of an important customer.*
  *Your failure to deliver the goods on time **resulted in** us losing an important customer.*
- *mean* + clause
  *Rising prices may **mean** that we will have to close the factory in Munich.*

Complete the memo with words or phrases from the box above.

To: Dispatch staff
From: Boris Vladev, Financial Director
Subject: Cost savings

Rising oil prices have **1** .... greatly increased transport costs. **2** .... that our profit margins are greatly reduced in those cases where we pay for delivery. **3** .... , we may have to raise prices, which could **4** .... our losing customers. Could I ask staff to:

- make sure all lorries leaving the factory are completely full. This will **5** .... a 5% saving on present transport costs.
- only use express delivery in really urgent cases. **6** .... , we will be able to save a further 6.5%.

Many thanks.

Grammar workshop 6 **117**

Sample answers to writing exercises

Unit 7 A stand at a trade fair

The International Food Exhibition

Writing

1 Sample email

> **Subject: International Food Exhibition**
>
> Hello Bill
>
> The organisers have given me the following information:
>
> - Stands cost between £120 and £200 per square metre. However, we have to pay a 50% deposit when we make our reservation. The balance must be paid one month before the exhibition begins.
> - The deadline for reservations is 1 September.
>
> Best wishes
>
> Frank

Preparing an exhibition stand

Writing 1

2 Sample email

> Dear Sirs
>
> We are interested in having a stand at the International Food Exhibition in London next March. Could you please give us an estimate of how much it would cost to build a stand of 30 square metres? I would also like to know when you can do it and when it would be possible for you to visit us to discuss the design of the stand if we like your prices.
>
> Many thanks
>
> Frank O'Donnell

Writing 2

2 Sample email

> Dear Mr Steel
>
> Thank you for your designs. In answer to your questions:
>
> 1 We have booked 40 m² of floor space.
> 2 Our stand is on a corner and we would prefer it to be open.
> 3 We would like to be able to accommodate up to 15 people at any one time.
>
> From the designs you sent us, the one we like the most is Number 3. We look forward to receiving your design and quotation.
>
> Best wishes
>
> Frank O'Donnell

4 Sample answer

> To: Sales staff
> From: Bill Cowley
> Subject: Stand at International Food Exhibition
>
> I'm pleased to inform you that the stand for the IFE is being designed at the moment. Could you please let me know what equipment you will need for the stand? Also, I suggest you start preparing the graphics you want to put on the stand.
>
> Many thanks
>
> BC

Unit 11 Starting up in a new location

Agents and distributors

Writing

Sample answer

> **Proposal for a choice of distributor in New Zealand**
>
> **Introduction**
>
> The purpose of this proposal is to compare two possible distributors for our products in New Zealand and to recommend which distributor we should choose.
>
> **Burford Electrical Distributions**
>
> This distributor has been in business since 1959 and they stock most major brands. However, this means they stock our competitors' products and will probably not be so interested in selling ours. Also, although they have a large, highly experienced sales force and offices throughout the country, they are also quite highly paid, which will make our products more expensive.
>
> Finally, they make daily deliveries. However, you have to pay extra for deliveries, which will also add to the cost of our products.
>
> **Choice Electrics**
>
> This company is relatively new. It was started in 2003, which means its sales force is not so experienced. On the other hand, they are young and keen and they have a reputation for dealing in high-quality state-of-the-art components like ours. Finally, they sell over the Internet and deliver by express courier the same day.
>
> **Recommendations**
>
> I strongly recommend that we choose Choice Electrics because they will sell our products more cheaply and because they seem more dynamic. I suggest we contact them to negotiate an agreement.

Unit 13 Business hotels and sales conferences

The results of a survey

Writing

2 Sample answer

> While 24% of respondents rated the Marriott chain as their favourite hotel chain, just 12% liked the Hilton best. However 7% chose Westin as their favourite.
>
> Forty-one per cent of the people who answered the survey considered the hotel's cost as very important, whereas 56% rated it as quite important. However, only 3% said it was not important at all.

Unit 15 Reports

A report on the use of private company jets

Writing

2 Sample answer

> **Report on the use of company aircraft by departmental directors**
>
> *Introduction*
> The purpose of this report is to describe how the company jet is used by senior staff (departmental directors and above) of Florentino International.
>
> *Number of flights per year*
> The number of flights per year has increased from 56 last year to 63 this year. This number is expected to increase by nearly 30% to 80 next year.
>
> *Reasons for flights*
> The main reason which was given for using the jet last year was customer meetings (56%). However, this has decreased to 40% this year. In contrast, company meetings, which constituted 35% of reasons for flights last year, rose to 45% this year. It is predicted that customer meetings will be the main reason for flights next year (60%), while company meetings are expected to decrease to just 30%.
>
> Other reasons for using the jet have remained almost the same over the three years at between 10% and 12%.
>
> *Conclusion*
> Use of the company aircraft is becoming increasingly popular, and customer meetings are the main reason for using it.

Unit 16 Business meetings

A survey of meetings

Talking point

2 Sample answer

> **Introduction**
> The purpose of this report is to summarise the findings of a survey on business meetings carried out in the United States.
>
> **Productivity of meetings**
> The survey found that, in successful companies, 25% of managers considered their meetings to be productive, whereas in unsuccessful companies this figure was only 2%. The average for all companies was 12%.
>
> **Time spent in meetings**
> The survey found that senior and middle managers spent 78% of their time in meetings and just 22% doing other things.
>
> **Number of meetings**
> In the United States in 1976, business people held an average of 11 million meetings a day. This has risen to the present figure of 25 million a day.
>
> **Conclusions**
> While meetings occupy a large amount of managers' time and are increasingly frequent, most managers consider them to be unproductive.

A business meeting

Writing

Sample answer

> Hello Barry,
>
> I would be happy to visit China during the first two weeks of June. I shall need to take about 100 leaflets, brochures and catalogues. I will also need a case containing samples of all our main products.
>
> Could you please let me know what expenses the company will pay for my trip?
>
> Many thanks,
>
> Sandra

Unit 18 Using the Internet

Upgrading a website

Writing

3 Sample answer

> Dear Ms Strauss,
>
> I'm contacting you because we would like to upgrade our company website www.businessbenchmark.com. We think that at present it is too complicated and that it requires more attractive graphics. I would be grateful if you could look at the website and send me an estimate for upgrading it.
>
> Many thanks
>
> Yours sincerely

Unit 19 A staff survey

A survey report

Writing

3 Sample answer

> **Report on staff survey into changes in the company's offices**
>
> The purpose of this report is to summarise staff opinions about changes to the company offices.
>
> **How to change our offices**
>
> Just under half our staff told me they were in favour of moving to new offices in this area, whereas just over a quarter of staff said that they preferred the idea of moving to new offices in the city centre. On the other hand, 23% of staff stated that they would like the existing offices to be modernised.
>
> **Office layout and lighting**
>
> Just over half the staff preferred the option of an open-plan office, while 20% thought that managers should have individual offices and the rest should be open plan. However, the vast majority (90%) told me that they wanted all workstations to have natural light.
>
> **Conclusions and recommendations**
>
> I recommend that we should move to new open-plan offices in this area, if possible in a building which allows all members of staff to work with natural light, as this will keep the majority of staff happy and boost staff morale.

Unit 23 Corresponding with customers

A letter about a new service

Writing

2 Sample answer

> Dear Mr Castle,
>
> **New Services from TopTen Leasing**
>
> As a valued long-standing client of TopTen, I am sure you will be interested to know that we are extending our leasing services to the whole of Europe. This means we guarantee to deliver the equipment you require anywhere in Europe within 24 hours of you placing the order. Also, for each seven-day lease, we will give you one free day.
>
> I enclose a leaflet detailing our service.
>
> As you already know, we make sure that all the equipment we supply is in perfect condition, so you can be certain to start using it as soon as it is delivered. Also, as a premium customer, you are not required to pay a deposit on the equipment you hire.
>
> If you would like to know more about this service, or if you would like to take advantage of it, please do not hesitate to contact me personally,
>
> Yours sincerely,

Preparing a letter of complaint

Writing

2 Sample answer

> Dear Mr Sarawi,
>
> **Late delivery of documents**
>
> I am writing to you to express my dissatisfaction with your document-delivery service.
>
> Last Monday, we asked you to deliver some important legal documents to our offices in Budapest in time for a meeting with company lawyers on Monday morning. The documents did not, in fact, reach them until 4 o'clock on Friday afternoon, with the result that we had to cancel the meeting and reschedule it for this week. This nearly resulted in us losing an important contract.
>
> I would like to remind you that we are a long-standing client of yours and that we rely on you to provide us with a trouble-free service. I must emphasise that we will only continue to use your service if deliveries continue to be problem-free in the future.
>
> Yours sincerely,

Exam skills and Exam practice

Contents

		Exam skills	Exam practice
About BULATS		122	
Listening Paper Part 4		124	125
Reading Paper Part 2 Section 2		127	128
Reading Paper Part 2 Section 3		129	131
Reading Paper Part 2 Section 4		132	133
Reading Paper Part 2 Section 5		134	136
Reading Paper Part 2 Section 6		138	140
Writing Paper Part 2		141	143
Speaking Test Part 1		144	
Speaking Test Part 2		145	147
Speaking Test Part 3		148	150

About BULATS

BULATS stands for Business Language Testing Service. It is a service for companies designed to help them find out the level of language skills among their staff, trainees or job applicants. It assesses language skills which are needed for the workplace, and for students and employees on language courses or on professional/business courses where foreign-language ability is an important element of the course.

BULATS provides tests for all learners of a foreign language. There is no 'pass mark'. Candidates are placed in one of six levels. These levels are expressed as ALTE (Association of Language Testers in Europe) levels, which are linked to the Council of Europe Framework (CEF) levels. This is explained in the table below.

ALTE levels	Council of Europe (CEF) Level	BULATS scores	Level description	Cambridge ESOL certificated examinations at these levels
Level 5	C2	90–100	Upper-Advanced	CPE
Level 4	C1	75–89	Advanced	CAE, BEC Higher
Level 3	B2	60–74	Upper-Intermediate	FCE, BEC Vantage
Level 2	B1	40–59	Intermediate	PET, BEC Preliminary
Level 1	A2	20–39	Elementary	KET
Level 0	A1	0–19	Beginner	–

The test is carefully designed to be suitable for a wide range of people at work – technicians, secretaries or managers, in banking, in education or in manufacturing, in administration, research or marketing. It does not require any previous business experience, and so it is also suitable for students who may need to use the foreign language in the future.

At the moment, four different types of test are offered: the BULATS Computer Test, the BULATS Standard Test, the BULATS Writing Test and the BULATS Speaking Test.

The BULATS Computer Test assesses your ability to use the foreign language by presenting questions via a computer. The computer test is adaptive. This means that according to your answers, the computer programme chooses each new question for you. (Your *Business Benchmark* CD-ROM allows you to practise for the Computer Test, but it is not adaptive: this means that you can try all the questions in the Computer Test, not just those chosen for you by the programme.)

Test Lengths

The Standard Test lasts 110 minutes and tests listening and reading skills, and knowledge of grammar and vocabulary. **The Computer Test** is shorter than the Standard Test because it chooses material at a suitable level for the candidate. The Computer Test usually lasts around 60 minutes.

The Standard Test

Skill	Part or section	Type of task	Number of questions
Listening	1	Understanding short conversations or monologues	10
	2	Taking down phone messages, orders, notes, etc.	12
	3	Listening for gist: identifying topic, context or function	10
	4	Listening to extended speech for detail and inference	18
Reading and language knowledge	1.1	Understanding notices, messages, timetables, adverts, graphs, etc.	7
	1.2	Gapped sentences	6
	1.3	Reading passage with multiple-choice questions	6
	1.4	Short reading passage; gap filling	5
	2.1	Four short reading passages; sentence matching	7
	2.2	Short reading passage; multiple-choice gap filling	5
	2.3	Short reading passage; gap filling	5
	2.4	Gapped sentences	6
	2.5	Long reading passage with multiple-choice questions	6
	2.6	Error correction	7

The Writing Test

	Part or section	Type of task	Time (approx.)
Writing	1	Short message/letter (50–60 words)	15 minutes
	2	Report or letter (180–200 words)	30 minutes

The Speaking Test

	Part or section	Type of task	Time (approx.)
Speaking	1	Interview	4 minutes
	2	Presentation	4 minutes
	3	Information exchange and discussion	4 minutes

Listening Paper Part 4: Exam skills

Part 4 consists of:

- three interviews, discussions or conversations with two or more speakers **or** a presentation or report with just one speaker
- six multiple-choice questions for each section.

You must choose **A**, **B** or **C**.

You practised similar skills in Unit 6 (page 32) and in Unit 18 (page 89).

This part of the exam tests:

- your ability to follow longer listening tasks
- your ability to interpret what the speakers say in order to choose the correct alternative.

> **Multiple-choice questions in the Listening paper**
>
> Each question has three alternatives. One is the correct answer, the others are 'distractors'. You have to distinguish the relevant information from the distractors. Be careful when you listen, because the speakers will usually mention something connected with the distractors. You must be alert in order to decide that they are the wrong answers.

Suggested exam technique

1 **Use the pause** between hearing the instructions and listening to the recording to:
   - read each question and underline the key words
   - study the alternatives for the first few questions and predict how these might be expressed.
2 The speaker will probably say something about all three alternatives. Listen carefully to discard the wrong alternatives.
3 Remember: the speakers will not use the same words as are used in the questions – you will have to listen for the **same meaning**.
4 Use the pause between listening the first time and listening the second time to check the questions which give you problems.
5 The Listening paper needs a lot of concentration. Make sure you keep **concentrating hard** until the end of the paper!

Exercises

1 a You are going to hear an interview with Frances Greene whose company supplies cosmetics to hairdressers and beauty salons. Before you listen:
   - underline the key words in these questions
   - check with a partner, and then discuss how Frances might express each alternative in the questions using other words.

12 b Listen and answer the questions.

   c Check in the transcript to see how each option is discussed and which one is correct.

1 How does Frances <u>measure customer satisfaction</u> in her business?
   A She employs a market research firm.
   B She carries out regular surveys.
   C She maintains informal contacts with all her customers.
2 What is the most common problem she has with customers?
   A They are late paying for goods.
   B They demand higher quality than she can give.
   C They only buy at certain times of year.
3 What is her most effective marketing tool?
   A Word of mouth
   B Her website
   C Direct mail

To try a real exam task, go to page 125.

Listening Paper Part 4: Exam practice

Section 1: Questions 33–38

- You will hear a discussion between Brian, the managing director of a company, and Judy, its finance director, about premises for a new head office.
- For questions **33–38**, circle **one** letter, **A, B** or **C**, for the correct answer.
- You will hear the discussion twice.

33 What is the location of the building that they are considering?
    A in a residential area
    B in the town centre
    C in the countryside

34 What do they agree needs to be done to the building?
    A Some internal changes should be made.
    B A great deal of repair work should be carried out.
    C An extension should be constructed.

35 What might cause difficulties?
    A the amount of parking space that is available
    B the entrance to the premises from the road
    C the distance from the site to the motorway

36 How much does Judy think the company should pay for the building?
    A £1,250,000
    B £1,500,000
    C £1,750,000

37 According to Judy, why do the owners of the building want to sell it quickly?
    A to purchase another company
    B to repay its debts to the bank
    C to invest in a new building venture

38 What do they decide to do next?
    A discuss the possible sale with colleagues
    B make an offer to buy the building
    C arrange a visit to the building

Section 2: Questions 39–44

- You will hear a radio interview with a man called Gary Waters about how advertising agencies can win new business.
- For questions **39–44**, circle **one** letter, **A, B** or **C**, for the correct answer.
- You will hear the interview twice.

39 New clients usually contact Gary's agency because
    A the agency has been recommended by another company.
    B they want to compare the prices of several agencies.
    C they are familiar with some of the agency's work.

40 Gary thinks the best way to start getting ideas for a proposal is to
    A become familiar with the product.
    B talk to somebody from the client company.
    C look at campaigns for the client's competitors.

41 Gary thinks that presentations and proposal packages written by several people may
    A give a poor impression of the company.
    B take too long to write and check.
    C leave out some important points.

42 Gary emphasises the importance in presentations of
    A speaking without hesitating.
    B seeing the audience's reactions.
    C keeping to what he has planned.

43 How does Gary prepare for difficult questions he may be asked at a presentation?
    A He gets his colleagues to ask him what the client might ask.
    B He asks the client in advance what they want to know.
    C He lists questions he thinks he might be asked.

44 Gary thinks the presentation should
    A last at least 20 minutes.
    B be entertaining.
    C focus only on the main points.

Section 3: Questions 45–50

- You will hear a radio news item about Ben Miller being appointed as the new European Chairman of GTR, a big advertising group.
- For questions **45–50**, circle **one** letter, **A**, **B** or **C**, for the correct answer.
- You will hear the interview **twice**.

45 According to the reporter, what action did Miller take last week?
  A He signed a contract with GTR.
  B He left his own agency.
  C He recruited a new partner.

46 Some people at GTR believe that
  A there was not enough consultation over Miller's appointment.
  B Miller's vision for the future isn't suited to the group's set-up.
  C Miller is unwilling to move to Europe.

47 When Miller was at Jackson Media, what was his working relationship with Mark West?
  A They were competing for the same business.
  B West was Miller's boss.
  C They collaborated on setting up the Manhattan office.

48 Why did Miller leave his job with Jackson Media?
  A He was held responsible for some financial irregularities.
  B He had a dispute with some of the company's biggest clients.
  C He found it difficult to work with his new boss.

49 How did Miller's agency, Hudson, get Yellowstone as a client?
  A Miller kept their account when he left Jackson Media.
  B Miller's contacts at Jackson Media had recommended him.
  C Miller had established a relationship with them while at Jackson Media.

50 What interest did the Outward Signs agency have in Miller?
  A They wanted him to become their chairman.
  B They wanted to take over his agency.
  C They wanted to collaborate with his agency.

Reading Paper Part 2 (Section 2): Exam skills

Part 2 Section 2 consists of:

- one text of about 100 words
- five multiple-choice gaps.

You must choose the best word, **A, B, C** or **D**.

You practised similar skills in Unit 1 (page 11) and Unit 13 (page 67).

This part of the exam tests your knowledge of:

- vocabulary
- dependent prepositions (e.g. *depend on*)
- grammatical structures which go with particular words (e.g. *make* + object + infinitive without *to*)
- expressions
- collocations.

> **Collocations**
> Collocations are words that are often found together, but which are not fixed expressions. Collocations may be:
> - adjectives with nouns, e.g. *You will have to work to **tight deadlines**.*
> - adverbs with verbs, e.g. *Prices have **risen sharply**.*
> - verbs with nouns, e.g. *He was unable to **repay his debts**.*

Suggested exam technique

1 Before looking at the alternatives, A, B, C and D, try to think which word will go in the gap – you may be surprised to find it's one of the alternatives!
2 The alternatives will have similar meanings: look for a dependent preposition or a grammatical structure which only goes with one of the alternatives.
3 Look for possible collocations: do you *do, achieve, succeed* or *provide* a service? (Answer: *provide*)
4 When you have finished, read the text again with your answers. Check and change anything which doesn't sound natural to you.

Exercises

1 Choose the best word for each of these gaps. In each case, the correct word is the only one which will go with the dependent preposition. (Note that the preposition is not always just after the gap.)

> When you **1** .... for an interview, your interviewers will **2** .... not just on your skills and experience but also your personality to see whether you will **3** .... comfortably into their organisation and do a good job.

1	A attend	B present	C give	D go
2	A look	B focus	C examine	D investigate
3	A match	B suit	C fit	D relate

2 Choose the best word for each of these gaps. In each case, the correct word will form a collocation.

> Although Bernard Lasky has a reputation for **1** .... a hard bargain after many years in sales, he **2** .... recommends negotiators to give clients a good deal. That, he insists, is the only way to ensure **3** .... long-term customers.

1	A forcing	B making	C driving	D fixing
2	A strongly	B strictly	C totally	D hardly
3	A faithful	B loyal	C friendly	D dependable

3 Choose the best word for each of these gaps. In each case, the correct word will depend on the grammatical structure of the sentence as well as the meaning.

> When launching a new product, you are **1** .... to carry out market research which will give you enough information to **2** .... you position your product correctly in the market. Moreover, it will help you **3** .... your promotional activities better.

1	A suggested	B advised	C insisted	D warned
2	A let	B allow	C permit	D facilitate
3	A produce	B plan	C invent	D create

To try a real exam task, go to page 128.

Reading Paper Part 2 (Section 2): Exam practice

Questions 1–5

- Read this article about an expanding company.
- Choose the best word to fill each space from the words below.
- For each question **1–5**, mark **one** letter, **A**, **B**, **C** or **D**, on your Answer Sheet.

Example:

He wants you to **(0)** .... him the reason.

0   **A** speak   **B** tell   **C** say   **D** talk

Answer:

| 0 | A ☐ | B ■ | C ☐ | D ☐ |

Molly Maid Expansion

Domestic cleaning specialist Molly Maid is responding to a huge increase in demand for domestic services by gearing up for a **(1)** .... expansion of their franchise network over the next five years.

Since the first Molly Maid UK franchise started in Essex in 1986, the company is now **(2)** .... in most parts of the country. But over the past decade, recruitment has now switched to other areas, although there are still many opportunities in the south-east.

The new drive is powered by fresh resources committed to the company since Canada-based Molly Maid International (MMI) **(3)** .... its direct investment in the UK at the end of 2002, when MMI **(4)** .... the UK Molly Maid franchised residential-cleaning operation from Agostpolar Group. Thanks to this, Molly Maid UK has undergone a significant **(5)** .... , particularly in regard to enhanced franchisee support services.

1   **A** main   **B** major   **C** chief   **D** core
2   **A** rooted   **B** grounded   **C** stood   **D** established
3   **A** rose   **B** developed   **C** increased   **D** grew
4   **A** acquired   **B** attained   **C** achieved   **D** collected
5   **A** amendment   **B** conversion   **C** transformation **D** modification

Reading Paper Part 2 (Section 3): Exam skills

Part 2 Section 3 consists of:

- one text of about 100 words
- five gaps which you must fill with one word.

You practised similar skills in Unit 7 (page 39) and Unit 11 (page 56).

This part of the exam tests your knowledge of grammar, especially:

- prepositions
- articles (*a, an, the*)
- auxiliary verbs
- pronouns
- relative pronouns
- grammar adverbs (*however, still, yet*, etc.).

> **What type of word?**
> The position of the word in the sentence will often tell you what type of word you need. For example:
> - between the subject and the main verb, you need an auxiliary verb, a modal verb or an adverb:
>   *Many businesses .... formed by serial entrepreneurs.* (auxiliary verb: *are*)
> - before a noun, you need an adjective, an article or a preposition:
>   *He noted that .... businesses are formed by serial entrepreneurs.* (adjective: *many*)
>   *Fewer than half of .... businesses formed by people under 25 are successful.* (article: *the*)
>   *Banks are ready to lend money .... businesses which have solid assets.* (preposition: *to*)

Suggested exam technique

1 Read the whole text first.
2 Look at each gap, sentence by sentence.
3 Consider what type of word you need – this will depend on the position of the word in the sentence.
4 When you know what type of word you need, think of alternatives and try them in the space.
5 Look carefully at the other words in the sentence, e.g. .... *interesting than* needs *more* to complete the comparative structure.
6 If you can't think of a word, leave it and come back to it later.
7 Don't leave any spaces blank – if you can't think of the correct word, guess: you may be right!
8 When you have finished, read the whole text again: does it read logically with the words you have chosen?

Exercises

1 Put each of these words into the table according to the type of word it is.

although	an	are	be	being	can
forward	have	it	much	so	than	the
they	to	what	who	with

Article	Pronoun	Relative pronoun	Auxiliary/ modal verb	Preposition

2 a Read the following sentences with a partner and decide what type of word would fit each space.

1 During .... most recent recession, house prices fell by 23%.
2 The consultancy firm Brace and Nichols has put .... a plan for a complete restructuring of the company.
3 In his speech to the AGM, Mr Ishiguro stated that the price of shares .... risen by more than 20% last year.
4 Recently, the company has been performing badly, and .... of the main reasons for this is high oil prices.
5 The firm Bahrain International Imports has reached an agreement .... Isoltis to set up a joint venture in the Gulf region.
6 Despite the buoyancy of the electronics market, new electronic consumer products are .... more likely to fail than to sell profitably.
7 Sales targets for this year have been set at higher levels .... last year.
8 He argued that such long-standing clients should have .... given a much higher discount.
9 John Corfield, ... previously worked in sales for General Electric, has been appointed CEO.
10 .... customers don't want is to be faced with too many choices.

b Write one word in each space in the sentences above.

3 Write one word in each space below. If you are not sure, decide what type of word you need, then choose from the words in Exercise 1.

How rational are your investment and other personal finance decisions? In many cases, something may **1** .... seemed a good idea at the time, but when you review your investment portfolio, the haphazard pattern could **2** .... embarrassing. It may also reveal how often you bought into shares or funds at **3** .... top of the market. This is the most obvious example of illogical investor behaviour. About 70 per cent of the UK's private investors admit that their investments are a mess, according **4** .... a recent survey. It found that 135 of investors did not even know **5** .... they had invested in.

All these examples of apparently bizarre activity **6** .... increasingly coming under a new microscope labelled behavioural finance. This is a branch of economic psychology that compares actual investor behaviour **7** .... the alleged purely rational approach dictated by classic economic theory.

4 Write one word in each space.

In 2004, Benton Electronics announced that **1** .... were moving their head office from the centre of Burton to a new purpose-built office building on a green-field site on the outskirts. At first, **2** .... were a number of protests from staff **3** .... thought their journey times to and from work **4** .... be significantly increased. However, when the move was made, **5** .... soon became apparent that the new offices were a success, not just with customers but **6** .... with staff. **7** .... customers and staff found the company offices' proximity to the motorway extremely convenient. **8** .... addition to the easy access, free parking in the company car park **9** .... an added bonus. Another factor contributing **10** .... the success of the new site has been the comfort of the offices and the views of the countryside.

To try a real exam task, go to page 131.

Reading Paper Part 2 (Section 3): Exam practice

Questions 6–10

- For questions **6–10**, read the text below and think of the word which best fits each space.
- Write only **one** word for each space on your Answer Sheet.

Example:
He is very interested **(0)** .... computers.

Answer:

0	in

Market leadership regained

The multi-functional Andrex UK team has achieved a dramatic turnaround for K-C Europe's most profitable brand, Andrex tissues. Faced **(6)** .... a declining share in an intensely competitive market, the team created a new, superior product which had increased softness and bulk. The improved product quality and lower price differential were a huge hit with consumers and, for now, they **(7)** .... reduced the reliance **(8)** .... promotions.

The change was successfully executed **(9)** .... of schedule and delivered a 25% increase in the baseline rate of sales. This means that **(10)** .... Andrex previously sold only when running special promotions is now a daily occurrence. Market share is back to 30%, and Andrex tissues is the UK's largest non-food grocery brand.

Reading Paper Part 2 (Section 4): Exam skills

Part 2 Section 4 consists of:

- six sentences with gaps.

You must choose the word or phrase, A, B, C or D, which completes the gap.

You practised similar skills in your Personal Study Book: Unit 14 (page 32) and Unit 20 (page 44).

This part of the exam tests your knowledge of vocabulary and grammar, especially:

- meanings of individual words
- collocations (see page 127).

Suggested exam technique

1 Decide if the question is asking you about vocabulary or grammar.
2 If it is asking you about vocabulary:
   - choose the word which sounds natural in the context
   - look for clues in the sentence: prepositions, etc.
   - If you don't know, discard the answers which you think are wrong and choose one of the others.
3 If it is asking you about grammar:
   - which word fits the grammar? For example, is there a verb + -ing (e.g. *hoping*) or an infinitive (e.g. *to hope*) after the gap? If there is a verb + -ing, perhaps the word you need is a preposition.
   - If you don't know, discard the answers you think are wrong and choose from the others.

Exercises

1 **In this exercise, all the alternatives have similar meanings, but only one is correct in the context. Work with a partner. Choose the alternative which is correct.**

1 Unless production is kept on ...., we will fall behind with our orders.
   A timetable   B schedule   C agenda   D programme

2 Toyota are planning to launch a new .... of their Lexus range in June.
   A make   B brand   C model   D trademark

3 He's a skilled negotiator who is known to drive a hard ....
   A bargain   B deal   C agreement   D contract

2 **Work with a partner. Choose the correct answers and say why the other alternatives are wrong. Where possible, say which preposition they would need.**

1 Comcam Ltd are looking for local suppliers in order to reduce their .... on imported components.
   A necessity   B requirement   C need   D reliance

2 One of the best decisions we ever made was to .... part of our profits in a new fleet of vans.
   A invest   B spend   C lay out   D buy up

3 If you're sending the goods by sea, it is essential to .... against any accidents which might happen during the journey.
   A guarantee   B cover   C insure   D assure

3 **Work with a partner. Choose the correct answer and say how you would need to change the sentence to make the other alternatives correct, e.g. *Despite their sales undergoing a record expansion, ...***

1 Comcam's profits in the last year were disappointing, ... their sales underwent a record expansion.
   A despite   B although   C however   D nevertheless

2 Dieter Schmidt has just taken over as managing director after working as head of human resources .... the last five years.
   A for   B in   C over   D during

3 We won't consider stocking their products .... them giving us a hefty discount.
   A providing   B unless   C without   D except

To try a real exam task, go to page 133.

Reading Paper Part 2 (Section 4): Exam practice

Questions 11–16

- Choose the word or phrase which best completes each sentence.
- For questions **11–16**, mark **one** letter, **A**, **B**, **C** or **D**, on your Answer Sheet.

11 Advertising should be sustained over time to .... creditable results.
   A collect
   B harvest
   C yield
   D earn

12 We can't hold the meeting externally .... Finance agrees that the company will fund it.
   A unless
   B without
   C despite
   D except

13 The new director has transformed the company by .... several brands.
   A detaching
   B loosening
   C demerging
   D shedding

14 They launched a new product in a .... to capture a larger share of the market.
   A proposal
   B bid
   C submission
   D tender

15 Desks need to be at least 1 metre wide to .... a monitor.
   A lodge
   B accommodate
   C house
   D contain

16 The plan that the board .... was received favourably by most staff.
   A put forward
   B went in front
   C pushed up
   D forged ahead

Reading Paper Part 2 (Section 5): Exam skills

Part 2 Section 5 consists of:

- one text of 450 to 550 words
- six multiple-choice questions where you must choose the best answer, **A, B, C** or **D**.

You practised similar skills in Unit 5 (page 29) and Unit 17 (page 85).

This part of the exam tests:

- your ability to read in detail
- your ability to interpret opinions and ideas expressed in the text rather than facts.

> **Skimming**
> Skimming consists of reading very fast to get a **general idea of the meaning and contents** of the whole text (for example, you get a long email marked *urgent* just before you are going into an important meeting and you have to decide what action to take very quickly).
> - When you see unfamiliar words or sentences you don't understand, do not spend time trying to understand them – continue reading.
> - Only worry about difficult vocabulary or sentences if you find there is a question about them.

Suggested exam technique

1 Skim the text first to get a quick, general idea of what it says.
2 Read the stem of the first question (the part before the alternatives A, B, C or D) and underline the key words.
3 Find where the question is dealt with in the text. Read the four alternatives and find which one is correct.
4 Remember: the words of the text will not repeat the words of the question. You will have to find the same idea expressed in a different way.
5 Make sure there is evidence in the text to support your answer.
6 The answers to the questions come in the same order in the text, so when you have answered one question, move on to the next part of the text to answer the next question.
7 Be careful about time. If you take too long with this part, you won't have enough time for other parts.

Exercises

1 Skim the following article (it is about half the length of an exam text, so take just a minute and a half to do this), then say which paragraph talks about:

1 how effective business books are
2 how you can make money from writing business books
3 what is wrong with most business books.

Why so many business books are awful

A If you want to profit from your pen, first write a best-selling business book. In few other types of book are the spin-offs so lucrative. If you speak well enough to make a conference of sleepy middle managers sit up, your fortune is made. 'You can,' says Mark French of Leading Authorities, an agency which finds speakers for conferences and other events, 'make a seven-figure income just from speaking.'

B Given this strong motivation to succeed, it is astonishing how bad most business books are. Many appear to be little more than expanded PowerPoint presentations, with bullet points and sidebars setting out unrelated examples or unconnected thoughts. Some read like an extended paragraph from a consultant's report (and, indeed, many consultancies encourage their stars to write books around a single idea and lots of examples from the clientele). Few business books are written by a single author; lots require a whole support team of researchers. And all too many have meaningless diagrams.

C The fundamental problem is that a successful business book needs a bright idea, and they, in the nature of business, come along infrequently. The dotcom boom brought some. Since then, new books have tended to focus on three areas: corporate governance, leadership, and how to make money out of bits of the business that were forgotten in the boom. It is hard to believe that many managers run their businesses differently as a result of their reading. Occasionally, however, a truly great business book will articulate an idea that helps them to explain what they are trying to do. It creates phrases – such as 'core competence' or 'emotional intelligence' – that fit the moment.

2 a Underline the key words in the stem of each question below, then answer the questions in five minutes.

1 In the first paragraph, the writer suggests that successful business books can <u>make an author rich</u> because:
   A there is a large market for such books.
   B they will result in new job offers.
   C they lead to other profitable activities.
   D the books command high prices.
2 The writer's main criticism of business books is that:
   A they are generally disorganised.
   B they are copied from things done at work.
   C they are not supported by examples.
   D they are insufficiently researched.
3 In the last paragraph, the writer suggests that business books have limited influence because they:
   A tend to concentrate on too few subjects.
   B do not change the way businesses are run.
   C are not published often enough.
   D only produce clever-sounding phrases.

b Compare your answers with your partner, and highlight the evidence in the text which supports your choices.

To try a real exam task, go to page 136.

Exam skills and Exam practice   **135**

Reading Paper Part 2 (Section 5): Exam skills

Questions 17–22

- Read this article about what makes a top company successful, and answer questions **17–22** on the opposite page.
- For questions **17–22**, mark **one** letter, **A**, **B**, **C** or **D**, on your Answer Sheet.

The Louis Vuitton Money Machine

If you look through the pages of the glossiest fashion magazines, you'll find pages and pages of top models displaying handbags and accessories from Louis Vuitton and its rivals Prada, Gucci and Hermes. At the glamorous end of the fashion market, Vuitton is great but not alone. So what makes it unique?

Well first, there's the relentless focus on quality. At all Louis Vuitton factories, employees work in teams of 20 to 30. 'Each team works on one product at a time, and team members are not only encouraged to suggest improvements in manufacturing, but they are also briefed on details about the product, such as its in-store price and how well it is selling,' says Stephanie Fallon, a former manager for Michelin who runs the Vuitton factory in Ducey, Normandy. 'Our goal is to make everyone as multiskilled and autonomous as possible,' says team leader Thierry Nogues.

The teamwork pays off. When a prototype for a new bag design arrived at Ducey last summer, production workers who were asked to make a test run quickly discovered that decorative metal studs were causing the zipper to bunch up, adding time and effort to the assembly process. The team alerted factory managers, and within a day or two, technicians had moved the studs a few millimetres away from the zipper.

Such efficiency helps compensate Vuitton for its decision to keep most manufacturing in France, one of the world's most expensive labour markets. Of the 13 factories that make Vuitton bags, 11 are in France, and the other two are across the border in Spain. The reason for this decision is simple, but is often asked about: 'The question gets raised all the time, and the answer is that we feel more confident of quality control in France,' says Head of Production, Emmanuel Matthieu.

Productivity alone won't sustain growth, so while most luxury groups cut their ad budgets last year, Vuitton boosted spending by about 20%, using top supermodels in the campaigns. Even so, Vuitton is so big that analysts reckon that it still only spends about 5% of revenues on advertising, half the industry average.

However, as Vuitton expands, hazards appear, with counterfeiting rising sharply in recent years. 'It's a menace we take very seriously,' says Bertrand Stalla Bardillon, Director of Intellectual Property.

But for Vuitton, the biggest challenge may be to keep this powerful machine under control. The company opened 18 stores last year, about twice the rate of store openings a decade ago. 'The temptation with a lot of brands is to immediately find new outlets, new sources of distribution, and price points,' says New York-based brand consultant Marc Gobe. 'But Vuitton are extremely disciplined,' Gobe says. Vuitton Chairman Bernard Arnault promises that Vuitton will never lose its discipline or focus on quality. 'That's what differentiates Louis Vuitton,' he says.

17 To help the Vuitton workforce become 'multiskilled and autonomous', they are given
    A opportunities to contribute ideas on product marketing.
    B information about the bags' retail performance.
    C training in enhancing product design.
    D experience of all the manufacturing processes.

18 How did a production team at Ducey make the production of a new bag more efficient?
    A They asked technicians to alter some of the parts that they had to assemble.
    B They redesigned the parts that opened and closed the bag.
    C They discovered the fastest way of attaching some decorative parts.
    D They reported that the position of some parts slowed production down.

19 What does 'the question' refer to in the fourth paragraph?
    A How many Vuitton factories are in countries that have high labour costs?
    B What are the disadvantages of manufacturing in France?
    C Which countries do Vuitton manufacture in, apart from France?
    D Why don't Vuitton manufacture their products somewhere cheaper?

20 What comparison between Vuitton and other similar companies is made in the fifth paragraph?
    A Vuitton had a smaller increase in advertising than most other companies last year.
    B Vuitton still spend less of their income on advertising than most other companies.
    C Vuitton need to run fewer campaigns than other companies because it is such a big brand.
    D Vuitton's advertising costs are lower than the costs of 50% of other companies in the industry.

21 Marc Gobe's opinion is that Vuitton
    A need now to focus on speeding up their brand expansion.
    B opened too many new stores last year.
    C have managed to resist the temptation to expand too quickly.
    D may have to sacrifice quality to sustain brand growth.

22 What is the writer's overall point in this article?
    A The luxury goods sector is showing others how to succeed.
    B Manufacturers can become more successful by opening their own outlets.
    C Success comes from concentrating on quality and attention to detail.
    D Every employee should benefit from a company's success.

Reading Paper Part 2 (Section 6): Exam skills

Part 2 Section 6 consists of:

- one text of 100–150 words; the text contains seven lines, each of which may contain one word which is not correct.

You must find the word which is not correct and write the correct word.

Some lines may be correct.

You practised similar skills in Unit 23 (page 110) of this book and Unit 11 (page 27) of your Personal Study Book.

This part of the exam tests:

- your ability to identify and correct errors in texts
- your knowledge of grammar.

Wrong words
You should look for 'grammar words'. Here are some examples with the wrong word crossed out. The correct word is in brackets at the end of the sentence:

- pronouns, e.g. *We put the product on the market last month and he is selling well.* (it)
- relative pronouns, e.g. *I'm happy to stock your product, but that I don't want is for it not to sell.* (what)
- conjunctions, e.g. *If we can sell the product immediately, we will withdraw it from the market without hesitation.* (unless)
- auxiliary or modal verbs, e.g. *Over the last five years, job cuts in the industry are lowered morale among workers.* (have)
- prepositions, e.g. *We need to concentrate in quality.* (on)
- small adverbs, e.g. *Running your own business is so a challenging job; it should not be undertaken unless you are prepared for hard work.* (such)

Suggested exam technique

1. Skim the text quickly to get a general idea of what it's about.
2. Although there will be an incorrect word in most lines, **read the text by sentences,** not by lines.
3. There will not be more than one wrong word per line.
4. Remember that **some lines are correct**, but read each sentence carefully to make sure.

Exercises

1. Some of the lines in this letter have a wrong word. Cross out the wrong word and write the correct word in the space provided. If a line is correct, put a tick (✔) in the space. All the wrong words are parts of verbs.

Dear Mr Inskip,	
Thank you for the visit you paid us last Monday. It was most interesting	1 ....✔....
to see your latest range of swimwear and I think it ~~would~~ do very well	2 ...will...
when the next season start.	3 ....
We would like to place an order for 2,500 items, which I list on the	4 ....
enclosed order form, as long as we may reach an agreement on payment	5 ....
terms. One of our managers have asked me if it is also possible to ask for	6 ....
different colours and patterns to being included in the range apart from	7 ....
the ones which are showing in the catalogue.	8 ....
I look forward to hearing from you shortly.	
Yours sincerely	
Fernando Delgado	

2 Some of the lines in this letter have a wrong word. Cross out the wrong word and write the correct word in the space provided. If a line is correct, put a tick (✔) in the space. All the wrong words are prepositions.

Memo:
To: All staff
From: CEO
Subject: Staff meeting

Management is considering changes ~~of~~ working practices, and we would welcome suggestions from staff. For this purpose, we will be holding a meeting at 4 pm on Wednesday 4 August by the staff canteen. You can either put your suggestions on an email to me, or you can make them at the meeting. Some ideas to think of include:
- career breaks for staff from over ten years' service
- flexitime, especially to parents with young children.

Many thanks

1 *in*
2 ✔
3 ....
4 ....
5 ....
6 ....
7 ....

3 Some of the lines in this letter have a wrong word. Cross out the wrong word and write the correct word in the space provided. If a line is correct, put a tick (✔) in the space. The wrong words are all the wrong type of word, e.g. an adjective instead of an adverb or a noun instead of a verb.

Dear Mrs Pereira

You may ~~memory~~ that we met at the Footwear International Fair in Santiago last year. At present, we are extreme active in developing our business with South America and are particularly interesting in expansion our imports of clothing products from all over the continent. I shall be in São Paulo brief next month and I would welcome the opportunity to meet you and discussion the possibility of us distributing your products in Europe (which you mentioned at the fair).
If you still find this possible of interest, please let me know, and we can arrange a meeting. My diary is already quite fill, so please let me know soon when you would find a meeting most convenient.

Yours sincerely,

Pierre Lauriac

1 *remember*
2 ....
3 ....
4 ....
5 ....
6 ....
7 ....
8 ....
9 ....
10 ....

To try a real exam task, go to page 140.

Exam skills and Exam practice **139**

Reading Paper Part 2 (Section 6): Exam practice

Questions 23–29

- A colleague of yours wants you to check this article for a company newspaper.
- In some lines there is one wrong word.
- If there is a wrong word, write the correct word on your Answer Sheet.
- If there is no mistake, put a tick (✓) on your Answer Sheet.

Example:

| One of the items you ordered from our catalogue | 0 | ✓ |

| is <u>temporary</u> out of stock | 00 | *temporarily* |

All change for new identity

Business sites throughout Exeline are busy implementing the changes to the company's
23 new identity. Work does accelerate in the coming weeks as the distinctive new logo and livery
24 spread for factory and office signs, vehicles, work wear and literature. Establishing the
25 new identity is seen as a vital element in the build-up of Exeline, and has been giving
26 priority attention. 'It was one of the first things we had to do because it was such
27 important,' says Don Watkins when he addressed the conference in Düsseldorf which
28 launched the identity. 'The two merged companies which created Exeline has a long and
29 illustrious past, with much to be proud at. But we were clear that Exeline must look
forward and outward, not backward and inward.'

Writing Paper Part 2: Exam skills

Part 2 consists of:

- either a letter or a report of 180–200 words.

You can choose to answer one of two questions.

You have approximately 30 minutes.

You practised similar skills in Unit 3 (page 20), Unit 15 (page 75), Unit 19 (page 93) and Unit 23 (page 111).

This part of the exam tests your ability to:

- use the correct format and appropriate register for the type of task
- use grammar and vocabulary accurately to express your ideas
- communicate clearly in writing.

Register

The register you use will depend on:
- the subject you are writing about
- who you are writing to.

For example, if you are writing a letter to an important customer, the register will be quite formal, but if you are writing to a close colleague, you may use quite an informal register.

Suggested exam technique

1. Read the instructions carefully, underlining key information in the instructions:
   - Is it a letter or a report?
   - Who will read it? (This will decide the register.)
   - What points must you include?
2. Write a quick plan. Make sure your plan covers **all the points you have been asked to include**.
3. Organise your plan in a logical way.
4. Write your answer from your plan using:
   - the correct format
   - an appropriate register (see above).
5. Use linking words and phrases to connect your ideas (e.g. *however, although, also, as a consequence, as a result*, etc.).
6. Check your answer for mistakes.

Exercises

1 Work in pairs.

a Read the task below and underline the key points, i.e. the things you must include in your answer.

A number of staff have recently told you that they are unhappy about the times when they start and finish work in your company. You have been asked to write a report for the managing director about this.

Write your **report**. Write about:
- why staff are unhappy with the times
- why it is important to keep staff happy
- what solutions your company should adopt for the problem
- any other points you think are important.

Write **180–200** words.

---

b Answer these questions about the task.

1. What things should you include in your answer?
2. What ideas or information will you have to invent?
3. What information can you include which will make your report sound more realistic?
4. Who is going to read the report? So what register should you use?
5. What format should your report have?

c Complete these notes for the task with your own ideas.

Introduction
Reason for report: ....

Problems with existing times
Working times at the moment: ....
Problems with these times: ....
....

The importance of keeping staff happy
1 Cost of recruiting new staff
2 ....

Solutions and recommendations
1 ....
2 ....

Exam skills and Exam practice

d Read the sample answer and answer the questions below.

Report on staff working times

Introduction

The purpose of this report is to analyse why our office staff are unhappy with the times when they start and finish work and to suggest solutions to the problem.

Problems with existing times

At present, office staff start work at 9 am and finish at 5.30 pm. A number of problems have arisen with this timetable:
- Staff have to travel during the rush hour, which means longer and more uncomfortable journeys. As a result, they arrive at work feeling stressed.
- Many of our staff find it difficult to leave their children at school (between 8 and 8.30) and arrive at the office on time to start work.

The importance of keeping staff happy

Staff turnover as a consequence of this problem has increased from 10% per year ten years ago to 20% last year. This in turn has caused an increase in recruitment costs for the company. Also, happy staff are more motivated, work harder and give better service to our customers.

Solutions and recommendations

I recommend that we offer staff a number of the solutions:
- They can have flexible starting and finishing times at work.
- Where possible, they can do some of their work from home.

---

1. Does the report contain the same ideas as you put in your notes (in part b)?
2. What do you notice about the layout of the report?
3. Does the report have a title?
4. What are the purposes of the first and last sections?
5. Find phrases which express results. (For more work on expressing results, look at Grammar workshop 6 (page 117) and Unit 23 (page 111).)
6. Has the writer completed the task? Is there anything which has been forgotten?

To try a real exam task, go to page 143.

Writing Paper Part 2: Exam practice

Task A

A number of visitors who recently visited your department complained about the quality of the hotel accommodation your company booked for them. The head of your department has asked you to write a report summarising the visitors' complaints and making a recommendation for the future.

Write the **report** for the head of your department.

Write about:
- the types of complaints visitors made;
- why it is important to use a good hotel for company visitors;
- which hotel your company should use instead

and any other points which you think are important.

Write about **180–200** words.

OR

Task B

You are unhappy with your company's current website. The head of your department has asked you to write a report making recommendations for setting up a new website.

Write the **report** for your head of department.

Write about:
- the problems with the current website;
- the kind of information a new website should contain;
- who should be involved in setting it up

and any other points which you think are important.

Write about **180–200** words.

Speaking Test

The Speaking Test lasts about 12 minutes. You are assessed by the examiner, and a recording is made, which is assessed by another examiner later.

In the test, you are given marks for:

- **accurate grammar and vocabulary**
- **range of language** (how much vocabulary and grammar you know)
- **discourse management** (how well you speak when giving longer answers; how fluent you are; and how well you organise what you say)
- **pronunciation**
- **interactive communication** (your ability to share and participate in a conversation with the examiner).

Speaking Test Part 1: Exam skills

Part 1 consists of:

- general questions which the examiner asks you about
  - where you are from/where you live
  - your interests
  - your job or your studies
  - your hopes for the future.

This part of the test lasts about four minutes.

You practised similar skills in Unit 1 (page 13) and Unit 2 (page 17).

This part of the exam tests:

- your ability to talk about yourself
- your ability to perform functions such as agreeing and disagreeing.

Suggested exam technique

1. Make sure, before you go to the Speaking Test, that you can:
   - describe what your job or your studies consist of
   - talk about your ambitions/hopes for the future
   - say what you like/dislike about your job/studies.
2. When you go into the interview, speak clearly so you can be heard.
3. Don't answer the questions with one or two words – answer with one or two sentences.
4. When you answer a question, give a reason for your answer or an example.

Some extra advice

- Try to speak naturally and confidently.
- Smile and look directly at the person you are speaking to.
- If you don't understand a question, ask the interviewer to repeat it.
- If you notice you've made a mistake, correct yourself.

Exercises

1. Complete these sentences about yourself. Then compare your answers with a partner.

   1. My job/studies consist(s) of ....
   2. The thing I enjoy most about my job/studies is .... because ....
   3. There are some things I don't like, for example ....
   4. I chose to do this job/this course because ....
   5. I use/expect to use English in my work in order to ....
   6. In the future, I hope to be working .... because ....
   7. I like this area for living/working because ....

2. a Work alone. Study the questions below and think how you could best answer them.

   - Can you give an example?
   - Can you add a reason for your answer?

   b Note down two or three words you would like to use when you are answering each question.

   1. Where do you come from?
   2. What do you like about the area where you live?
   3. Is this a good area to work in?
   4. What does your job consist of? / What do you study?
   5. What do you most enjoy about your work/studies?
   6. Is there anything you don't enjoy?
   7. Why have you been studying Business English?
   8. How important is English in your job? / How important do you think English will be for you in the future?
   9. What would you like to be doing in, say, ten years' time?

3. a Work with a partner. Take turns to interview each other using the questions from Exercise 2.

   b When you have finished, discuss how you could improve your answers.

Speaking Test Part 2: Exam skills

In Part 2:

- You are given a page with three topics printed on it. Each topic begins *Talk about …* or *Describe …* (for example: *Talk about how your company markets its products or services*) and ends *Give reasons for your answer.*
- Some questions are printed below each topic to help you.
- You are asked to choose one of the three topics.
- You have one minute to prepare your answer and make notes.
- You must speak for one minute about the topic.
- When you have finished, the examiner will ask one or two questions about your talk.

This part of the exam tests:

- your ability to speak for a longer period of time, as you might have to do when giving a presentation or speaking at a business meeting
- your ability to communicate a series of ideas clearly
- your ability to structure your speech and connect your ideas.

This part of the text lasts about four minutes.

You practised similar skills in Unit 24 (page 114).

> **Interview nerves**
>
> It is natural to feel a little nervous about this part of the interview. Overcome them by telling yourself:
> - you have something interesting and important to say
> - the examiner wants to hear your ideas
> - he/she would be equally nervous if he/she had to give a talk in your language!
>
> Above all, **keep speaking**. If you dry up, take a breath and start again. Don't worry if you repeat something you have already said.

Suggested exam technique

A You have **one minute** to prepare. Use it to:
  1 choose the topic you think is easiest
  2 think how you give longer answers to the questions by:
     - giving reasons
     - giving examples
  3 make brief notes while you are thinking
  4 note down key business vocabulary you want to use.
B If you can, **use your own experience** to answer the question.

C When speaking:
  1 refer to your notes, but **look at the examiner**
  2 introduce your talk by saying what topic you have chosen
  3 sequence your talk by saying *firstly*, *secondly*, *finally*, etc.
  4 signpost your talk with phrases like *this is because*, *for example* and *as a result of this*
  5 watch the time and try to finish your talk with a brief concluding sentence at the end of the minute.

Exercises

1 a Work in pairs. Study Topic 1 below and discuss how you could answer it. Take two or three minutes to do this and take notes.

  b Change partners and give your talk. Your partner should listen and, at the end, ask you one or two questions about your talk.

  c When each of you has given your talk, give feedback on what you did well and what you could improve.

  d Do the same for Topics 2 and 3.

---

1 Talk about the meetings you have to attend in your company.
  You should say:
  - how often you go to meetings
  - what sort of meetings you have to attend
  - how effective the meetings are
  How could the time spent at meetings be improved in your company? Give reasons for your answer.

---

2 Describe how your company promotes its products or services.
  You should say:
  - what promotional activities your company uses
  - who decides which activities to use
  - how effective you think these activities are.
  What changes would you like to see in the way your company promotes its products or services? Give reasons for your answer.

---

3 Talk about a job you have applied for.
  You should say:
  - what the job was
  - why you applied for the job
  - what happened during the application process.
  Was your application successful? Why? Why not? Give reasons for your answer.

2 a Complete this talk by writing one of the words or phrases from the box in each space.

> A further point   Another important thing is
> But, to conclude   Firstly   For example   I mean
> So   This way

Well, I'm going to talk this evening about what is important when setting up a new business. **1** .... , it may depend on the type of business you are thinking of starting up, but if it's a small business with just one or two employees, management experience is not absolutely essential. What is far more important is knowledge of the product. **2** .... , if you're going to open a clothes shop, you should have some experience of working in a clothing outlet and know a lot about clothes.

3 .... a knowledge of the market. You should know who your competitors will be, and you will have already identified your target customers and perhaps even spoken with some of them before launching your business. **4** .... you will feel reasonably confident that someone is going to buy your product. **5** .... , you don't want to invest your life savings in a business, only to find that it doesn't interest anyone!

6 .... is that you must have a reasonable working knowledge of finance, so that you can produce a sales forecast. You should estimate your costs and make a cashflow prediction. **7** .... , you'll be able to persuade a bank to give you a loan or overdraft.

8 .... , the most important thing is interest in the product and your customers.

14 b Check your answer by listening to Martin, a small business advisor, giving a talk to business students at an adult education college.

3 In his talk, Martin does the following things. Read what he said in Exercise 2 again and find where he did them.
1 He introduces his talk.
2 He makes three main points.
3 He gives an example.
4 He explains what he means using other words.
5 He concludes his talk.
6 He uses business vocabulary.

To try a real exam task, go to page 147.

Speaking Test Part 2: Exam practice

> **INSTRUCTIONS**
>
> Please read all THREE topics below carefully.
> Choose **ONE** which you feel you will be able to talk about for one minute.
>
> You have one minute to read and prepare your talk.
> You may make notes.

Topic A

Talk about how your company assesses the performance of its staff.

You should say:
- how often staff performance is assessed;
- who is responsible for assessing performance;
- how performance is assessed.

How is performance rewarded in your company? Give reasons for your answer.

Topic B

Describe how the Internet has affected your company.

You should say:
- how it has affected communications;
- what effect it has had on business;
- how staff feel about using it.

Will the Internet become more important for your company? Give reasons for your answer.

Topic C

Talk about a business trip you have been on.

You should say:
- where you went;
- why you went there;
- who you met there.

Was the trip a success? Give reasons for your answer

Speaking Test Part 3: Exam skills

In Part 3:
- you are given a card with a role-play situation
- you ask the examiner questions to get the required information
- you must then give your opinion about the information the examiner has told you
- you then discuss a related topic with the examiner.

This part of the exam tests:
- your ability to ask questions
- your ability to express opinions
- your ability to agree and disagree.

This part of the test lasts about four minutes.

You practised similar skills in Unit 8 (page 41) and Unit 20 (page 97).

Asking questions

You can ask questions directly by saying things like *How much does it cost?* or *When will you be able to deliver it?*
You can also ask questions more indirectly by saying *Can you tell me how much it costs?* or *I'd like to know when you will be able to deliver it.*
It's a good idea to practise asking both types of question before you go to the speaking test.
For more work on asking questions, go to Grammar workshop 1 (page 27).

Suggested exam technique

1 Read the card carefully before you start speaking.
2 Greet the examiner and introduce the questions before you ask them, e.g. *Good morning, I'd like to ask you a few questions about ...* The examiner will answer with something like: *OK, what would you like to know?* You can then sequence the questions, e.g. using *Firstly, Secondly* and *Finally.*
3 Make sure to ask the questions correctly. (You did work on asking questions in Unit 2 (page 15), Unit 3 (page 20) and Unit 8 (page 41).)
4 Listen carefully to the examiner's answers and at the end give your opinion about what he/she says.
5 Be ready to disagree with the opinions or ideas the examiner expresses. (For language of agreeing and disagreeing, see Useful language on page 10.)

Exercises

1 **Read the task sheet and complete the questions below it with one word for each space.**

TASK SHEET

Car suppliers

Your company has decided to buy a new fleet of cars for its executives. The examiner is a representative of a firm which supplies cars for companies. She/He is visiting you to discuss the matter.
Find out this information:
1 types of car available
2 prices
3 terms of payment.

Question 1:
- What types of car ....?
- .... you tell me what types of car ....?

Question 2
- How much .... the cars ....?
- I'd like to know how much ....

Question 3
- What .... terms of payment?
- What terms of payment .... offer?

2 a **Study these ways of sequencing questions and introducing indirect questions.**

Ways of sequencing questions	Ways of introducing indirect questions
First	I'd like to ask ...
First of all,	I'd like to know ...
Another thing	Can you tell me ... ?
Also	I was wondering ...
One last thing	Could you tell me ... ?

b **Combine phrases from the table above to ask questions for this task sheet.**

TASK SHEET

A business hotel for a conference

Your company is looking for a business hotel for a conference they are going to hold in your city. You are visiting a hotel in the area. The examiner is the manager of the hotel.
Find out this information:
1 facilities available at hotel
2 prices of rooms
3 discount for group booking.
You will then be asked to give your opinion about this information.

3 a Combine a comment from each column to form ways of expressing an opinion.

I like the price, but …	I don't think you are offering me a big enough discount.
The price is a bit high, but …	the facilities sound excellent.
I think the price is fine, and …	I'd prefer a hotel with more facilities for business people.

b Read the information below, which would be given by the examiner. What opinion(s) could you express about it?

- Facilities at hotel: bar, restaurant, discotheque and business centre. No Internet connection in rooms.
- Price: $150 per night (single room), $200 double room
- Discount for group booking: 10% on groups of ten or more

4 Work in pairs. Student A should take the role of candidate and Student B should take the role of examiner.

Student A (candidate)

Read this task sheet. Find out the information and give your opinion when the examiner asks for it.

TASK SHEET

Advertising in a newspaper

Your company is interested in advertising its products in a regional newspaper. Your examiner sells advertising space in the newspaper. He/She is visiting you to discuss the matter.
Find out this information:
1 types of space available
2 price of full page
3 number of readers of newspaper
You will then be asked to give your opinion on this information.

Student B (examiner)

Look at Student A's task sheet and answer with the information below. When Student A has finished asking, find out his/her opinion about the information. You can ask *So what do you think of the information I have given you?*

1 Types of space available: full page, half page and smaller sizes.
2 Price of full page: $6,000 per day
3 Readers: 50,000 a day

5 Work in the same pairs and change roles.

Student A (examiner)

Look at Student B's task sheet and answer with the information below. When Student B has finished asking, find out his/her opinion about the information. You can ask *So what do you think of the information I have given you?*

1 Spaces available: 50
2 Rates: 20% discount on normal price for one-year contract
3 Security: People park cars in car park at their own risk. Car park has no insurance.

Student B (candidate)

Read this task sheet. Find out the information and give your opinion when the examiner asks for it.

TASK SHEET

Car-parking facilities

Your company is considering renting car-parking facilities in a public car park near the office for office workers. The examiner is the manager of the car park. He/She is visiting you to discuss the matter.
Find out this information:
1 Number of spaces available
2 Special rates
3 Security in car park
You will then be asked for your opinion on this information

To try a real exam task, go to page 150.

Speaking Test Part 3: Exam practice

Air-Conditioning System

Information Exchange

Your company has decided to install air conditioning in its offices. The examiner is a sales representative of a firm which supplies these systems. She/He is visiting you to discuss the matter.

Find out this information
1. types of system available
2. cost
3. terms of the service agreement

You will then be asked to give your opinion on this information.

Discussion

Now discuss this topic with the examiner.

How important is a comfortable working environment?

Answer keys

UNIT 1
Staff development and training

Recruitment brochure
Vocabulary

1 skills   2 qualifications; ability   3 course; degree
4 certificate; knowledge; experience   5 development; training
6 trainee; hands-on

Reading

1   1 f   2 c   3 d   4 e   5 a   6 b
3   1 B   2 A   3 C   4 B   5 D   6 C   7 A   8 D   9 B   10 C

Training course
Listening

1 e   2 f   3 d   4 a   5 b   6 c

Deloitte Touche
Reading

1 Sample answers
Paragraph 1: Why I chose Deloitte
Paragraph 2: Help and support with my studies
Paragraph 3: Internal training
Paragraph 4: You can choose your training method
Paragraph 5: Passing on skills in the company
Paragraph 6: Help with obtaining professional qualifications
2   1 F   2 C   3 B   4 A   5 E   6 D

Vocabulary

1 in the fast lane to promotion   2 on-the-job training and development
3 has gone out of his way   4 monitors   5 internal training
6 core skills   7 graduate trainees   8 appraisals   9 peers
10 fully funded   11 workload

UNIT 2
Job descriptions and job satisfaction

Getting started

1 Chief Executive Officer   2 Chief Information Officer
3 Personal Assistant   4 Human Resources Manager
5 Director of Research and Development   6 Public Relations Officer

Vocabulary

1   1 b   2 c   3 a   4 e   5 g   6 f   7 d
2   1 performance   2 launched   3 recruitment (of new staff)
   4 accountant   5 easing   6 project teams   7 targets
   8 budgets   9 meeting deadlines

What I like about my job
Listening

3   1 b   2 f   3 c   4 a

The management accountant
Reading

1   a   How hard do you have to work?
   b   What do you like about your job?
   c   How long have you been in your present job?
   d   What are your ambitions for the future?
   e   What does your job consist of?
   f   When were you first attracted by accountancy?
2   1 f   2 b   3 e   4 a   5 d
3   1 False: She came to the UK to study English.
   2 True: *Following her graduation, with a first-class BSc Honours degree, she joined IMI as a trainee accountant.*
   3 True: *… at school, where I was the class treasurer for four years.*
   4 False: She's also involved in new product launches, IT system introductions, etc.
   5 True: *I have two divisional management accountants reporting to me.*
   6 True: *I supply financial information to all levels within the organisation, from local management to the board of directors.*
   7 False: She thinks the extra work should be seen as something that comes with a managerial position.
   8 False: She'd like to progress from a local office to a job at headquarters with responsibility for various offices.

A human resources manager
Listening

1   1 h   2 g   3 f   4 e   5 b   6 d   7 c   8 a
2   1 A   2 B   3 C   4 C   5 B   6 B

UNIT 3
Letters of enquiry and applications

Job satisfaction at EMI
Reading

2   1 Helen   2 Deby   3 Deby   4 Sally   5 Mark   6 Sally   7 Mark
   8 Helen

Vocabulary

1 in house   2 (added) bonuses   3 a nine-to-five kind of person
4 standing over   5 take over   6 loads of   7 venues   8 entry level

A letter of enquiry
Writing

2   1 d   2 g   3 e   4 f   5 c   6 b   7 a
3   1 I would like to know whether I have the right qualifications.
   2 I would be most grateful if you could send me information about what opportunities exist in EMI Music.
   3 Could you also tell me how I should apply?
   4 I'd be interested to know when the final date for applications is.

Advice on job applications
Listening

1 Sample answers
   a Attach a picture to your letter or email so they can see what you look like.
   b Send your application electronically so that it gets there quicker.
   c Your letter of application should not be too long, as it will take too long to read.
   d Mention the things you like doing in your spare time, so that they can get a better idea of what sort of person you are.
   e Ask someone to look at your application before you send it, as mistakes will make a bad impression.

f After you have sent your application, call the company to check they have received it.
  g Don't tell lies in your application, as they may find out later.
  h Include contact details for your referees, so that the company can get in touch with them easily.
3 1 d 2 b 3 g 4 e 5 f

An email of application
Writing
1 1 I am 2 in application 3 post 4 curriculum vitae
   5 current position 6 practical experience 7 held 8 extensively
   9 attending 10 attended 11 I am 12 represent 13 seeking
   14 have the experience of managing regional sales
   15 curriculum vitae 16 available for 17 employers 18 supply
   19 look forward
2 Her CV   b
   A summary of relevant work experience   b
   Details of her academic background   b
   Her availability for interview   e
   Reasons for applying for this job   d
   References from her employers   e
   The reason for writing the letter   a
   Where she saw the advertisement   a
   The job training she has received   c

UNIT 4
Telephone skills

Telephone language
Listening
2 1 Rubenstein 2 Top Flight 3 Meeting room 4 Job interviews
   5 18 May 6 Coffee (for interviewers and interviewees)
3 1 can I help 2 This is 3 calling from 4 give me your
   5 can you tell me 6 would you 7 would you like 8 let me know

A telephone quiz
Reading
1 B and C are normal if the call has been routed through a switchboard; D would be appropriate if you are a receptionist, for example. A is just unhelpful because the caller doesn't know if he or she has reached the right person or company.
2 All three are possible.
3 B
4 C
5 A and C are both correct, but B is not.
6 A is quite formal, B is informal and C is neither correct nor polite.
7 C is formal, A is informal and B sounds rude.
8 A and B are both correct, although you would only use A with someone you know well.
9 A and B are both correct.
10 B and C are both correct, depending on what information you are looking for.

Enquiring about a job
Listening
1 1D, 3B, 4C, 10B
2 1 mornings (only) 2 bookkeeping 3 beginning of 4 by email

Grammar workshop 1
Comparison of adjectives and adverbs
1 1 more challenging 2 more economical; further/farther
   3 more highly 4 longer; greater 5 friendlier / more friendly
   6 strongest; more impressive 7 most motivating
   8 less than; harder

Present perfect and past simple
1 1 present perfect 2 past simple 3 present perfect
   4 past simple
2 1 have worked 2 went; haven't gone/been
   3 was; left; have not seen; went 4 have changed; started; finished
   5 posted; has been; has got married; (has) started

Simple questions
1 Sample answers
   1 Did you have
   2 Will/Would working in this city
   3 How long / How many years have you worked
   4 What do you
   5 What would you

Complex questions
1 1 Could you tell me how long you have been a product manager?
   2 I'd like to know if/whether you have studied abroad.
   3 I wonder when you first became interested in this profession.
   4 I'd like you to tell me what you enjoy doing in your free time.
   5 Can you predict what you will be doing in ten years' time?

UNIT 5
Promotional activities and branding

Getting started
1 1 c 2 h 3 e 4 g 5 a 6 f 7 d 8 i 9 b

Promoting AXE
Reading
1 Promotional activities: a slogan, online game, free samples, point-of-sale displays, media advertising, PR, a house party, direct mailing, online publicity, leaflets, advertisements in magazines, website, television show, free CD
2 1 B (young men's natural interest in pretty girls ... appeal to American male youth culture)
   2 D (... young men to log on to the Internet to play a video game on the AXE website ... If the player reached a certain level, he entered a lottery to win a trip to the party.)
   3 C (AXE focused on the intrigue and discovery of the party)
   4 A (It was all about getting into the mind of the 20-something guy)
   5 B (To our knowledge, nobody had ever taken a consumer promotion and turned it into a television show)
   6 C (a 22% increase in general brand awareness among males aged 11 to 24)

Vocabulary
1 k 2 i 3 g 4 e 5 f 6 h 7 b 8 j 9 a 10 d 11 c

Supermarkets' own brands
Listening
2 1 C 2 A 3 B

The power of brands

Reading

2
1 A *A logo was a straightforward guarantee of quality and consistency.*
2 D *Old-fashioned market-research methods help explain such mistakes. Focus groups, for example, are poor at discovering the real reasons why people like brands*
3 C *… to sell a lifestyle or a personality …* + *'Our product is a personality,' he claims. 'We like certain people, but some people are just more fun and interesting.'*
4 C *Clever, simple ads are dreamt up long before the product is produced.*
5 B *… they switch products more often.*
6 A *… consumers were, quite rationally, prepared to pay a premium.*
7 C *As one company president says of his product, it is its sense of humour, rather than its taste, that is the reason for its success.*
8 B *Brands now face competition from the most unexpected quarters.*
9 D *Firms such as Coca-Cola and McDonald's, complacent from past success, find it difficult to admit that their customers are changing to newer products.*
10 A *Brands also helped consumers to buy efficiently* + *'People want to simplify their lives.'*

Vocabulary

1 logo 2 pay a premium 3 multiply 4 switch 5 approach
6 task 7 complacent 8 reinvent themselves 9 appeal

UNIT 6
New product development

Developing and launching 'chai'

Listening
3 1 A 2 A 3 B 4 B 5 C

Reading
2 1 H 2 C 3 G 4 F 5 A 6 E

Vocabulary
1 entrepreneurial skills 2 up-market 3 founding 4 prohibitive
5 soared 6 takings 7 a niche product 8 take off 9 stocking
10 outselling 11 new lines 12 projected turnover

Launching and promoting a new product

Listening
2 She says market research is important to make sure that there is a market for your product. She used her tea bars to test the market.

4/5
1 ✔ to raise awareness
2 ✔
3 ✔
4 ✔ so that people will know how it tastes, there are lots of people
5 because she doesn't have a big budget
7 ✔ to become well-known in other markets
9 because these cost too much – about £100,000
10 ✔ to keep momentum and sell in the warmer months

Grammar workshop: Expressing purpose

1 Sample answers
1 … they would write articles about my product.
2 … get invited to *The Good Food Programme*.
3 … give people a chance to taste chai.
4 … it's important to get people talking about the product.
5 … we employed a professional web designer.

2 1 B, C 2 A, D

UNIT 7
A stand at a trade fair

Getting started
1 This is a trade fair, where companies hire space and set up stands. Company representatives and sales people are talking to potential customers who visit their stands. People visit trade fairs to identify possible products and potential suppliers.
2 Sample answers
Potential customers can see and handle the products on display. They can talk to sales staff.
Companies can invite potential customers to visit them at their stand.
A good stand can give a company prestige.
It gives the company an opportunity to promote its products to its competitor's customers.

The International Food Exhibition

Reading
1
1 A memo is an internal note circulated to people in an office (nowadays usually by email) containing information or instructions, possibly about a new policy or activity.
2 Directly, with the subject of the memo. If you wish, you can finish it with *Many thanks* (or something similar) and your initials or your signature.
3 Start with the name of the addressee and finish with *Thanks* or *Best wishes* and the name of the writer.
4 Contact the organisers of a trade fair to find out information about setting up a stand.

3 a ✔ b ✔ c ✘ d ✔ e ✔ f ✘ g ✔ h ✘

4 We are a small company from the Republic of ~~the~~ Ireland specialising in ~~the~~ producing and exporting typical and regional foods from our country.
We are interested in the ~~having~~ possibility of exhibiting at the International Food Exhibition in London ~~during~~ next March and we would like answers to the following ~~these~~ questions:
• How much would it cost ~~for~~ to hire a space for a stand at the exhibition?
• Can you tell us when ~~do~~ we would need to make a booking?
We ~~are~~ look forward to hearing from you, and thank you in ~~the~~ advance for the information.

Listening
2 1 floor space 2 in writing 3 by cheque 4 floor plan
5 guaranteed

Answer keys 153

Writing

1 Sample email
Subject: International Food Exhibition
Hello Bill
The organisers have given me the following information:
- Stands cost between £120 and £200 per square metre. However, we have to pay a 50% deposit when we make our reservation. The balance must be paid one month before the exhibition begins.
- The deadline for reservations is 1 September.

Best wishes
Frank

Grammar workshop: Forming questions

2 1 How much does a ticket to the exhibition cost?
2 Can you tell me how much a ticket to the exhibition costs?
3 Could you tell me how many visitors came to the exhibition last year?
4 How many exhibitors were there at the exhibition?
5 I would like to know how far the exhibition centre is from the centre of London / how far from the centre of London the exhibition centre is.

Preparing an exhibition stand
Writing 1

2 Sample email
Dear Sirs
We are interested in having a stand at the International Food Exhibition in London next March. Could you please give us an estimate of how much it would cost to build a stand of 30 square metres? I would also like to know when you can do it and when it would be possible for you to visit us to discuss the design of the stand if we like your prices.
Many thanks
Frank O'Donnell

Reading

2 1 A 2 B 3 B 4 C 5 B 6 A 7 C
3 1 B 2 C 3 A 4 D 5 A 6 D 7 C
4 1 As you will see   2 You should let us know   3 at any one time
4 If you would be so kind as to supply us with this information …

Writing 2

2 Sample answer
Dear Mr Steel
Thank you for your designs. In answer to your questions:
1 We have booked 40 m² of floor space.
2 Our stand is on a corner and we would prefer it to be open.
3 We would like to be able to accommodate up to 15 people at any one time.
From the designs you sent us, the one we like the most is Number 3. We look forward to receiving your design and quotation.
Best wishes
Frank O'Donnell

4 Sample answer
To: Sales staff
From: Bill Cowley
Subject: Stand at International Food Exhibition
I'm pleased to inform you that the stand for the IFE is being designed at the moment. Could you please let me know what equipment you will need for the stand? Also, I suggest you start preparing the graphics you want to put on the stand.
Many thanks
BC

UNIT 8
Establishing relationships and negotiating

Establishing a business relationship
Listening

1/2

	Who would express it?	Correct order
Asking about the other person's journey	S	3
Saying they like the stand	V	1
Asking the other person where they are staying	S	5
Saying how busy the fair is	V	7
Offering refreshment	S	8
Saying how nice the city is	V	4
Offering to show their products	S	6
Thanking the other person for the invitation	V	2

3 1 this 2 meet 3 too 4 thanks 5 talk 6 trip 7 Lovely
8 staying 9 get 10 Busy 11 either 12 with

Asking questions about a product
Reading

2 1 easy to keep 2 does it weigh 3 would we be 4 would* you; it
5 could you get 6 Does it come; to pay
* *could* is also possible here, although *would* is on the recording.

4 1 Questions 1, 2, 6   2 Questions: 3, 4, 5
5 1 d 2 h 3 e 4 b 5 f 6 a 7 c 8 g

Terms and conditions
Vocabulary

1

Discount	Payment terms	Delivery date
€19.95 on each item if you place an order now 5% on bulk orders $2 if you order within one week 7.5% on 100 or more	at sight 30 days 90 days	by courier within two weeks of receiving the order dispatched immediately

2 Better for the buyer: 90 days
Better for the seller: at sight

Negotiating
Listening

1 Scales: 500 on sale or return, €80 per unit, 5% discount on sales over 500 for repeat orders, 30 days payment (to be renegotiated for subsequent orders)

Grammar workshop: First conditional

2 Sample answers
1 … we'll place a larger order straight away.
2 … you guarantee me the same terms and conditions.
3 … you agree to buy at least 500.
4 … we won't make a profit.
5 … our mark-up is too low.

154 Answer keys

Grammar workshop 2

Countable/uncountable nouns

1

Countable	Uncountable	Both
advertisement	advertising	business
budget	advice	cost
euro	direct mail	experience
job	information	innovation
leaflet	marketing	profit
product	money	promotion
qualification	news	
trip	office furniture	
	progress	
	publicity	
	sponsorship	
	transport	
	travel	
	work	

2 1 some 2 any/much/a 3 much; any/much 4 an; much
5 a; a 6 some; a; a 7 Some/Many/Few; a
3 1 **an** advertisement; **a** new sales director 2 *correct* 3 **a** higher advertising budget 4 ~~a~~ direct mail 5 *correct* 6 ~~a~~ work; **a** job
7 ~~an~~ experience; ~~a~~ wholesale business 8 ~~a~~ business success
9 *correct* 10 ~~an~~ information

-ing forms and infinitives

1 1 training 2 dealing 3 to get 4 advertising; to invest
5 developing; to be 6 leaving; to start 7 to develop; lending
8 Studying; to be

The first conditional

1 e 2 g 3 b 4 c 5 f 6 d 7 a

UNIT 9
Going it alone

Why start your own business?

Listening
2 1 g 2 b 3 f

Vocabulary
1 1 go 2 running 3 entrepreneur 4 started 5 competition
6 outlet 7 franchise 8 looked 9 fees 10 marketing
11 profits 12 starting

Buying into a franchise

Reading
1 1 They wanted to run their own business and franchises are 90% successful.
2 It was a business they thought they would feel a passion for.
2 1 G 2 F 3 B 4 A 5 D 6 C

Vocabulary
1 f 2 b 3 a 4 c 5 d 6 e 7 g

Grammar workshop: Time clauses

1 1 B 2 C 3 A 4 A 5 A 6 B
2 1 opened 2 meet 3 comes 4 starts 5 have been; decided
6 deal / are dealing 7 rings 8 found / had found

Financial terms

Vocabulary
1 1 b 2 g 3 d 4 a 5 c 6 f 7 e
2 1 turnover 2 costs 3 profit 4 interest rate 5 asset 6 tax
7 liability

A letter to a franchiser

Reading
2 1 ✔ 2 was 3 time 4 ✔ 5 the 6 these 7 is 8 for
9 ✔ 10 will 11 for 12 the 13 to 14 will 15 an 16 salary
17 so 18 ✔

UNIT 10
Financing the start-up

Getting started
1 d 2 b 3 a 4 c 5 e

Start-up opportunities

Vocabulary
1 raise finance / money / a loan
borrow money
carry out market research / a business plan
launch a company
cover overheads
write a business plan
repay a loan / money
2 1 launch a company 2 carry out market research
3 raise finance/money/a loan / borrow money
4 write a business plan 5 repay your/the loan
6 cover (your) overheads

Setting up a food consultancy

Listening
2 1 exhibitions 2 start-up 3 business plan 4 clients
5 (more) enthusiastic 6 part-time 7 pay back

Raising finance

Reading
3 1 A *Banks don't care whether or not your business has great profit potential. They are only interested in the business's ability to cover the principal and interest payments.*
2 B *You should prepare a written agreement*
3 B *Don't be embarrassed to show financial statements, tax returns or whatever else they want to see.*
4 C *They are best known for financing high-tech firms*
5 C *only be interested in entrepreneurs who have experience of successfully starting up businesses.*
6 A *Banks like to use assets such as premises, motor vehicles or equipment as collateral (or security) against loans.*

Setting up a multimedia company

Listening
2 1 A 2 A 3 C 4 B 5 C

Talking point
2 Luck, knowing where you want to go, having a good business plan, good people with a track record, vision, business skills (understanding market, financial projections, understanding cost base)

UNIT 11
Starting up in a new location

Getting started
2 Suggested extra information:
- how much BioBok is willing to invest
- number of staff
- where the staff will come from

A new location in Scotland
Listening
2 1 and offices   2 60   3 recruited locally   4 government grants

Reading
2 1 Edinburgh (*the Science Triangle*)
   2 Edinburgh (*to encourage active collaboration*)
   3 Glasgow (*remains above the Scottish rate*)
   4 Edinburgh (*has excellent transport links*)
   5 Glasgow (*a student population ... second only to London*)
   6 Glasgow (*the largest city in Scotland*)
   7 Edinburgh (*with world firsts*)
   8 Glasgow (*ranks second in Europe in terms of offering value-for-money office space*)

A proposal
Reading
1 1 to   2 which   3 the   4 because/as/since   5 one   6 for
2 1 It's divided into sections with headings; it contains bullet points; it has a title.
   2 The existing situation may be mentioned, but the proposal concentrates on suggested future courses of action.
   3 The first states the purpose of the proposal. The last contains recommendations and a suggested action plan.
   4 Examples of formal phrases: **The purpose of** *this proposal is to* … / **I suggest that we should** *recruit people.* / *Property prices* **appear to be** *lower.* / **Our next steps should be to** *…*, etc.

Making recommendations
Writing
1 Other phrases which introduce recommendations:
   It would be a good idea to …
   I strongly recommend that …
   Our next steps should be to …
2 Sample answers
   1 It would be a good idea to find premises close to the airport.
   2 I strongly recommend that we design our own building.
   3 I suggest that we contact Edinburgh University.
   4 Our next step should be to advertise for staff in science magazines.

Grammar workshop: Contrasting ideas
2 1 although
   2 However/On the other hand
   3 on the other hand/however
3 Sample answers
   1 Although our factory is rather old, it's still highly productive.
   2 We have a very small training budget. However, we still manage to recruit some of the most highly skilled staff in the industry.
   3 We do not pay our staff as much as our competitors. On the other hand, we give them very generous holiday leave.
   4 Our new CEO has made the company very successful although he has only been with us for two years.
   5 The business was not very profitable last year. However, this year's interim results are promising.

Agents and distributors
Talking point
1 1 Joint-ventures   2 Distributors   3 Agents
2 Advantages and disadvantages which may come up in discussion:
   Joint-ventures
   Advantages
   Firms participating may benefit from complementary expertise (e.g. knowledge of local markets on the one hand, and technical or production facilities on the other).
   May be a cheaper way of breaking into a new market than setting up a local operation.
   You have (joint) control over the operation in the new country.
   Disadvantage
   Co-operation with a separate company, negotiating and reaching agreement on how to manage and develop the joint-venture.
   Distributors
   Advantages
   Local knowledge, established sales force and distribution system etc.
   Disadvantage
   Unless good agreements have been negotiated, lack of control over how the product is marketed, pricing policies, motivation of local sales teams etc.
   Agents
   Similar to distributors, but, while distributors work on a profit margin, agents take a commission on sales.

Writing
Sample answer

Proposal for a choice of distributor in New Zealand
Introduction
The purpose of this proposal is to compare two possible distributors for our products in New Zealand and to recommend which distributor we should choose.
Burford Electrical Distributions
This distributor has been in business since 1959 and they stock most major brands. However, this means they stock our competitors' products and will probably not be so interested in selling ours. Also, although they have a large, highly experienced sales force and offices throughout the country, they are also quite highly paid, which will make our products more expensive.
Finally, they make daily deliveries. However, you have to pay extra for deliveries, which will also add to the cost of our products.
Choice Electrics
This company is relatively new. It was started in 2003, which means its sales force is not so experienced. On the other hand, they are young and keen and they have reputation for dealing in high-quality state-of-the-art components like ours. Finally, they sell over the Internet and deliver by express courier the same day.
Recommendations
I strongly recommend that we choose Choice Electrics because they will sell our products more cheaply and because they seem more dynamic. I suggest we contact them to negotiate an agreement.

UNIT 12
Presenting your business idea

Getting started
2 1 data projector   2 laptop   3 screen   4 pointer   5 flipchart
   6 handouts   7 samples of product   8 remote control
   9 speakers

Structuring a presentation
Talking point
1 c 2 e 3 d 4 f 5 b 6 g 7 a

Signalling the parts of a presentation
Listening
1 1 b, j 2 h 3 k 4 c, e 5 a, d, i 6 f 7 g
3 1 advertising 2 drivers 3 traffic conditions 4 main road 5 leasing 6 2,000 7 premium rates 8 500,000

Making the most of presentations
Reading
2 1 A (*some basic training*)
2 D (*speak slowly*)
3 C (*recording and listening to yourself*)
4 D (*make eye contact with members of the audience as often as possible*)
5 B (*prepare*)
6 A (*Rehearsing the presentation will greatly reduce anxiety.*)
7 B (*which things it is worth knowing about in case anybody asks you about it*)
8 D (*put any lengthy detail into a handout*)

Grammar workshop: Modal verbs
1 These should be 2 you must 3 it might be 4 people can

Grammar workshop 3
Tenses in time clauses
1 have written 2 were giving / gave 3 had given
4 receive / have received 5 finishes / has finished 6 launched
7 had built 8 was trying 9 closed / had closed 10 comes / has come

The second conditional
1 1 weren't 2 would start 3 paid 4 could work 5 would take
2 Sample answers
1 If I spoke perfect English, I could get a job with the San Francisco branch.
2 I wouldn't work so hard if I didn't enjoy my job so much.
3 If they don't give me promotion, I'm going to start looking for another job.
4 If I started my own business, I would have to work much longer hours than I do now.
5 If I needed money to start a business, I'd have to get a bank loan.
6 I'll study another language if I think it will help my career.

Comparing and contrasting ideas
1 1 although 2 Although 3 Despite / In spite of 4 However 5 However / On the other hand 6 Although 7 although 8 despite / in spite of 9 Although
2 Sample answers
1 I am successful despite not working very hard.
2 I've made progress learning English, although my pronunciation is still weak.
3 Although I enjoy some aspects of my work, there are some things I find really boring.
4 In spite of working hard, I still haven't been promoted.
5 Money is important to me. On the other hand, there are things that money can't buy.
6 I like the town where I live, in spite of the fact there is too much traffic.

Modal verbs
1 You should rehearse your presentation before you give it.
2 You should / ought to put complicated details on a handout.
3 You must speak loudly and clearly so that everyone can hear you.
4 Giving presentations to senior managers can be very frightening.
5 You can/may pause to drink water if your mouth is dry.
6 People may/might interrupt your presentation with questions.
7 You can/may tell them to save questions till the end.

UNIT 13
Business hotels and sales conferences
The results of a survey
Writing
1 1 we 2 as/was 3 as 4 most
2 Sample answers
While 24% of respondents rated the Marriott chain as their favourite hotel chain, just 12% liked the Hilton best. However 7% chose Westin as their favourite.
Forty-one per cent of the people who answered the survey considered the hotel's cost as very important, whereas 56% rated it as quite important. However, only 3% said it was not important at all.

Business accommodation
Reading
2 1 E 2 D 3 F 4 H 5 A

Vocabulary
1 subscribers 2 logged on (to) 3 chain 4 staffer (*American English*) 5 attentive 6 consistency 7 singled out 8 rivals 9 tweaked 10 the bottom line

Conference problems
Listening
2 1 E 2 D 3 F 4 H 5 B
3 1 should have sent 2 should have practised 3 should have hired
4 1 Candice 2 Igor 3 Paola

Planning a lively sales conference
Reading
1 C 2 A 3 B 4 B 5 D 6 D 7 C 8 A 9 C 10 D 11 B 12 D 13 C 14 A 15 D

UNIT 14
Business conferences
Arranging conference facilities
Listening
2 1 partners 2 guest speakers 3 opening ceremony 4 (company) logo 5 microphone 6 (own) laptop(s) 7 on request 8 reception area 9 (Free) refreshments

A conference programme

Reading

1. Dr Bowden-Kerby (*will talk about practical examples from work he has done*)
2. Roger Poulton (*This will be your chance to gain more insight into the challenges facing international air travel and how they will affect your business.*)
3. Wally Stone (*will cover the recent success story of Tourism New Zealand's '100% Pure Brand'*)
4. Roger Poulton (*changing face of aviation*)
5. Catherine DeVrye (*Good Service is Good Business*)
6. Mike Tamaki (*reinventing the way in which Maori culture is presented to the tourism market*)
7. Dr Bowden-Kerby (*tourism can be a 'good neighbour', especially in terms of its impact on the fragile coastal environment*)
8. Wally Stone (*the formula for success is a business based on a powerful mix of indigenous people, culture, heritage and environment*)

Vocabulary

1 c 2 a 3 f 4 b 5 h 6 e 7 d 8 g

Networking at a conference

Listening

1 1 g 2 a 3 b 4 c 5 e 6 d 7 h 8 f
2 1 f 2 d 3 e 4 h 5 a

A destination management company

Listening

1 C 2 C 3 B 4 B 5 C 6 A

UNIT 15
Reports

The Forest Conference Centre

Reading

1 1 off 2 of 3 a 4 so 5 ✔ 6 down 7 on 8 reached 9 ✔ 10 near 11 not 12 were 13 ✔ 14 now 15 in
2 1 It has a title and is divided into sections with section headings.
   2 A proposal.
   3 A report is more likely to concentrate on findings, or results of research, whereas in a proposal the emphasis is on suggestions for future action. Reports may contain recommendations where appropriate.
   4 Increased costs.
   5 Formal. It is written for the Board of Directors. Notice the impersonal style, use of passive, no contractions, formal vocabulary, etc.

Grammar workshop: Using the passive

1 Other examples of the passive: *is used, is expected, is predicted, is forecasted*
2 1 is not equipped
   2 is seen
   3 has not been provided / is not provided
   4 be used
   5 have been vacated / are vacated
   6 be cleaned
   7 be removed
3 It is predicted that; this figure is forecasted to fall

4 1 believed that profits are rising
   2 forecasted that this figure will fall
   3 predicted to decrease
   4 is expected to increase
   5 predicted that visitor numbers will fall

Vocabulary and speaking

1 1 rose: increase, went up
   2 fell: decrease, drop, (suffering)

A report on the use of private company jets

Listening

2 1 G 2 B 3 D

Writing

1 Sample answers
   1 Report on the use of company aircraft by departmental directors
   2 Introduction, Number of flights per year, Reasons for flights, Conclusion
   3 Formal: it will be read by the CEO.
2 Sample answer
   Report on the use of company aircraft by departmental directors
   Introduction
   The purpose of this report is to describe how the company jet is used by senior staff (departmental directors and above) of Florentino International.

   Number of flights per year
   The number of flights per year has increased from 56 last year to 63 this year. This number is expected to increase by nearly 30% to 80 next year.

   Reasons for flights
   The main reason which was given for using the jet last year was customer meetings (56%). However, this has decreased to 40% this year. In contrast, company meetings, which constituted 35% of reasons for flights last year, rose to 45% this year. It is predicted that customer meetings will be the main reason for flights next year (60%), while company meetings are expected to decrease to just 30%.
   Other reasons for using the jet have remained almost the same over the three years at between 10% and 12%.

   Conclusion
   Use of the company aircraft is becoming increasingly popular, and customer meetings are the main reason for using it.

UNIT 16
Business meetings

Getting started

1 1 e 2 d 3 h 4 g 5 f 6 c 7 a 8 b

Talking about meetings

Listening

1 1 e 2 c 3 a 4 f 5 g 6 d 7 b
2 1 Jenny: 3   2 Darron: 6   3 Shirley: 2   4 Paul: 1

A survey of meetings

Talking point

2 Sample answer
   Introduction
   The purpose of this report is to summarise the findings of a survey on business meetings carried out in the United States.

Productivity of meetings
The survey found that, in successful companies, 25% of managers considered their meetings to be productive, whereas in unsuccessful companies this figure was only 2%. The average for all companies was 12%.

Time spent in meetings
The survey found that senior and middle managers spent 78% of their time in meetings and just 28% doing other things.

Number of meetings
In the United States in 1976, business people held an average of 11 million meetings a day. This has risen to the present figure of 25 million a day.

Conclusions
While meetings occupy a large amount of managers' time and are increasingly frequent, most managers consider them to be unproductive.

Think before you meet

Reading
1 C   2 A   3 B   4 C   5 B   6 A   7 C   8 D

Vocabulary
1   1 cornerstone   2 what they set out to do   3 spontaneous
    4 outcome   5 tedious   6 advocates   7 scepticism   8 huge
    9 frame   10 enlist
2   1 to   2 into   3 in   4 in   5 out

Grammar workshop: *Too* or *enough?*
1   All the ideas except item 3 are expressed in the article.
2   1 too   2 too   3 enough   4 enough   5 enough   6 too; enough

A business meeting

Listening
1   Agreeing: 4, 7, 9   Asking someone's opinion: 1, 8
    Disagreeing: 3, 10   Introducing your own opinion: 2, 5, 6

Writing
Sample answer
Hello Barry,
I would be happy to visit China during the first two weeks of June. I shall need to take about 100 leaflets, brochures and catalogues. I will also need a case containing samples of all our main products. Could you please let me know what expenses the company will pay for my trip?
Many thanks,
Sandra

Grammar workshop 4

While and *whereas* for contrasting ideas
1   While/Whereas the Marriott Hotel is situated in the city centre, the Hyatt Hotel is located near the airport.
    The Marriott is situated in the city centre, while/whereas the Hyatt Hotel is located near the airport.
2   While/Whereas the Expo Hotel caters for business people, the Bali Hotel looks after tourists.
    The Expo Hotel caters for business people, while/whereas the Bali Hotel looks after tourists.
3   British Airways offers business class and tourist class, while/whereas EasyJet only has one class.
    While/Whereas British Airways offers business class and tourist class, EasyJet only has one class.
4   Forty per cent of business travellers choose airlines because of their price, while/whereas 35% of business travellers choose them for their schedules. While/Whereas 40% of business travellers choose airlines because of their price, 35% of business travellers choose them for their schedules.
5   While/Whereas the Hilton Hotel has excellent conference facilities, the Paradise Hotel is quiet, small and family-run / is a quiet, small, family-run hotel.
    The Hilton Hotel has excellent conference facilities while/whereas the Paradise Hotel is quiet, small and family-run / is a quiet, small, family-run hotel.

Modal verbs: perfect forms
1 could/should have asked   2 could/should have stayed
3 could have rested   4 might have been   5 might have made
6 might/could just have dialled   7 could/should have told

Passives 1
1   has been sent to head office.
2   will be opened by the Minister for Trade and Industry.
3   must be submitted by 19 March.
4   have been taken by the Board of Directors this morning.
5   are being interviewed for the job at the moment / for the job are being interviewed at the moment.
6   of finished articles are rejected as substandard.

Passives 2
1   expected to fall next year due to increased competition.
2   are expected to rise by 50% in the next six months.
3   been announced that profits have reached record levels.
4   reported to be losing money.
5   thought (by most people) to be an excellent personnel director.
6   expected to meet its deadlines.

Too/enough
1 too   2 enough   3 enough   4 too much   5 too many; enough
6 enough / too much (especially in American English)

UNIT 17
New technologies and change

Getting started
1   1 d   2 b   3 g   4 a   5 f   6 c   7 e

New technology
Grammar workshop: *Used to*
A

Talking point
Sample answers
1   In the past, colleagues used to work in the same location, or had to travel to see each other. Now, colleagues can work in teams at different locations using video conferencing, Messenger and other applications.
2   Relationships between businesses and customers used to be slower and not so exact. Now they can exchange information, order products, view products and review schedules more quickly using the Internet. Correspondence used to take place by letter or telephone. Now email has made correspondence more instantaneous.
3   Need for constant retraining and readiness to adapt to change, the possibility that employees can be contacted 24 hours a day through mobile technology, etc., the replacement of workers by machines.

Grammar workshop: The definite article

1 the 2 – 3 the 4 – 5 – 6 the 7 – 8 – 9 the 10 the

The Internet and change

Reading

1 1 C (*That places a premium on sites that are able to offer one-stop shopping with the lowest prices.*)
   2 B (*… it saves money. The customer does the work once done by an employee*)
   3 C (*Many people research travel options in cyberspace and then book their trip through a retail travel agent.*)
   4 B (*And they do all of this with no human employees in sight.*)
   5 D (*The top two categories among its three million classified ads in any given month are for job vacancies (23%) and accommodation (21%).*)
   6 A (*companies rent software*)
   7 D (*All the money still comes exclusively from employers advertising job vacancies*)
   8 A (*Training usually takes hours rather than weeks*)

Vocabulary

1 licence fees 2 applications 3 hardware 4 web browser
5 home loans 6 track packages 7 a decade 8 roughly
9 stumbling blocks 10 places a premium on 11 spouse
12 sense of community

Changes at work

Listening

1 1 A 2 F 3 D
2 1 D 2 C 3 B

Change at Adobe Systems

Reading

1 1 Adobe's main products: Adobe Acrobat, Adobe fonts, Adobe Photoshop, Adobe After Effects
   2 Main motivation: employees feel proud of what they are doing – it has an impact on the world.

3 1 A (*By that time, we had already refocused our business.*)
   2 C (*It's always been about developing, designing, marketing, selling software to help people to communicate better.*)
   3 D (*The biggest growth opportunity for Adobe is around documents … We believe at least 60 million of them want to send reliable documents*)
   4 B (*So the people who chose to stay really saw the potential in this company*)
   5 D (*The fact that we have had **that** kind of impact on society – and the belief that we could continue to have that impact on society – is, I believe, what has motivated our employees more than anything else*)

UNIT 18
Using the Internet

Getting started

2 1 c 2 b 3 f 4 e 5 d 6 g 7 i 8 a 9 h

E-shopping at Tesco.com

Listening

2 1 local store 2 five 3 more contact/communication
   4 front/home page 5 recognised

Vocabulary

1 1 task bar 2 URL/Internet address 3 link 4 scroll bar
   5 banner ad 6 pop-up box 7 status bar
2 1 link 2 URL/Internet address 3 task bar 4 status bar
   5 scroll bar 6 pop-up box

Website design

Reading

2 1 By making sure no page is more than three clicks away and by providing site maps so people know where they are.
   2 Once every three seconds.
   3 It takes a lot of time and effort. Complicated sites are often done quickly.
   4 To consolidate brand identity and start a relationship with the target audience.
   5 When the emphasis is on information.
   6 When you want to consolidate your brand's identity.
   7 It will attract criticism, and people will pass on their criticism.
   8 Because people visit favourite sites often, and time passes fast on the web.

Vocabulary

1 straightforward 2 consolidate 3 target audience 4 redundant
5 gizmos 6 itchy 7 velocity 8 updated

Websites and business

Listening

2 1 B 2 C 3 C 4 C 5 A 6 C

Upgrading a website

Writing

3 Sample answer
Dear Ms Strauss
I'm contacting you because we would like to upgrade our company website www.businessbenchmark.com. We think that at present it is too complicated and that it requires more attractive graphics. I would be grateful if you could look at the website and send me an estimate for upgrading it.
Many thanks
Yours sincerely

UNIT 19
A staff survey

Getting started

2 1 a optional part-time working b career breaks
     c flexible working hours
   2 Benefits of the changes:
     For the company:
     Staff may be less stressed by outside factors, and therefore more efficient/effective.
     Possibly less sick leave and other absences.
     May be easier to retain staff, who, due to external circumstances might otherwise leave.
     Easier to recruit staff.
     Generally, lower costs.
     For staff:
     Less stress.
     Better work-life balance.
     Ability to combine working life with family commitments.

A working party
Listening
2/3

	Job	Benefit/ problem
1 Linda	H	N
2 Brian	A	P
3 Olga	C	J
4 Dan	F	K
5 Martin	D	M

Reading a report
Reading
1 1 A 2 B 3 D 4 C 5 C 6 D 7 B 8 D 9 C 10 B
2 1 This makes it easy and clear to follow. The reader can see the structure and contents very quickly.
 2 No, these are summarised. Normally a report would be accompanied by tables with the figures.
 3 Yes.
 4 The company should go ahead with the changes (under Recommendations).
 5 Yes, also in Recommendations.

Expressing numbers
Vocabulary
1 1 a smaller percentage 2 a large majority 3 a significant number
2 1 g 2 f 3 e 4 c 5 a 6 b 7 d

Grammar workshop: Reported speech
2 1 found travelling to work at peak times stressful and time-consuming.
 2 the new scheme was introduced, he/she hoped he/she would be able to take a career break.
 3 had always wanted to travel round the world.
 4 could provide on-site nursery care for pre-school children.
 5 had used flexitime, and it had been very successful.
 6 we introduced these/the changes, he/she might decide to work part-time

Grammar workshop: Reporting verbs
1/2

Must have indirect object	Can't have indirect object	Both
tell	say	ask
order	state	request
inform	think	promise
	predict	
	demand	
	enquire	
	answer	

3 Sample answers (others may be possible)
 1 'Prices will rise by 5%.'
 2 'Carry out a security check, (please).'
 3 'There will be budget cutbacks in the next financial year.'
 4 'Could/Can/Would you book the flights? / Would you mind booking the flights, (please)?'
 5 'We want our money back!'
 6 'How much do the flights cost?'
 7 'I'll meet the deadline. / I promise to meet the deadline.'
 8 'I'll look into the problem as soon as possible. / I promise to look into the problem as soon as possible.'
 9 'We have no plans to close the factory at present.'

A survey report
Writing
Sample answer

Report on staff survey into changes in the company's offices
The purpose of this report is to summarise staff opinions about changes to the company offices.

<u>How to change our offices</u>
Just under half our staff told me they were in favour of moving to new offices in this area, whereas just over a quarter of staff said that they preferred the idea of moving to new offices in the city centre. On the other hand, 23% of staff stated that they would like the existing offices to be modernised.

<u>Office layout and lighting</u>
Just over half the staff preferred the option of an open-plan office, while 20% thought that managers should have individual offices and the rest should be open plan. However, the vast majority (90%) told me that they wanted all workstations to have natural light.

<u>Conclusions and recommendations</u>
I recommend that we should move to new open-plan offices in this area, if possible in a building which allows all members of staff to work with natural light, as this will keep the majority of staff happy and boost staff morale.

UNIT 20
Offshoring and outsourcing

Getting started

Advantages

The company	• May reduce costs (e.g. labour, land, premises)
	• May benefit from more flexible working practices
	• More advantageous labour laws
	• May be closer to markets
The receiving country	• Employment
	• Taxes
	• Generation of wealth
The customers	• Goods may be produced at lower prices

Disadvantages

The company	• May be more vulnerable to political changes
	• May find offshore operations more difficult to manage/control
	• May attract negative criticism
	• May have higher transport costs due to its operations being more widespread
The receiving country	• May be vulnerable to changes in company policies, external market factors
The customers	• Customer services may not be so efficient

Can outsourcing work for small businesses?
Reading
1 Yes, especially for specialised back-office operations such as payroll, as well as tax advice, graphic design work and computer systems help. However, offshoring may be too expensive unless the operation is of a certain size.
2 1 C (*Olinger … doubts he could find overseas workers with the right expertise for his business*)
 2 A (*less than half the cost of an employee*)
 3 B (*it wouldn't be wise to offshore customer-care contact centre operations unless the contact centre is going to employ 50 people or more.*)

Vocabulary

1 sticking with   2 expertise   3 payroll operations   4 hire
5 call centres   6 foreseeable future

What should we offshore?

Listening

1/2 Information systems   Keeping company secrets
     Administrative work   Management may take more time
     Customer services   Training

3 **Asking for clarification**
Sorry, could you explain that again?
What do you mean by that?
Asking someone else's opinion
Don't you think so?
What do you think?
Agreeing
True.
You could be right.
Disagreeing
Possibly, but …
That's true, but …
Yes, but …
Asking for more suggestions
What else could we outsource?
What else?
Making suggestions
We could consider …
Being non-committal
Maybe.
You could be right.
I suppose so.

4 1 do you mean   2 you think   3 could be   4 Yes   5 What else
   6 true   7 else   8 True

Offshoring from Britain

Listening

1 1 a   2 c   3 b   4 g   5 j   6 d   7 e   8 h   9 i   10 f
2 1 D   2 E   3 C
3 1 made redundant   2 (labour) costs   3 more efficient   4 factories
   5 components   6 (retail) prices   7 quality

Grammar workshop 5

Used to

1 1 used to complain; gave   2 used to watch   3 was; didn't you use to find   4 used to use; have installed; don't do   5 used to dictate; used to type
2 Sample answers
   1 … write everything by hand, as we didn't have computers.
   2 … send text messages to each other.
   3 … spend so long in front of a screen.
   4 … be so expensive.

Articles

1 1 an   2 -   3 a   4 a   5 -   6 -   7 an   8 an   9 an   10 A
2 1 an   2 the   3 -   4 -/the   5 the   6 -/the   7 The   8 a   9 the
   10 the   11 the/an   12 the/a   13 an   14 the   15 -   16 -   17 the
   18 -   19 a   20 -   21 a   22 -   23 -   24 -   25 -

Reported speech

1 Sven said the computer system had been installed the week before.
2 Sven said he hoped to have all the technology up and running the following week.
3 Gabriella informed them that their investment in the new systems would reduce staff costs.
4 Rajiv told us they had been working on the new project since the previous year / the year before.
5 Marionella admitted that they couldn't afford her prices.
6 Arnaldo told the staff that the work they had been doing might be outsourced to India the following / the next year.
7 Max complained that Martin had sent them the wrong invoice the day before / the previous day.
8 My boss told me to print it out when I had finished writing it.

UNIT 21
Customer loyalty

Getting started

Vocabulary

1 h   2 f   3 j   4 i   5 d   6 c   7 g   8 b   9 k   10 a   11 e

From satisfaction to loyalty

Reading

2 Factors mentioned in the article which make customers loyal to a company:
   • good relationships between your employees and your customers
   • the value of the product they are buying
   • ease of doing business
   • your staff's responsiveness, integrity, trust and professionalism
   • having staff who are highly motivated, highly engaged
   • staff have necessary customer-service skills

3 1 C (*when your customers have a strong bond to you*)
   2 B (*people are your key competitive advantage*)
   3 B (*the impact that customer loyalty can have on your bottom line*)
   4 D (*The top factor is value: 'Is this company's product or service having a positive impact on my business? Do I have a strong return on investment?'*)
   5 A (*it's hard to be different from your rivals because best practices spread across an industry very rapidly*)
   6 D (*empowerment, which means that organisations need to empower employees to make decisions and take risks*)

Grammar workshop: Relative pronouns

1 1 which/that/-   2 which/that/-   3 which/that; which
   4 who/that   5 which/that/-   6 which/that   7 where

A supermarket and customer loyalty

Listening

1 1 service desk   2 comment card   3 loyalty card
   4 (local) schools   5 rural areas   6 computer equipment
   7 sample shop   8 shopping experience

UNIT 22
Communication with customers

Getting started

1 1 email bulletin   2 company newsletter   3 visiting sales rep
   4 operator at call centre   5 website   6 leaflet
   7 advertisement

162 Answer keys

Communicating with customers at Espresso

Listening
2   1 (freephone) helpline   2 email (bulletin)   3 (trained) engineer
    4 business development   5 subscription(s)   6 dialogue
    7 new material(s)

Turning complaints to your advantage

Reading
3   1 to   2 ✔   3 of   4 the   5 ✔   6 yet   7 ✔   8 are   9 with   10 to
    11 ✔   12 for   13 it   14 to   15 ✔

Customer communication at Not Just Food

Listening
2   1 B   2 B   3 C   4 A   5 B
3   1 By giving a discount when it costs less to do the work than they originally quoted, and by swallowing the cost when it costs more.
    2 By being fair (see answer to previous question) and by helping small clients who initially made them little money, but who then grew.

Vocabulary
1 b   2 f   3 e   4 c   5 h   6 a   7 i   8 d   9 g

Training in customer communication skills

Reading
2   1 D (*More and more companies are setting up customer helplines as the quickest and most convenient way of establishing customer contacts.*)
    2 C (*Word of mouth is the cheapest and most effective way of marketing your business and extending your customer base.*)
    3 A (*you will learn how email can be used for effective communication with your customers*)
    4 B (*enabling a confident return to the workplace*)
    5 A (*You will learn ... how non-verbal communication is interpreted by customers*)
    6 C (*learn how to handle awkward customers appropriately*)
    7 B (*the skills to exceed that expectation*)
    8 C (*To address your customers' needs, you must be able to think like them, respond to whatever they throw at you*)

Vocabulary
1 rapport   2 non-verbal communication   3 project   4 a must
5 front-line staff   6 workplace   7 word of mouth   8 people skills
9 retain customers   10 handle awkward customers

UNIT 23
Corresponding with customers

A letter about a new service

Reading
1   1 B   2 A   3 C   4 D   5 A   6 B   7 D   8 B   9 A   10 D
2   1 The letter has a heading after *Dear Mr Sloane*. Note: in the US, the heading normally comes before *Dear Mr Sloane*; in Britain, a comma (,) is used, while in the US a colon (:) is used; in the US, titles like *Mr.* and *Mrs.* are written with a full stop.
    2 *valued*
    3 *we shall be offering the same level of service*
    4 *reliability, trouble-free*
    5 *contact me personally*

Writing
2   Sample answer
    Dear Mr Castle,
    New Services from TopTen Leasing
    As a valued long-standing client of TopTen, I am sure you will be interested to know that we are extending our leasing services to the whole of Europe. This means we guarantee to deliver the equipment you require anywhere in Europe within 24 hours of you placing the order. Also, for each seven-day lease, we will give you one free day.
    I enclose a leaflet detailing our service.
    As you already know, we make sure that all the equipment we supply is in perfect condition, so you can be certain to start using it as soon as it is delivered. Also, as a premium customer, you are not required to pay a deposit on the equipment you hire.
    If you would like to know more about this service, or if you would like to take advantage of it, please do not hesitate to contact me personally,
    Yours sincerely,

A letter from a dissatisfied customer

Reading
1   1 ~~Referring~~ Following   2 ~~of~~ with   3 ~~Past~~ Last   4 ~~who~~ which
    5 ~~of~~ to   6 ~~an~~ the   7 ✔   8 ~~Although~~ However   9 ~~putting~~ placing
    10 ~~why~~ which   11 ~~it~~ this/that   12 ✔   13 ~~more~~ extra
    14 ~~being~~ been   15 ~~in~~ over   16 ~~another~~ other   17 ✔   18 ~~it~~ which
2   1 Yes: when, where, the exact nature of the problem.
    2 Yes: and especially if it caused injury, cost money, lost customers.
    3 Yes, this is essential, otherwise there's no point in writing the letter.
    4 Not unless it is related to the problem which occurred.
    5 Perhaps, but you should be careful about not angering people by threatening too much, and you should not make absurd threats which you will never carry out.
    6 Yes, if this is true.
    7 Not necessary.
3   1 (paragraph 2); 2 (paragraph 3); 5, 6 (paragraph 4)

Grammar workshop: Expressing results
Sample answers
1   You delivered the wrong model. As a consequence (of this), we had to send it back.
2   Some of the goods were damaged. As a consequence (of this), we lost an important order.
3   You were late sending the information. This meant that we missed an important deadline.
4   There were several mistakes in the invoice. As a result, we had to spend a day sorting it out.
5   You sent the components to the wrong factory. This meant that we had to stop the production line for an hour.
6   Two of the pieces were broken. Consequently, we had to return the entire consignment.

Preparing a letter of complaint

Listening
1 Remind them   2 five days   3 the results   4 problem-free

Writing
Sample answer
Dear Mr Sarawi,
Late delivery of documents
I am writing to you to express my dissatisfaction with your document-delivery service.

Last Monday, we asked you to deliver some important legal documents to our offices in Budapest in time for a meeting with company lawyers on Monday morning. The documents did not, in fact, reach them until 4 o'clock on Friday afternoon, with the result that we had to cancel the meeting and reschedule it for this week. This nearly resulted in us losing an important contract.

I would like to remind you that we are a long-standing client of yours and that we rely on you to provide us with a trouble-free service.

I must emphasise that we will only continue to use your service if deliveries continue to be problem-free in the future.

Yours sincerely,

UNIT 24
A business seminar

Speakers at a business seminar
Listening

1 1 A   2 F   3 E   4 H   5 D
2 a 3 b 3 c 5 d 3 e 1 f 2 g 1 h 4 i 5 j 3 k 1 l 1 m 2
3 **Sequencing**
   And another thing …
   Firstly …
   His next point is …
   The first is this …
   Then next …
   Introducing a surprising fact
   In actual fact …
   Introducing your own experiences
   In my experience …
   In retrospect …
   Introducing an example
   Just to give you one instance …
   Advising
   You really must …
   You've got to …
   Saying something is not useful
   It's no good …
   It's not worth …

A short talk
Listening

1 in actual fact, firstly, and another thing, just to give you one instance, in my experience, it's no good
2 1 plastic components   2 the Internet   3 management level   4 socialise

Grammar workshop: *It's not worth, it's no good*, etc.

1 1 *-ing* form   2 noun
2 Sample answers
   1 asking / applying to   2 applying/(trying)   3 attending / going to / holding / having / calling   4 preparing / putting together   5 buying / investing in

Advertisement for a business seminar
Reading

1 D 2 B 3 A 4 C 5 B 6 A

Grammar workshop 6
Relative pronouns

1 1 He joined the firm 15 years ago when Mr Patel was the managing director.
   2 The report, which was sent by express courier two days ago, has not arrived. / The report which/that was sent by express courier two days ago has not arrived.
   3 I've visited the website where you advertise your products.
   4 I started working for the company in 1998 when it only had 15 employees.
   5 She works at your main office where your central administration is located.
   6 Garsons Ltd, whose parent company is Garfield International, has just announced record profits.
   7 He's the new recruit whose CV impressed us so much.
   8 Do you remember the customer who called last week (and) who wanted a replacement?
   9 He called to say you sent a replacement which/that was faulty.
2 1 which/that   2 which   3 where   4 which/that   5 which/that   6 whose   7 which/that   8 when   9 which/that   10 which/that   11 which/that   12 who   13 whose   14 which/that   15 What   16 when

Expressing causes

1 1 The reason why   2 caused   3 resulted in / led to
   4 due to / as a result of / owing to / because of
   5 leads to / results in / will lead to
2 1 As a result of new technology, companies can keep large databases about customers.
   2 Companies are theoretically able to target individual customers owing to their ability to exploit large databases. / Owing to their ability to exploit large databases, companies are theoretically able to target individual customers.
   3 The reason why companies think they can give customers personalised treatment is that/because they have the ability to target individual customers.
   4 The introduction of new technology has led to customers expecting personalised treatment.
   5 Companies have more information than they can manage on their databases, which causes them to be unable / which means they are unable to give personalised treatment to customers.
   6 The inability of companies to meet customers' expectations results in customer dissatisfaction.

Expressing results

1 meant / resulted in
2 This means
3 As a result / As a consequence of this / Consequently
4 mean / result in
5 mean / result in
6 As a result / As a consequence of this / Consequently

Exam skills and Exam practice

Listening Paper Part 4: Exam skills
1b 1 B 2 C 3 A

Listening Paper Part 4: Exam practice
33 A 34 A 35 B 36 A 37 C 38 B 39 C 40 B 41 A 42 B
43 A 44 C 45 B 46 A 47 B 48 C 49 C 50 B

Reading Paper Part 2 (Section 2): Exam skills
1 1 D 2 B 3 C
2 1 C 2 A 3 B
3 1 B 2 A 3 B

Reading Paper Part 2 (Section 2): Exam practice
1 B 2 D 3 C 4 A 5 C

Reading Test Part 2 (Section 3): Exam skills
1

Article	Pronoun	Relative Pronoun	Auxiliary / Modal verb	Preposition	Other
an the	it they	who what	are be being can have	to with	although forward much so than

2 1 the 2 forward/together 3 had 4 one 5 with 6 much/far
 7 than 8 been 9 who 10 What
3 1 have 2 be 3 the 4 to 5 what 6 are 7 with/to
4 1 they 2 there 3 who 4 would 5 it 6 also 7 Both 8 In
 9 was 10 to

Reading Test Part 2 (Section 3): Exam practice
6 with 7 have 8 on 9 ahead 10 what

Reading Test Part 2 (Section 4): Exam skills
1 1 B timetable for flights, courses, etc.; agenda for meetings; programme for conferences, etc.
 2 C Toyota is the make or brand; the trademark is the logo
 3 A collocations are: *drive a bargain, make/sign a deal, reach an agreement, sign/negotiate a contract*
2 1 D *necessity, requirement* and *need* **for**
 2 A *spend/lay out* **on**; *buy up* has no other preposition
 3 C *guarantee* and *assure* do not have the right meaning; *cover* **for**
3 1 B *despite* + gerund/noun; *however* and *nevertheless* start a new sentence
 2 A *in, over* and *during* mean *for part of the last five years.*
 3 C *providing* and *unless* need a clause; *except* + *for / that.*

Reading Test Part 2 (Section 4): Exam practice
11 C 12 A 13 D 14 B 15 B 16 A

Reading Paper Part 2 (Section 5): Exam skills
1 1 C 2 A 3 B
2a 1 C 2 A 3 B

Reading Paper Part 2 (Section 5): Exam practice
17 B 18 D 19 D 20 B 21 C 22 C

Reading Paper Part 2 (Section 6): Exam skills
1 1 ✔ 2 ~~would~~ will 3 ~~start~~ starts 4 ✔ 5 ~~may~~ can 6 ~~have~~ has
 7 ~~being~~ be 8 ~~showing~~ shown
2 1 ~~of~~ in 2 ✔ 3 ~~by~~ in 4 ~~on~~ in 5 ✔ 6 ~~from~~ with 7 ~~to~~ for
3 1 ~~memory~~ remember 2 ~~extreme~~ extremely
 3 ~~interesting~~ interested 4 ~~expansion~~ expanding 5 ~~brief~~ briefly
 6 ~~discussion~~ discuss 7 ✔ 8 ~~possible~~ possibility 9 ~~fill~~ full 10 ✔

Reading Paper Part 2 (Section 6): Exam practice
23 ~~does~~ will 24 ~~for~~ to 25 ~~giving~~ given 26 ~~such~~ so 27 ✔
28 ~~has~~ have 29 ~~at~~ of

Writing Paper Part 2: Exam skills
1a A number of staff have recently told you that they are unhappy about the times when they start and finish work in your company. You have been asked to write a <u>report for the managing director</u> about this.
 Write your report. Write about:
 - <u>why staff are unhappy with the times</u>
 - <u>why it is important to keep staff happy</u>
 - <u>what solutions your company should adopt</u> for the problem
 - <u>any other points</u> you think are important.
 Write <u>180–200</u> words.
1b 1 You must include the underlined points.
 2 Why staff are unhappy, why it's important to keep staff happy, solutions to the problem.
 3 Statistics
 4 The managing director, so a formal register.
 5 A title and sections with section headings.
1d 1 Students have their own answers to this question.
 2 It has a title, is divided into sections with section headings and it uses bullet points.
 3 Yes.
 4 The first section introduces the purpose of the report. The last section recommends solutions to the problem.
 5 Phrases which express results: *means, as a result, as a consequence of*
 6 Yes. Nothing has been forgotten.

Writing Paper Part 2: Exam practice
Sample answers
Task A

Report on accommodation for company visitors

<u>Introduction</u>
The aim of this report is to summarise the complaints visitors to our department have made about the accommodation we provided and to recommend changes.

<u>Visitors' complaints</u>
Several visitors complained that the Queen's Hotel, where we normally lodge visitors, is too far from our offices and that they spend too much time travelling here. Also, it is situated in a very noisy part of the city, and several people complained about difficulties in sleeping.

<u>The need for a good hotel</u>
Most of our visitors are important, lucrative clients, so it is essential for them to have the best possible experience of their visit to our company. By providing them with excellent accommodation, we will improve our company image.

<u>Recommendation</u>
I have investigated hotels in the area and found a new five-star hotel, the London Palace, which has recently opened just five minutes' walk from our offices. It is situated in a quiet area surrounded by gardens. I recommend we contact the hotel and negotiate special rates. I also suggest that in future we provide a taxi service for all visitors from the airport to the hotel and from the hotel to our offices.

Task B

Report on the company website

Introduction
The purpose of this report is to outline the shortcomings of the company website and to suggest improvements to make it more suitable.

Problems with the website
I have identified two main problems. Firstly, the website is in only two languages: English and Spanish. However, more than 50% of our customers are either Chinese or Japanese, and the website should also be available to them in their own languages. Secondly, although the website provides a full catalogue of our products, we do not include prices. This means potential customers have to contact us to obtain this information, which generates extra work for us.

Changes to the website
I recommend we make the website available in Japanese and Chinese. I also think it would be a good idea to include the prices of all the products listed on the site. In order to do this, we will have to:
1 engage a specialist translation service to provide a full translation of all pages of the site;
2 contact the web-design company we normally use and ask them to include the information about prices and set up the Chinese and Japanese versions when these are available.

Speaking Test Part 2: Exam skills

2a 1 Firstly   2 For example   3 Another important thing is   4 So
5 I mean   6 A further point   7 This way   8 But, to conclude

Speaking Test Part 3: Exam skills

1 1 What types of car are available?
      Can/Could you tell me what types of car are available?
   2 How much do the cars cost?
      I'd like to know how much the cars cost.
   3 What are your terms of payment?
      What terms of payment can you offer?

Transcripts

UNIT 1

02 Listening page 12
WJ = Wendy Jones; CS = Carol Sharp

WJ: Skills Development College. Wendy Jones speaking.
CS: Hello, my name's Carol Sharp. I'm calling from Forrest Insurance to make enquiries about the company training courses you run.
WJ: OK. What sort of course are you looking for?
CS: Well, we're interested in knowing if you run courses in advanced computer skills. This is for a number of graduate trainees we have.
WJ: Yes, we do. We have standard courses, which are four hours a week for ten weeks. In this case, your trainees would be mixed in with students we have from other places, and they wouldn't just be people working in insurance. Or we can offer you tailor-made courses adapted for your particular staff.
CS: Yes, that sounds more the thing.
WJ: Right, well, these can have the length and the programme you require, depending on what your learning goals are.
CS: Good. Well, all the goals we have are very specific, and the price you quote will obviously have to be compatible with our training budget. All the training you give is hands-on training, isn't it? I mean, it's not just theoretical?
WJ: No, it's all very practical, very hands-on. All the trainees will work on their individual computer. Of course, we teach background theory where necessary, and we do give a certificate at the end.
CS: OK, well, what we need is, I think, a one-month course for 15 members of staff. They're all basically computer literate – I mean, they have the core skills, but in a highly computerised industry like ours, we want to have them working efficiently as soon as possible.
WJ: Of course. Can I suggest we send round our director of studies to do an analysis of your needs and then we can design a course to suit you and give you a quotation of how much it would cost?
CS: That would be great. When can your director come?

UNIT 2

03 Listening page 15

1 *Jane Milton*
I love being able to work out what a client needs and … and do it. And I love, you know, having an idea for a new food product for them and then seeing it, you know, in a supermarket, or, um, writing something and then having loads of emails from people because they've used that recipe so much and they can't believe how easy it was, or a whole lot of different things.

2 *Lewis Bronze*
I enjoy, now, the company is five, six, seven years old, I enjoy seeing the vision being executed. I enjoy seeing how the company has grown, we've attracted some excellent people to work here. I think we have a very strong culture in the company which supports the excellence of what we're trying to do across a whole range of disciplines.

3 *Amanda Hamilton*
I absolutely thrive on the freedom, just being able to make, you know, my own choices. It is, as you said, a lifestyle choice, although you probably end up working slightly more hours than you did working for a corporation. I used to work for the BBC prior to that, so it was a very structured environment, but you sort of somehow don't mind those longer hours because it's fulfilling. It's your own project, your own baby and there's also a sense of pride, I think, when you can make your own decisions.

4 *Maxine Macpherson*
As the UK representative, I'm in contact with the agents who organise the conference incentive events overseas, so that's what I like most about the job, meeting people and selling the services that we provide abroad and trying to explain what we do.

04 Listening page 17
I = Interviewer; C = Christina Bunt

I: What do you most like about your job?
C: I suppose the most enjoyable for me is training because it's what I started out doing, so it's, er, the bit that I enjoy most … Um, there's not many things that I dislike, to be honest. I suppose, um, the most challenging part of it is when you're talking in the area of discipline or, um, sometimes the firing part … Um … That's one of our major considerations is getting the right people in the right job to start with. If you, if you employ the right people, you don't have a problem managing them once they're in the … the workplace. Um, our cashiers, obviously customer service is our … our major selling point when it comes to our company. Um, if you employ a cashier who is naturally friendly, naturally smiles, naturally polite, it's not a problem. If you try and teach them to be polite and to smile, it doesn't necessarily work …
I: And how did you get into this line of work?
C: Um, … I originally worked, er, trained as a nurse, um, … when my daughter was born, needed a part-time job and, um, took a part-time job with Tesco. I used to work nine hours a week on the checkouts, er, covering lunch reliefs. And then they offered me an evening checkout supervisor's job which I took, and then … I took a full-time job, went into training about 15 years ago. I've worked with them for 22 [years], so, yeah, about 15 years ago I went into … as … into a job as a training manager, which is a kind of natural progression into personnel. So I did the training job for about four or five years, and then took my first role about ten or 11 years ago.
I: And where do you think you might be workwise in ten years? Where would you like to be?
C: Where would I like to be? I actually would like to still be working in personnel. Um, the career progression within my firm does tend to try and take senior team through to store management, but it's actually something that I'm not particularly interested to do. Um, I prefer the people side of the business and I would like to either be still in a personnel role in store or in a regional role as personnel.
I: Now, if someone came to you and said, 'I've … I've got a job interview, what should I try and make sure I do?' … can you give three tips for good interview technique?
C: Um, I suppose the first thing is to keep in mind that the first impression sticks, um, and I'm not looking for people to turn up to interview with me with … in a three-piece suit looking

Transcripts 167

as if they've just stepped out of a fashion plate, but ... tidy but comfortable, um, and that first step towards the person who's going to interview makes a huge difference if you're quite prepared to smile and be open and shake a hand, and sometimes for young people that can be really difficult because they're not used to a formal greeting ... And to be totally natural and not try to put yourself forward as something that you're not. Because it's too obvious in an interview situation when you're, when you're trying to pull the wool over someone's eyes. ... Um, talk about the things that you like, talk about the things that you're good at, because you do that naturally, if there's something that you're really interested in, even if it's got nothing to do with the job role that you're actually going into, the enthusiasm will come across. Um, I'll always know that I'm talking to somebody that's going to be enthusiastic about whatever I put in front of them, because they're enthusiastic about things that they like in their normal life.

UNIT 3

05 Listening page 20

Presenter: So, finally, let's have some advice from each of you about how to go about getting that first job, the one you've studied so hard to prepare for. Samuel?

Samuel: My advice is this: especially with the first job, prospective employers want to get a complete picture of you, not just what you've been studying and your holiday jobs. So include a section in your CV for the things which you like doing in your free time. These say a lot about you, and may make you a lot more interesting than all those other kids who just spend their evenings going to the pub or listening to music.

Presenter: OK. Marta?

Marta: I was reading somewhere that, in the US, more than 80% of applications nowadays are made electronically – personnel officers don't want the trouble of having to file lots of applications, so what comes by snail mail goes straight in the bin. What goes into the computer is there in front of you at the click of a mouse.

Presenter: Thanks for that, Marta. Salim, what's your advice?

Salim: Well, I agree with everything I've heard so far, but one thing I'd like to emphasise is that you've got to make yourself as attractive as possible to a potential employer, so make your good qualities stand out. On the other hand, don't ever tell a lie, because it'll catch up with you in the end – you know, you'll be found out. And when that happens, the only thing you'll achieve is a feeling of embarrassment.

Presenter: That's good advice. Yukari, it's your turn to offer some words of wisdom.

Yukari: Words of wisdom!? Mine's just plain common sense, Harry, and comes from long experience of non-native speakers writing applications in English. Get someone to look it over before you send it, someone who speaks the language well, preferably a native, because it's such a pity to lose that all-important chance for a job interview because of some slight grammatical mistakes – and they do make a difference to the impression you're giving.

Presenter: Good point, Yukari, and I couldn't agree more. What about you, Ivan?

Ivan: Frankly, I agree with everything that's been said in the last five minutes. You know, I get pages and pages of applications every week, and I find it hard to sort people who are genuinely interested in working for us from the ones who just send the same application to every company on the Internet. So, though they all have names and addresses, they don't all get replies. My advice is follow up that application with a call to ask if your application has been received and to show that you really are interested. It makes all the difference, and chances are you'll get invited in for a chat.

UNIT 4

06 Listening page 22

R = Receptionist; J = Jack

R: Flemings Hotel. How can I help you?

J: Good afternoon. This is Jack Rubenstein, and I'm calling from New York. I want to book a meeting room while I'm there in London.

R: OK, sir. Let me get your details first. Could you give me your name again, please?

J: Yeah. My name's Jack Rubenstein, that's R-U-B-E-N-S-T-E-I-N.

R: Fine, Mr Rubenstein. And can you tell me the name of your company, so I can put it on the invoice?

J: No problem. The name of my company is Top Flight International.

R: OK, and what size room would you like? We have meeting rooms for up to 15 people, 20 people and 30 people.

J: The smallest one for 15 people will be quite large enough. We'll be using it for job interviews, and there'll only be three of us plus the interviewees.

R: When would you like the room for?

J: I was hoping for May 18 – that's in a month's time.

R: Right, sir. I'm just checking availability. Yes, that's fine.

J: Good. Could you let me know the rates, please?

R: Meeting rooms are taken by the hour, sir, and we charge £25 an hour.

J: OK, well, I'd need it all morning actually, from 9 o'clock to 1 o'clock, if that's all right.

R: Yes, that's fine, sir. And would you like any extra services while you are here, Mr Rubenstein?

J: Well, I'm going to be interviewing four candidates for a job, so if you could provide coffee during the morning for interviewers and interviewees, that would be great. Some of them will be travelling down from outside London.

R: No problem. We look forward to seeing you then, Mr Rubenstein.

J: Thanks. Bye.

R: Goodbye.

07 Listening page 24

J = Jack; M = Monica

J: Burfords Engineering.

M: Hello. Could I speak to Jack Burford, please?

J: Speaking.

M: Good morning. My name's Monica Pereira. A friend of mine suggested I phone you because she told me you might have a vacancy for an office administrator.

J: Yes, that's right. We haven't advertised it yet, but we'll be needing somebody.
M: I see. Do you mind if I ask you some questions about the job?
J: No, not at all. Can you just hang on a sec while I get the details of the job up on the screen. That's it. Now, what would you like to know?
M: Can you tell me if the job is full time or part time?
J: Well, we haven't finalised details yet, but I imagine it'll be mornings only. Would that suit you?
M: Yes, very much. I'm interested in finding a job for while my children are at school. And what would the job consist of?
J: Basic office administration, typing letters and reports, bookkeeping, that sort of thing. Do you have any experience of office work?
M: Yes. I worked in an office for ten years. When would the job start?
J: Let's see. At the beginning of September, I imagine.
M: OK, and how should I make my application?
J: Could you make it by email, please? It's so much easier to process that way.
M: Yes, of course. Could you give me your email address then, please?

UNIT 5

08 Listening page 30

Tesco were actually the first supermarket to introduce an own brand, and it was Tesco tea, um, when … and that was before the supermarkets … um, the main reason for it, I would imagine, er, started off as overheads … if you're not paying a premium to another supplier to produce that brand. You also have much better control over the brand, the product that's going into the packet, and you also get recognition, so if Tesco produce a particularly good biscuit or a particularly good kind of coffee, you're building up all the time customer loyalty, because they've got that Tesco brand in their cupboard, and it's good, and they'll go back to that store to get it … Some are cheaper, some are more expensive. Tesco Own Brand Finest, for instance, may be more expensive than a similar product, but it'll be much better quality, and Tesco will be able to control that quality. Um, our value brands are branded specifically to be at a better price, and we can do that because we're a large business that, you know, has an awful lot of product going through it.

UNIT 6

09 Listening page 32

I = Interviewer; A = Amanda

I: Now, just explain exactly what chai is and how you came about it.
A: Chai, um, is actually a generic word for 'tea', and in India, chai has been drunk for centuries in the same way that we would drink a normal cup of tea. It's a blend of spices … mixed with milk, sugar and black tea, and in India it's traditionally boiled on the side of, um, train stations in huge woks where they've freshly boiled the ingredients and offer chai to thirsty commuters coming into the train station. In America, as they do, they've westernised the chai recipe and created many chai latte flavours, ready-to-drink chai options, um, and you can get chai in most groceries, delis and cafés in the US. The reason I'm mentioning the US is because that's where I discovered chai, not in India, and I … I should probably go back a step in that I actually had created mobile tea bars, um, at train stations in the south-east … So the idea was to create upmarket tea bars where commuters could have coffee, but have a nice range of maybe fruit teas, herbal teas, and this chai was the perfect addition to our diverse menu.

We researched the market a lot and found very, very few people selling it in this country, um, but the only people that were were importing it from America. Problem was, it cost a fortune to exp… imp… import, and the supply chain kept breaking down and so customers would, you know, get … get very annoyed with us. So really, the … the … decision to try and create my own chai was born out of just supplying my own tea bars, not really anything wider than that …
I should say it took a year in development … Some of the early recipes were horrible, you know, and the beauty of having the tea bars was that you had a mini market-testing tool and that I could take the recipes straight to the tea bars and let the customers decide because they're the most important people … we'd reached the point where the customers either couldn't tell the difference between mine and the … the US version, or they preferred it and that was good enough to me. We stopped the US supply, and I started solely supplying my own tea bars … if I was producing chai for my customers and they were enjoying it, why could that not be expanded on a glo… you know, wider scale, um, possibly selling to other café bars or, you know, even retail in supermarkets, so I decided to, um, to just approach supermarkets and just see what they thought, sent in samples to, er, Tesco, really not expecting much back … and, um, got a call back to say that they absolutely loved the samples and would be interested in meeting me, and so last summer we went in to have the meeting with the buyer and pitched, you know, my, my research in the US and how I thought it would be placed in the UK, and he offered, um, 230 stores nationwide straight away, at which point my mouth dropped rather like yours is now, and, um, that was a massive turning-point obviously because at that point I had to get a brand and packaging like really quickly in about six weeks, and I didn't have a designer, and it was all just full on for that period of time.

10 Listening page 34

I = Interviewer; A = Amanda

I: What do you think was most important, or is most important when launching a new product?
A: Checking, testing that there's a sufficient market for it. I mean, are … are enough people going to want your product? Because there's no point in launching something that you're not going to have customers for, so that's why the tea bars were a perfect market-testing tool for me because I could have launched a flavour or drink that I thought might, you know, have been nice, but had not tested it on any customer base, so although it was a small market-testing tool, it was effective.

11 Listening page 35

I = Interviewer; A = Amanda

I: How would you go about attracting new customers? What promotional activities have you done?

A: We've had, um, brilliant coverage actually in the press. Um, we've had write-ups in, um, *Slimming* magazine, *Delicious* … most of the women's magazines, um, the food pages have written positively about the product, which is … which is great. Um … I've had a number of articles, like business-led, um … in the *FT* this weekend there was a piece, um … about me, which was great. Well, me … the product, which, um, is just … is just … it's just awareness. Um, I mean that's obviously a really high-profile newspaper, so, um, it's just all about, you know, raising awareness to try and, you know, increase sales … Er, in terms of, er, getting new customers, we have one strategy, and that is sampling. Um, the more people that can try the drink, er, the more, you know, customers we'll get because it is unique taste and … and people, you know, they're not sure of how it … how it tastes. So we do, um, a number of, um, sampling shows; we did the BBC Good Food show last … last year, er, and sampling out on the road. I'm looking at the moment at getting one of those jet packs … sample packs where you, um, hike them on your back like a rucksack and can sample both hot and cold drinks from the back, and pick, you know, festivals or … er, large areas where there's lots of people … It's just sampling, sampling, sampling … I don't have big budgets for advertising, so, um …

I: I mean presumably you use your website a lot. I mean, the Internet must have made a huge difference to business start-ups, would you say?

A: Mm yes, yeah, absolutely. It's like, um … it's like your shop window, um … to … to the world, really and you … and actually I've had some interest from overseas now as well in some Scandinavian markets where chai is actually a lot more well known … in Germany, chai has really taken off actually. Erm, and so because, you know, the Internet brings us all together, you can receive interest and possibly … hopefully orders from …

I: What about things like, um, a sachet … an add-on with a food magazine; they could strap a couple of sachets to the front cover.

A: Yeah, yeah it's just …

I: All that sort of thing, it's just, I suppose, having the budget.

A: It's so expensive. I looked at that … that … that sachet on magazine thing and you're looking at sort of over a hundred thousand for a … for a run, so it's just all a bit, um … you know, you think about, you know, Cadbury's and some of the big players, they just have so much marketing spend and my product is sitting on the shelf next to these big players. How do you compete? It's a real challenge to … to compete with, you know, a moderate budget. But you can be clever, you can … you can be creative, it's really important to … to push … to push with PR. I recently did a … a show at, um, the London Food Fair where we did some sampling of 'ice chai', actually because, um, it's all very well launching a hot drink, but then, you know, what do you do come the warmer months? It's very important to keep a momentum, so we had 'ice chai' and I created, er, a 'chill-out zone', …

UNIT 7

12 Listening page 37

Frank: Pop-the-Cork Marketing Department. How can I help you?
Mandy: Hello. Can I speak to Mr O'Donnell, please?
Frank: Speaking.
Mandy: Hello. It's Mandy Price here from Showfood.
Frank: Oh, Showfood. I was wondering when I was going to hear from you.
Mandy: Yes, we've been having a bit of trouble with our server after that big power cut in London.
Frank: Oh, right.
Mandy: Anyway, you sent me an email the other day asking about prices. I thought I'd just ring you to give you the information.
Frank: Right. Fine. Let me just note it down then.
Mandy: Here it is. Floor space at the exhibition, which runs from the 13th to the 16th of March, costs between £120 and £200 a square metre, depending on where your stand is situated.
Frank: OK.
Mandy: You have to reserve your space in writing by the 1st of September of this year.
Frank: Fine, and do I have to pay a deposit?
Mandy: Yes, that's 50% of the total amount.
Frank: Fifty per cent. And how do you like us to pay?
Mandy: Er, the easiest way is by cheque along with your written reservation.
Frank: Not a money transfer?
Mandy: We prefer not.
Frank: OK.
Mandy: So I'll fax you through a floor plan where you can see the spaces which are still available; er, the sooner you choose and reserve one the better.
Frank: But didn't you say by the beginning of September?
Mandy: Yes, but for actual locations, we work on a first-come-first-serve basis.
Frank: Ah, I understand. And when do we have to pay the full amount?
Mandy: The deadline for that is one month before the exhibition starts, er, in other words the 13th of February. After that, your reserved space can't be guaranteed.
Frank: OK. I've got all that. Thanks, Mandy. I'll discuss this information with my boss and get back to you. Can I have your phone number, please?
Mandy: Yes, it's 01399 445378.

UNIT 8

13 Listening page 40

Jack: Hello. Good morning. Tessa Marcovitz? My name's Jack Lemming, and this is my colleague, Susie Chen.
Tessa: Hello. Nice to meet you. So you got my letter? That's great.
Jack: Hello.
Susie: Hello. Nice to meet you too. So this is your stand? Very smart, and thanks for inviting us, by the way.
Tessa: Well, we've been wanting to talk to you people for some time, and we like to let people know when we've got a stand at a fair. Did you have a good trip?

Jack: Yes, thanks. Very good.
Susie: Yes, the airport's so convenient for this fair. Lovely city, isn't it?
Tessa: Yes, lovely. Where are you staying?
Susie: We're staying at the Ritz, in the city centre.
Tessa: Good. They say it's the best hotel in town. When did you get in?
Jack: Just last night, but not too late.
Tessa: Oh, good. Now, can we show you a few of our products? Take a seat if you like.
Jack: Thanks. Busy, isn't it?
Tessa: Incredibly, and it's been like this all week. This fair is getting more popular every year. Would either of you like a cup of coffee or a cup of tea before we get started?
Susie: Yes, please. I could really do with a cup of coffee myself. What about you, Jack?
Jack: Er, tea for me, please.
Tessa: Fine. I'll just send one of our people out for it. Sam! Can you bring two cups of tea and one cup of coffee, please?
Sam: Sure.

14 Reading page 41

Tessa: So, which of our products are you most interested in?
Susie: A whole lot of them. We saw quite a few of them on your website, but it would be good to actually handle them and …
Jack: Yeah. Then we can see if they're really the sort of things we can stock in our stores.
Tessa: That's right. A lot of our stuff is for people with disabilities and the elderly.
Susie: Right. Let's have a look at the kitchen products first. What have you got here?
Tessa: This is our talking kitchen scale, which is ideal for people who have problems with their sight. All they have to do is put the food in the bowl and it will tell them how much it weighs.
Jack: Is it easy to keep clean?
Susie: Nice design – I always think that if a gadget looks good, it'll sell well.
Tessa: You're right there, and this is very popular. To wash it, you just pop the bowl in the dishwasher, and the rest of the apparatus can be cleaned with a damp cloth.
Jack: Not very heavy, is it? How much does it weigh?
Tessa: No, it's very light. Let's see. It weighs less than half a kilo.
Susie: And how is it operated? Do you need to plug it into the mains?
Tessa: No, no. It has one small 9-volt battery. Look, it works like this:
Electronic voice: 250 grams.
Jack: Great! Now, if we stocked this product, how much would we be able to sell it for, Susie?
Susie: I think it would retail at around €149.
Jack: OK, and what price would you supply it to us at?
Tessa: At €100, so you've got a 50% mark-up.
Susie: Yes. We wouldn't want to carry a lot of stock. How quickly could you get them to us if they were selling well?
Tessa: Well, we do carry stock because we sell plenty of these in North America, so we could get them to you pretty quickly. Within the week if necessary. But obviously if you put in a biggish order, we'll give you an extra discount.

Susie: That could be interesting. Jack, I think you ought to note that down as a good possibility.
Jack: Right. Let's think about it, and then we'll come back to you on that to sort out the details if we think it's what we want. OK?
Tessa: Fine.
Susie: Now, what else have you got?
Tessa: Well, there's this wine-bottle opener. This really does sell well.
Jack: One more question about the talking weighing machine. Does it come supplied with a battery, or do customers have to pay extra for that?
Tessa: No, it comes with the battery included.
Jack: Good. Now, what about this bottle opener. It looks smart, but is it an innovation?
Tessa: Look, I know it's a bit early for opening bottles of wine …
Susie: Never too early!
Tessa: … but I'll show you how it works and I'm sure you'll see what a great product we've got here …

15 Listening page 43

Tessa: Hello. Back again!
Jack: Yes, we've been doing a bit of thinking, and we've decided some of your products could interest us, that is, if the terms are right.
Tessa: That's good news. Which items were you thinking about in particular?
Susie: Let's start with the talking kitchen scale, shall we, Jack?
Jack: I think we might be able to sell a few of those, if only for the novelty value.
Tessa: I'm sure you'll have no difficulty in selling a pretty good number. How many were you thinking of?
Jack: Well, we thought we'd start with 50 or so to see how they go.
Tessa: Just 50? I think 500 would be a better number.
Susie: Five hundred!
Tessa: Sure, because I think you'll find they sell like hot cakes. Look, I'll tell you what: if you take 500, I'll take back whatever you haven't sold after six months at the price you paid for them. How does that sound?
Susie: Five hundred on sale or return? Yes, we'll accept that if we can agree on the other details.
Tessa: Great!
Susie: I'm a bit worried about the price you're asking, because if we buy the scales at €100 each, we won't make a decent profit. Our overheads are enormous, you know.
Tessa: So, what do you suggest, Susie?
Susie: We'd like to pay €70 a unit.
Tessa: I could do €80 if you are thinking of buying other products from us as well.
Jack: Yes, OK. I think €80 will be fine if you can give me a discount of 5% on sales of over 500.
Tessa: You mean, if you place a repeat order, you'll want a 5% discount on the price we've just agreed?
Jack: That's it.
Tessa: Agreed. Is that all?
Susie: Not quite. Can you tell us your payment terms?
Tessa: Yes. Payment at sight with new customers.
Susie: We generally pay at 90 days. We're a well-known and reputable company.
Tessa: Mm. That's far too long, I'm afraid, especially with the discount I've already given you.

Susie: OK. How about 30 days on this order, and then we'll renegotiate it if we place subsequent orders?
Tessa: Thirty days it is, then.
Jack: That's great. I think we've got a deal.

UNIT 9

16 Listening page 46

Presenter: Good evening. Tonight on *Building your Future* we talk to three women who have made a go of starting their own businesses. We talk to them about the excitements and risks of running your own business and find out what it takes to be an entrepreneur in the 21st century. But first we ask them why they started up their businesses in the first place. First you, Lisa. Why did you decide to take the plunge?
Lisa: Well, you know, my mother was Italian, although I was born and brought up here in Wales, and I'd always preferred to make my own food rather than buy ready-made food from supermarkets. Anyway, it struck me that in my home town there's nowhere you could buy handmade home-made pasta – you know, it's so much better than the stuff which comes out of packets – and anyway my friends had always said that they like my pasta better than anything they could get in the shops. So, I thought, here's my opportunity – no competition and a really good product – why not open my own outlet?
Presenter: Why not indeed? And you, Naiara? What inspired you to become an entrepreneur?
Naiara: I'd worked for an airline for 20 years in marketing, and then in 2001, September 11th happened, and I was made redundant. Suddenly, in my forties, I found myself, you know, with nothing to do. I mean, I found that pretty traumatic and I thought 'I don't want this to happen to me again. Perhaps I'd better take charge of my own future.' So with my redundancy money I bought into this, you know, this franchise which is actually a travel agent's, as a matter of fact, and since then, I've got to say, I … I've never looked back.
Presenter: Gone from strength to strength.
Naiara: That's right. Best thing I ever did.
Presenter: Can you explain, for those listeners who need it, what a franchise is?
Naiara: Sure. Basically, it's your own business, but you buy the right to sell the products of a large franchising organisation – you know, you pay fees and part of your profits and you use their logo and benefit from their marketing. McDonalds, the fast-food chain, is one example. Each restaurant is, in fact, a small business.
Presenter: Thanks, Naiara. And you, Marcelle, why did you decide to go it alone?
Marcelle: I'll tell you. I'm one of those people who is ready to work really hard, but quite honestly, I'm not prepared to work hard to increase someone else's profits. Frankly, I want the profits for myself. I know I'm just starting out, but I think I'm good enough to make a lot of money and I think that money should be for me, not for some fat-cat shareholders who I'll never meet!
Presenter: So, Marcelle, if I can continue with you, how did you go about setting up your business? Where did you get the idea?

UNIT 10

17 Listening page 51

J = Jane Milton; I = Interviewer

J: My name is Jane Milton and my business is called Not Just Food.
I: And what does your company do?
J: Gosh. We … we do a mix of food-related marketing things from recipe-writing to preparing food for photographs to organising exhibitions …
I: And what market research did you do before launching your company, and how did you go about it?
J: Gosh. I was quite lucky, actually. I, um, was told about an organisation called The Training and Enterprise Council at that time, um, who ran business start-up courses, and I went on one of those, primarily really because at the end of it, they would help you to get any funding you needed, and you stood a better chance of getting money from a bank if you'd done one of their courses. Um … and I had a great, the two men who tutored me through the eight weeks, I think, of one or two hours at a time, um, they were incredibly rigorous about the setting up of my business and how realistic my business plan was, and they made me phone … cold-call companies to ask if they would use my services if I did this kind of work. And I nearly made myself ill doing it, I really hated the idea of doing it. But I phoned people and said, 'I'm not trying to sell you anything, I'm trying to do some research. Can you give me five minutes to answer some questions.' And some people said, 'Phone back another time,' and at that time I phoned back and about 50% of those initial people that I interviewed became clients when the business started. So it was a great system.
I: So really there's nothing to beat doing your own … doing your own market research rather than employing someone else to do it?
J: I think that's probably right, I mean, I'm sure a market-research company could have done some, but even in the office when somebody else answers the phone and explains what we do, they are less successful at getting work than I am because I am just much more enthusiastic about it, I think. And I think that … that helps.
I: And, um, what options were open to you for raising finance to start up?
J: Um, initially I got a small business start-up loan at a very competitive rate with one of the banks, um, through this scheme that I'd been on, but, um, I didn't need much to start. I borrowed a laptop computer from somebody, um, and I just, you know, made do and I set up office in my spare bedroom and so my overheads weren't that high initially, and I also took a part-time job at first, so that I had enough income just to pay my most basic bills while I got started.
I: What do you think is important when looking for finance for a start-up?
J: I think you have to be realistic about how much money you need, and also realistic about how much you can afford to pay back, 'cos obviously nobody lends you it without wanting it back, and so you have to be sure that whatever you borrow, you could meet the monthly repayments …

18 Listening page 53

L = Lewis Bronze; I = Interviewer

- **L:** I'm Lewis Bronze and I'm the chief executive of Espresso Education Ltd.
- **I:** And can you just tell me what does your, what does Espresso do, and where did you get the idea for the company?
- **L:** We make what are called digital educational resources, so we supply digital materials for teachers and pupils to use, particularly in primary or elementary schools, to support their lessons across the whole curriculum. The idea came from, um, it came out of my head really, er, it was an idea I had when someone came to me and talked about a technology being developed to allow the movement of large data files by satellite, um, and, er, I thought of an application which would be to use video in those files and then to build a wrapper around it which would be educational. So that was where the original idea came from.
- **I:** And did you do any market research before launching?
- **L:** No. Er, we did everything the way that it shouldn't be done, probably, if you're starting a company. It was a gut instinct that this was a good idea, the technology was coming along, I'd been a school governor, er, and I knew what schools needed to use, so I wanted to combine television, computing and the Internet to create a new kind of educational resource. And that's what we've done.
- **I:** And did … did you have to raise finance?
- **L:** Oh, yes. We started off by raising finance through a European Space Agency initiative called ARTES-3 … Basically, ARTES-3 was a programme looking for applications of the use of space in either medicine or education, and we wrote a proposal to the European Space Agency … And we were successful in winning a grant of about £400,000 from the European Space Agency in 1998, and that was central to the start of the business. We then had to raise a lot of money subsequently from the private venture-capital market in London and from individual investors in order to sustain the business in its early days.
- **I:** If you had not got funding from them, were … were there other options open to you?
- **L:** Um, not really. It was a very, er, it was a very interesting and original idea, and there was no precedent for having done it. It was complicated to execute, and you could not have gone to a bank or to even an angel investor with a blank sheet of paper and said, 'This is my idea, would you fund me?' I think without the European Space Agency initial grant, the business never would have got off the ground.
- **I:** So what do you think's important when looking for finance to start up a business?
- **L:** Luck. Er, you need to be very lucky. You need to know, you need to think quite carefully about where you want to go. You have to obviously, you know, there's all the advice you can read about having a good business plan and so on and so forth, but in our case the business plan – we had one – but it was really written in sand because no one had tried this kind of business before. There are many things about our company which is quite new, very few companies had ever tried to sell to English schools a product on a subscription basis, and in fact the chief executive of the largest company in this space told me point blank in 1999 that schools don't like subscriptions and it would never catch on. I'm glad to say that our instinct was correct and it has caught on. A lot of what we wanted to do defied a conventional business plan, so it needed, um, the faith that the European Space Agency had in the people. So what do you need? You need luck, you need a very good idea, you need very good people with some kind of track record to indicate that they can execute, and you need a vision.
- **I:** But what do you think are the risks of starting up on your own?
- **L:** Well, you have to try and not do too much too soon. Er, it's important if you can to restrict your costs, not to splash out in any big way in terms of hiring staff or fancy premises until you can see, er, revenues coming into the company and be fairly sure that they're going to be guaranteed over a period.

19 Talking point page 53

L = Lewis Bronze; I = Interviewer

- **I:** So what do you think's important when looking for finance to start up a business?
- **L:** Luck. Er, you need to be very lucky. You need to know, you need to think quite carefully about where you want to go. You have to obviously, you know, there's all the advice you can read about having a good business plan and so on and so forth, but in our case the business plan – we had one – but it was really written in sand because no one had tried this kind of business before. There are many things about our company which is quite new, very few companies had ever tried to sell to English schools a product on a subscription basis, and in fact the chief executive of the largest company in this space told me point blank in 1999 that schools don't like subscriptions and it would never catch on. I'm glad to say that our instinct was correct and it has caught on. A lot of what we wanted to do defied a conventional business plan, so it needed, um, the faith that the European Space Agency had in the people. So what do you need? You need luck, you need a very good idea, you need very good people with some kind of track record to indicate that they can execute, and you need a vision. I think those are the basic criteria. On top of that, you can lay a, all the business skills, like having, like understanding the market, like doing very good financial projections and so on and so forth, understanding your cost base. All of those things, of course, have to come, but they come second to those other criteria I mentioned.

UNIT 11

20 Listening page 54

C = Charles; A = Alicia

- **C:** Charles Langley.
- **A:** Hi, Charles. It's Alicia here, Alicia Flores.
- **C:** Oh, hello, Alicia. How are you doing?
- **A:** Fine, thanks, Charles, and you?
- **C:** Very well. And what can I do for you?
- **A:** Well, it's about your email. I have a few questions I thought I'd better just clear up quickly before I get down to investigating.
- **C:** OK, and what are they?
- **A:** Well, it would be useful to know what sort of investment you're thinking of making in Scotland.

Transcripts 173

C: Well, this is all a bit hush-hush at this stage, so I didn't want to put it in an email straight away, but we're thinking in terms of two million pounds in the first year – that's for laboratories, equipment and offices.

A: Wow! A major move, then.

C: Sure, but for biotechnology, Scotland's one of the places to be at the moment, and we've got to keep up with what's happening there.

A: So there'll be quite a lot of people employed there, I take it.

C: We thought that we'd start with ten drawn from different divisions around the world, and then, if things go well, we'd build up to about 60 people.

A: All recruited from our other divisions?

C: A few, because we want a bit of cross-fertilisation of ideas – that's one of our objectives – but mainly recruited locally.

A: OK, that sounds interesting.

C: And we're hoping that there'll be someone suitable from your division to head up the new operation, so keep your eyes open for that, too.

A: Right.

C: And one last thing, Alicia.

A: What's that, Charles?

C: I hear that in some regions in Europe they offer government grants for companies thinking of moving there. Can you check and see if any are available for Scotland? It could save us some money if there are not too many strings attached.

A: Sure, I'll get onto all this right away and let you have a proposal in a few days' time.

C: Great stuff, Alicia. I look forward to that. Bye.

A: Bye.

UNIT 12

21 Listening page 59

Good morning, and welcome to the Adelphi Hotel. Thank you all very much for coming; some of you have travelled a long way to hear us today, and I hope you've all had good journeys. So let me introduce myself: my name's Peter Furlong and this is my partner, Mark Davies.

The purpose of this presentation, as you know, is to explain our business plans to you and hopefully to get you interested in investing in Clock Options Express.

In my presentation, I aim to do three things. First, I'll give you a short summary of our main business idea. Then I'll tell you the findings of the market research that we've been conducting, and finally I'll outline our financial requirements and plans, which should show you what a sound and exciting investment Clock Options Express represents. If you have any questions you'd like to ask, I'll be happy to answer them at the end of the talk.

So let's start with my first point – our main business idea: information and advertising display panels. This idea arose from the observation that in this city and in surrounding towns, there's a definite need for reliable and accurate information to drivers and other travellers concerning the time, traffic conditions, parking and the public-transport situation, and that this information could be displayed on public display panels strategically situated on main road accesses to the city, at railway stations …

… which would be paid for by leasing advertising space on the same public display panels. Now to move on to my second point: market research. We started last year by conducting a survey of over 2,000 motorists who travelled in this area over a two-month period. Simultaneously, we commissioned a study of public-transport users. The findings of these two investigations can be seen on this chart, which clearly shows not only that the display panels would attract interest arising from travellers' need for reliable information, but that they would also be a major focus for advertisers who would be prepared to pay premium rates for leasing space …

… as you can see, our products have considerable market potential. I think that just about covers the market research, so now let's deal with the third part of my presentation, which is to explain our financial requirements and plans. In this chart, you can see a breakdown of our initial costs into five main areas: suppliers, premises, equipment, staff and marketing costs. Now, you will notice that although we have tried to keep our requirements to a minimum …

… and I hope you'll agree that our concept is very valid and represents an extremely interesting investment opportunity.

Now, if I can just summarise the main points again, they are these: first, we have an interesting and useful product which, in this area, is not on the market at the moment. Second, our market research both with travellers and potential advertisers shows a clear demand for our product and a readiness to buy into it. Finally, our initial financial requirements of just £500,000 in the first year are modest and the potential return on investment makes this a very attractive opportunity for involvement in the start-up of a new business.

So, finally, I'd like to finish off by saying that it's been a pleasure talking to you all and thank you for your patience and interest in listening to me. Now, if you have any questions, please feel free to ask them.

UNIT 13

22 Listening page 66

Mark: Right, I've called this quick meeting because I've got to organise the annual sales conference this year and I want to avoid a few of the pitfalls. I know you've all been to a good number of conferences of one kind or another over the years, so I'd be grateful for a bit of advice if you can. What can go wrong, do you think, Candice?

Candice: Well, I really look forward to conferences, meeting colleagues from other offices and old friends who've moved to other jobs and other organisations, and it gets me out of the office in my working time, so what I really look forward to is going somewhere exotic, somewhere I couldn't afford to go to if it was me who was paying, but I can remember a really awful conference held in some ugly industrial town just because it was easy for most delegates to get to, when what we really wanted was, you know, somewhere a bit more unusual – they should have sent us to South America or the Far East or something – I mean, it didn't even work out cheaper in the end.

Mark: Good point. What about you, Igor?

Igor: I can remember a one-day conference which got off to a dreadful start because the woman who was going to give the first speech, very distinguished she was too, just couldn't handle the technology – you know – I think she had a PowerPoint presentation prepared, but

	she couldn't make it work. Mind you, it wasn't the computer or anything like that – it was her, and she got nervous and lost her place and started repeating herself and it spoilt the whole day, got everyone in a bad, unco-operative state of mind. She really should have practised a bit beforehand. It's not that difficult.
Mark:	OK, thanks, Igor. And you, Paola?
Paola:	I can tell you about a conference they held in an old 19th-century hotel in Oslo, and the place was really not suited to the sort of conference this was supposed to be. It was a lovely old hotel, but the keynote speech was in the dance hall, for instance, with everyone sitting on plastic chairs and nowhere to take notes. They should have hired one of those purpose-built conference centres. The organisers, I mean – much better: decent air-conditioned lecture theatres, comfortable padded seating …
Mark:	Yes, but more expensive, I guess.
Paola:	Sure, but it gives a better impression.
Harry:	You're right about that, but I can tell you what most upset me.
Mark:	What's that, Harry?
Harry:	It was the people.
Paola:	The people? But you go to a conference to meet people, Harry, be reasonable!
Harry:	No, the people hired to run the conference, you know, the stewards and receptionists and that lot. This was that sales conference, a number of years ago now. You might remember it. You were there, but they were all so rude and offhand. I just don't think they'd been given any training in customer service, so we were lost and fed up. It completely ruined the four days we were there, and you know, it was a lovely place. Should have been a great conference.
Mark:	So, we have to make sure we get the right people. Finally, you, Susan.
Susan:	It's hard to remember actually.
Mark:	What?
Susan:	I mean it's hard to remember a good conference, in my case. I hate them all. But, you know, being in a wheelchair doesn't help. It's not the lifts or things like that. It's staying in hotels – somehow, they're never quite right for someone like me. I just find the rooms unsuitable, too hot or too noisy, things like that, and I find it difficult to sleep in a strange bed.
Mark:	There are several things there which I'll have to bear in mind. Thanks, Susan. So what other advice can you all give me before I go off and start emailing people?

UNIT 14

23 Listening page 68

Conversation 1

Martin:	South Pacific Tourism Organisation. How can I help you?
Sally:	Good morning. Can I speak to Martin Forbes, please?
Martin:	Speaking.
Sally:	Oh, hello Mr Forbes. This is Sally McBride from South Pacific Events.
Martin:	Good morning. Call me Martin, by the way.
Sally:	OK, and I'm Sally.
Martin:	Right, Sally. What can I do for you?
Sally:	I was just wanting to clear up a few details of the conference events we're organising, and then we can send you an estimate.
Martin:	Right. What do you need to know and I'll see if I can tell you.
Sally:	Yes, well, first I've got to have numbers – delegates, delegates' partners, husbands, wives and so on – for the transport as much as anything else.
Martin:	So far we've got 550 who've booked up. I don't think there'll be any more, because the closing date was last week.
Sally:	Does that include partners?
Martin:	No, I'll email you the number of partners because I haven't counted them yet.
Sally:	Fine.
Martin:	And there'll be eight guest speakers.
Sally:	Eight?
Martin:	Yes, who'll want picking up from the airport by car, not in your fleet of buses.
Sally:	Right. You'll let me know when they're arriving in due course, won't you?
Martin:	Just as soon as *I* know.
Sally:	Now, special events: you wanted a Maori poi dance for the opening ceremony, didn't you?
Martin:	That's what we talked about. It would be great – everyone enjoys those.
Sally:	Because we'll have to fly them in specially.
Martin:	Sure.
Sally:	And then at the umukai feast, there are going to be fireworks, I see in my notes.
Martin:	Yes, but you'll have to liaise with Air New Zealand about those – they're sponsoring them.
Sally:	So we'll send the bill direct to them for those?
Martin:	You could do, but it's important to talk to them because they'll want the company logo if they're paying for all that.
Sally:	Sure. Well, I think that's all my queries for the time being.
Martin:	Well, if you need anything else, just pick up the phone or drop me an email.
Sally:	I will. Thanks. Bye.
Martin:	Bye.

Conversation 2

Hannah:	Rarotonga National Auditorium.
Sally:	Hello. Can I speak to Sam Fingal, please?
Hannah:	He's not in the office at the moment. I'm Hannah, his assistant. Perhaps I can help you instead?
Sally:	Sure. Let's try at least. My name's Sally McBride from South Pacific Events, and I'm ringing to find out about equipment at the auditorium for the conference in October.
Hannah:	OK. What would you like to know?
Sally:	Can you tell me what you've got in the main conference room?
Hannah:	Well, it's quite big, so there are no flipcharts or anything like that – delegates wouldn't see them. Basically, a screen and a projector.
Sally:	That's a data projector, is it, not a slide projector?
Hannah:	No, data projector.

Transcripts **175**

Sally:	You say the place is big. Will speakers be able to make themselves heard, I mean, without shouting?
Hannah:	There's a microphone, of course, for those who want it.
Sally:	And what about a computer in case people want to do a PowerPoint presentation?
Hannah:	We find that people generally bring their own laptops, so you should advise your speakers to do that.
Sally:	OK – bring own laptops – I'm sure they will. They're all old hands on the conference circuit.
Hannah:	Good. Anything else?
Sally:	Yes. What about in the smaller meeting rooms? What equipment have you got there?
Hannah:	Basically flipcharts, though we can put in screens and data projectors on request.
Sally:	I'd better note that down for the information sheet – on request – otherwise people will come without having requested things.
Hannah:	That's right.
Sally:	Just out of interest, you know that several companies will be wanting to put up exhibition stands at the conference. Where are they going to be?
Hannah:	We've got a large reception area where we normally put those things.
Sally:	Good. And what's the weather like in October? Pretty hot, I suppose.
Hannah:	Quite warm if you're not used to it.
Sally:	So, will people be able to get refreshments – cold drinks – that sort of thing?
Hannah:	Oh yes. We always offer free refreshments round the clock to delegates at conferences. It's part of our hospitality policy.
Sally:	Wonderful.
Hannah:	Anything else you'd like to know?
Sally:	No, I think that's just about everything on my list. Thanks. You've been very helpful.
Hannah:	It's my pleasure.
Sally:	Look forward to meeting you at the conference, then. Goodbye.
Hannah:	Me too. Goodbye and have a good day!
Sally:	Thanks. Bye.

24 Listening page 70

1

Man:	You know it's a pretty intractable problem, the one we've got.
Woman:	I know. We had something similar a few years ago, and actually we went to Ireland and Strong. You know, they're based in Boston and they're not cheap, but actually they sorted out the financial implications pretty quick, so I'd suggest trying them. If you're interested, I could give you their number, and I'll tell you who we found was really efficient actually …

2

Woman:	What you're talking about is exactly the sort of thing we specialise in!
Man:	That's what I thought, and actually, you were recommended to me by Jerry Linklater, so if you'd like to do the job, we'd be delighted to give it to you, and we'd pay you more than the market rate, I guess, though I'd have to clear those details with my colleagues, of course.

3

Man:	No, I feel that after five years in this job, it's time I was moving on and doing something a bit more challenging.
Woman:	Well, for the sort of work you're looking for, I'd have thought Lyle Parkers would be ideal. In fact, I know someone in human resources there, and if there's an opening in marketing, I'm sure he'd know. Would you like me to give him a ring? It would be better than you cold calling …

4

Woman:	Hi, Bill.
Man:	Maria! This is great. Just the person I was wanting to speak to. I was thinking of calling you and arranging a meeting, but somehow I never seem to get round to it. You know what it's like. Have you got ten minutes? Or better still, let's have lunch together later!

5

Man:	Well, I think your ideas are really interesting! We should talk about this some more.
Woman:	I'd be happy to. And I'm sure we could do some pretty profitable business together. How about fixing something up where we talk about this properly – it's too noisy here, and there are too many other people around. Are you going to be in Amsterdam soon? Otherwise I could fly over to London. It's not that far, and it would be a pity to let an opportunity like this slip.

25 Listening page 71

I = Interviewer; C = Charlotte

I:	Can you describe, um, Pacific World to me … what exactly is it?
C:	Pacific World is a destination management company, um, they have offices all across Asia, South-East Asia and China. Um … a destination management company is a company that basically, when you go on holiday or you organise an event in Asia, they are the people that handle all of the ground arrangements, so if you were on holiday and arranging, um, tours, transfers, hotel accommodation, they are the people behind the scenes that organise those.
I:	And are they also for business travellers?
C:	Uh, not so much business travellers, but for event management agencies … if you are an event management agency in the UK organising a conference or incentive over there, you will always use a DMC – destination management company – to do that because they have all the local relationships, they organise all the dinner venues, they organise all the creative ideas to make your event special.
I:	What sort of company might use you?
C:	Um, someone like, uh, World Event Management or, um, various different companies … probably names that wouldn't be that well known because they're agencies, usually about … maximum 100 people, um, so it could be marketing agencies with an event-management side to them. But the people using those are people like pharmaceutical companies, IT companies who would, um,

use an event-management agency to organise their annual conference for their staff or incentive for their sales staff, um, that kind of thing …

I: What's the biggest, um, event or conference that you've organised?

C: We're just working at the moment on a conference to … it's a corporate company that have come to us to organise a conference for all of their worldwide staff in Shanghai … it's for 1,500 people. So for them, we then have to … because they don't know, um, China, they don't know Shanghai, and they know that we do, um, we've then sourced all of the accommodation and the meeting space, so you're talking about several hotels for that size group, all within close proximity to the convention centre, um … I think China, more than anywhere, is based very much on relationships, nothing … no business is done on a phone call or an email, you can't phone up and say: 'Have you got availability for this …?', they will … you have to take them out for lunch and talk weeks in advance, um, for things. So, um, so I think in that sense, China is one of the places where you absolutely have to use a destination management company, you can't get in through another angle, um, but yes, so for them, apart from organising all the meeting facilities, all the, um … then you'd have to do transfers from the … all the hotels, a social programme, which will involve different, um, evenings' entertainment with a big … I think they've got a big 'welcome' dinner on the first night and a big gala dinner on the last night, um, but because it's all different nationalities as well, we'll organise translators, English-speaking staff … any kind of documentation that you need while you're there, um …

I: Why have they chosen Shanghai?

C: Um, they were looking at Shanghai and Europe. Shanghai has got huge, um, facilities for large meetings because it is booming, um, and the hotels go up so quickly; everything is built so quickly that it can cater to that size. Also, Shanghai is such a modern up-and-coming city, it is *the* place to go at the moment. It's expensive; the rates are very high because they can do … just like Hong Kong was not so many years ago, that's what Shanghai is now, um, so I think prestige, actually, more … it's an exciting, exotic place to go and it's a … and it also very much … it's a huge financial centre that is booming and so, in that sense, to a finance company, which this is, it's incentivising to their staff in they see the sort of affluence of a destination and that gives you a big … buzz.

UNIT 15

26 Listening page 74

Mariano: My name's Mariano Merano, and I'm Senior Production Engineer with Florentino International. The reason I favour the company jet is simply convenience. Normally, when I fly, I'm on my way to solve some production problem, and I never know before I arrive how long it's going to take, so by having the aircraft waiting, I don't have to depend on the departure times of commercial flights.

Pascuala: I'm Pascuala Fernández, Senior Account Manager. I should say that about 75% of the time I'm in the office is spent in meetings. If I can get some of those done while I'm flying, it leaves time for other work when I arrive. On commercial flights, they're just impossible.

Nicole: My name's Nicole Lefranc and I'm Chief Sales Director for Florentino International. I take the private jet simply because it's quicker, and since in our business time is very definitely money, it probably saves money as well.

UNIT 16

27 Listening page 76

Consultant: So, the purpose of this workshop today is to talk about some of the problems you people have with meetings and to see if we can find our way to solving some of them and making your working life just a little happier and perhaps a bit more productive. So let's just get a few ideas of the sorts of problems you have with meetings. Let's start with you. Your name is …?

Jenny: Jenny.

Consultant: OK, Jenny, tell us a problem.

Jenny: Well, this one's a fairly typical one in this company. I was sent an agenda for the meeting a week before, I spent a lot of time preparing for it – you know, getting together a presentation for my part, doing a bit of research, finding statistics and so on, and then I got a phone call saying my boss had suddenly had to go off on an urgent business trip to Paris and could I ring everyone to say it wasn't happening. The meeting still hasn't happened, and that particular boss has left the company.

Consultant: How frustrating!

Jenny: Utterly!

Consultant: And you …?

Darron: Darron. Well, to tell you the truth, I find some meetings so stressful that about two months ago, there was this meeting, and I decided I just couldn't take it and I didn't go. When they asked me afterwards why I wasn't there, the only thing that occurred to me to say was that I was terribly sorry, but I'd just forgotten.

Consultant: What is it that makes meetings so stressful in this company?

Shirley: Oh, I can tell you that. My name's Shirley, by the way. What makes meetings so stressful is that we never seem to reach any decisions. I'm probably especially to blame for this because I run a lot of meetings myself, and it's really my job to get the participants to reach a conclusion, but, for example, the one I held yesterday ended in chaos with everyone talking at once.

Consultant: Well, that's a problem we can certainly work on. Now, finally you?

Paul: Paul.

Consultant: OK, Paul, what problem would you like to mention?

Paul: Well, I'm an assistant office manager, and one of my jobs is to get people to go to meetings, and find a time when everyone can make it. The trouble is, everyone's so busy, that it's sometimes nearly impossible. Take a meeting I was arranging last week for senior managers: I spent nearly an entire morning calling them and emailing them until I finally found a time they could all meet.

Consultant: Well, we've certainly got a good range of problems here. So let's continue by looking at some potential solutions …

28 Listening page 78

Barry: Well, hello everyone. Let's start, shall we? Now, you've all seen the agenda which I circulated to you last week, so you've had time to think about this. Just the one question: we want to be in the Chinese market: how do we get there? Sandra, what do you think?

Sandra: Well, Barry, I think we should start by finding a distributor. Perhaps we should visit the country and meet a few possible distributors first. Get the feel of the place.

Patrick: Yes, and do some market research while we're about it.

Mark: I'm not sure.

Barry: Mark?

Mark: Um, personally, I feel that market research is something best left to market researchers, not to export department managers like ourselves who don't even speak the language …

Sandra: Yes, but the distributors will have a pretty good idea of the market, don't you think?

Mark: If you know them, and if you know that they aren't exaggerating things. Frankly, I think that first we need an independent market-research firm to tell us what we can sell, how much we can sell and how to sell it.

Barry: That's right. We've got the money for it, and it's what we'd do if we were going to develop and market a new product in this country.

Patrick: That's true. So let's begin with market research.

Mark: Still, I think your idea, Sandra, of visiting the country and getting a feel for it is a good one. Would you like to volunteer for that?

Sandra: Sure, and [fade] perhaps you'd like to come with me, so we can get a different point of view …

UNIT 17

29 Listening page 84

Christina Bunt

We had, we had a pretty major management structure change. Our management structure was quite top-heavy. We tended to have a store manager, an assistant store manager, a personnel manager, a customer service manager, every department had a manager, every department had a deputy manager and then we had supervisors. So we went through a process where we really refined the management system, and it's now a store manager, in a normal-sized store, store manager, two trading manager, managers, customer service manager, personnel manager and then each department in the store has a section manager.

The only, I suppose the only difficulty that we've got is that there is the danger that the section manager has got such a large number of staff that you lose that day-to-day contact, and because we're 24 hours and we've got people that work, you know, short shifts, they may not see their manager very often.

Jane Milton

I don't know, people often suggest to me that, you know, because of the Internet I could live in Scotland again and still do the job that I do, but I couldn't, because London is where many of the head offices of companies are and people still want to see you face to face, and I would be going up and down all the time on planes, and also a lot of the ingredients that I use wouldn't necessarily be available to me there, and OK, they would be if I planned ahead and got them three days later and, but … ah, for me also London is full of inspiration for me because it's such a multicultural place and because it's so cosmopolitan that a lot of my inspiration comes from seeing new things here which I wouldn't get if I was in a remote Scottish hillside village with my laptop.

Lewis Bronze

We're looking at putting some of our content onto a PDA. That's quite exciting for us, and I think that's probably the next area of development. A PDA is a Personal Digital Assistant, um, so these are mini-computers with screens that are big enough to run videos, small screens, but you can run video on them. Er, and we're looking for educational applications. We think it's possible that this device could really give a child access 24/7 to the Internet to learning resources. So they might be lying in bed, they might be sitting on the bus and they might be doing some research, doing some homework, and we want to make sure that we have Espresso resources available.

UNIT 18

1 Listening page 86

I = Interviewer; C = Christina Bunt

I: In what way does Tesco use the Internet, because surely the Internet has made the biggest change to everything?

C: Online shopping was us … We have specific stores within each area that are dot-com stores, and our system it, it, it's purely and simply it's somebody else doing your shopping for you. They're shopping from your local store, but they shop for you. They put it into a van and they bring it to your house … It's a huge business and it's expanding. Only a couple of years ago, we had, I think, two dot-com stores in Cornwall. We've now got five to my knowledge, so we cover all of Cornwall now.

I: What are the advantages for a business of having a website?

C: I suppose it's just always more contact, it's just a different way of contact. People want to talk to us. People want their feelings to be felt, to be heard, they want, if they've got a problem with something, they want to let us know.

I: So what would you say was the, um, would be the characteristics of a really good company website?

C: I suppose it's got to be simple. You've got to be able to find it easily. Tesco is a recognisable name anyway, but it's, it's, you've got to be able to get into that, er, website quite easily, you've got to be able to find what you want, you need a front page which gives you everything that you want to know, so whether you want your flowers delivered to your loved one tomorrow, whether you want to pick up your shopping next week, whether you want to get car insurance, home insurance, whatever. It needs to be all there on that front page and easy to get at.

I: What sort of people do their shopping by the Internet?

C: All sorts of people. You've got the, um, you've got the busy working woman, but you've also got the pensioner who hasn't got access to public transport and maybe widow/widower who doesn't drive. It's everybody across the spectrum.

I: Would you shop, um, by the Internet if you didn't work in store?

C: I do shop by the Internet and I do work in the store … Well, if you've been working in a supermarket all day, one of the last things that you want to do is to walk around and do your own shopping, because apart from everything else, you're recognised as a member of staff while you are doing your shopping and get asked all sorts of questions. So it's much better to order it on the … on the Net.

2 Listening page 89

I = Interviewer; J = Jane Milton

I: So, how important do you think the Internet is for your business?

J: It's hugely important. We get about 70 or 80 real emails a day. We probably get a couple of hundred junk ones, unfortunately, but we do, and we email everything and stuff that I used to have to send by bike leaves my office by email and is with somebody else five minutes later. And whenever it's down, I really notice how much I use that. But the web, too, is great for researching things, for finding things. We've just recently done a promotional job and we ordered lunch boxes, American-style ones, from the States, which we found on the web, and we'd never have accessed them any other way.

I: How would you have done your job without the Internet?

J: We use a sourcing company which we still use, who'll find us, you know, exactly the right width of ribbon with our company's, client's name written on it, or will find somebody that can do it and that kind of thing, and it was more about your contacts before, and now I can nearly always find somebody who could if I didn't know the answer, but I mean, just you build up a great database of all those sorts of things. And that's how we would have managed before, but, I mean, to research an article before, you'd have had to go to the library, you'd have had to go to the Institute of Marketing, you'd have had to go, and it's all at your fingertips, so it does save us a huge amount of time.

I: What do you think are the characteristics of a well-designed company website?

J: I think it's got to tell people what you want them to know. A lot of people can't decide whether their website is something that tells consumers about their company or tells other people in the trade about their company. I think you have to be very clear before you set it up what you want it to do, and then I think it's got to be quick and simple to use. Um, we've recently simplified ours and taken loads of information off it so that you don't have to scroll down pages, 'cos what we really want to do is whet people's appetite and then have them contact us, and so it's to give them enough to let them know that it's worth doing that, really. And also that it's well connected to all the search engines and things.

I: Do you think, can you predict that there're going to be other new technologies coming out that will change business in the future in the same way that the Internet has?

J: I'm sure there will be. I'm not very good at imagining what the next thing will be. But, you know, I mean, ten years ago, I would never ever have believed that the web would change what I do so much, and it really does. I mean, you know, looking for birthday presents and all sorts of stuff, too, that would have taken you away from work, would have meant you had to go out for an hour and go and sort, I mean you can source them and have them wrapped and sent without even seeing them. It's phenomenal.

UNIT 19

3 Listening page 90

Assistant: What do you think of these proposals, Linda?

Linda: What do I think? Well, I'm all in favour if I can tie it in to my work. I mean, if I can get out to the customers with their orders when they want them, you know, well, it would be great not to have to do any driving at peak times, and I'd find the job a lot more relaxing – know what I mean? I get really uptight having to drive through the rush hour.

Assistant: Thanks, Linda. Now, Brian, your turn. What do you think?

Brian: Well, it's going to take a bit of organising and getting used to on the shop floor, especially for me, as I have to do all the organising and keep our output up to schedule, but it should make the staff happier and that would be great because there are far too many people taking sick leave at the moment, and, er, I think it's worth trying, just to reduce that.

Assistant: So you're in favour, despite what might be the extra workload for you.

Brian: On balance, yes.

Assistant: And what about you, Olga?

Olga: I think it's great because between my husband and me, we'll have more time for being with the kids. In my case, at the moment, I come in at nine every day and finish at five, but my boss works very flexible hours – sometimes he doesn't come in until just before a board meeting, sometimes he works till ten at night, especially if he's video conferencing with the president of the American office, so I don't see why I shouldn't have an equally flexible timetable.

Assistant: OK, and what about you, Dan?

Dan: I have to be flexible anyway, so I don't reckon much to them, personally – I mean, I have to come in when something breaks down and repair it, even if it's the middle of the night. But I reckon that if flexibility keeps the staff happy so they don't go off and find another job, that'll be a good thing, because too many of my problems are caused by inexperienced new staff.

Assistant: That's a very good point, and I can see it would save money if it helped staff retention. Er, what do you think, Martin?

Martin: I think they're a great idea. I've got this idea that I'd like to take some time out. I've always wanted to travel and see a bit of the world, and have a break from spending all day with figures, balance sheets, profit and loss, cash flow – just for a year or two while I'm still young enough. These proposals might just give me that chance.

Assistant: Thanks, Martin. Thanks for your input, everyone. I'll put together a report …

UNIT 20

Listening page 95

M = Margaret; J = Jeremy

M: Things are getting expensive in this country, and there's no doubt that we could do things more cheaply if we offshored some of our activities.

J: What do you mean by that? Moving parts of the business abroad, or outsourcing parts of the business to overseas companies?

M: I'm not sure, really. Perhaps outsourcing to companies abroad would be easier and more logical. What do you think?

J: You could be right. But which parts of the business should we outsource?

M: Well, we could outsource the IT department. Lots of companies do that.

J: Yes, but the problem with that is confidentiality.

M: But there are ways of dealing with that, just like we have to protect confidentiality inside our company.

J: I suppose so. What else could we outsource?

M: Perhaps some of the back-office administrative work – for example, the salaries and other parts of the accounting.

J: Maybe. Nowadays it's easy to keep in contact – with intranets and email – although it may be a bit more time-consuming giving instructions or sorting out mistakes.

M: Possibly. But you just have to pick up the telephone and call them.

J: That's true. Anyway, it's worth looking into.

M: Mm, I think so. What else?

J: We could consider outsourcing the customer service department. You know, they do all their work by telephone anyway, so nowadays with cheap telecommunications and so on, it should be possible to get someone abroad to do the same thing much more cheaply.

M: That's true. But they'd have to be given courses …

J: Including pronunciation courses.

M: True. There's just something that worries me, though.

J: What's that?

M: How are we going to break the news to the staff?

J: Yes, that could be a problem.

M: A major problem, I reckon. I'm really not sure what the best way is to tackle …

Listening page 97

Reporter: So, Molly Tyler; first, can you tell us the thinking behind this move?

Molly: Well, just let me say from the start that I fully sympathise with all those people who are going to be made redundant, and I just want to give an assurance that we'll do everything possible to help them find other employment within the organisation. But for us, this move is absolutely necessary – the saving in costs, especially labour costs, and the chance to locate half our IT operation on the other side of the world mean that the company will be so much more efficient. You see, with half the IT over there, we'll be able to run the systems 24 hours a day – 12 in India and 12 here. That's going to make the shareholders happy, too, and you must remember my prime responsibility is to them, I mean, to generate profits for them.

Reporter: I see.

Molly: Also, by doing this, our own investment both in terms of capital and in terms of human resources will be reduced, so that if there's a downturn in the market, we won't be so exposed.

Reporter: Yes, I can see that. And, Arthur Brown, do you think this is a good move?

Arthur: It makes me and my people feel a bit insecure, you know. They're moving some of their IT activities to India, and some of their back-office activities as well. My worry is that before we know it, the factories will be going there, too, or to somewhere equally far away, and then they'll find someone on that side of the world to provide them with the components they need, and we'll be left high and dry, so while I understand why they're doing it, I can't say I'm happy about it.

Reporter: Karen Weinberg. Your reaction?

Karen: Well, I don't share Arthur's dismay. I'm hoping that the cost savings will be transmitted through to their final retail prices, which can only be good for us. I do worry, though, that the quality of the services they offer will not be of the same level. Frankly, there's a lot of competition out there, and they need to know that if they're going to maintain their client base, they can't cut costs at the expense of quality.

Reporter: Thanks to all three of you, and now for a government reaction, I turn to …

UNIT 21

Listening page 103

We've got, well, we've got a huge customer relations department at Head Office, who deal with customers … What we like to do is to try and ensure that our customer-service-desk staff will sort out your comment for you, um, so if you've got, if you feel there's something wrong with the service that you've had, we like to think that our customer-service desk can … staff can deal with that and send you away happy. But sometimes it'll be something that they can't sort out, so we have a system where, we have a system of customer comment cards, so customers are invited to fill out a customer comment card, they get looked at first of all in store to see if it's something quite simple we can sort out.

We're one of the first companies to bring in the loyalty card, so the Tesco Clubcard points are quite well known, and it … I mean it … it works. People like getting their Clubcard vouchers; um, but you've also, we … we also try to do quite a lot within the community wherever the store is, so the personnel manager and customer service manager will quite often have links with local schools, um, different local groups that we, um, … we go out and talk to people, um, … We run community buses to get people in from rural areas into the store. And of course there's 'Computers for Schools' where, depending on how much you spend, you get given a computer voucher, and those computer vouchers, your children can take to school with them, and the school collect them and then trade them in for computer equipment.

We have, um, we do a number of things around the way that the store is perceived. We have a mystery-shopper system, where, um, we will get … somebody will come into the store once every four weeks and do a sample shop, and we then get a report back from Head Office to say what they've seen, so they will comment on anything from the tidiness of the car park and being able to get a trolley, through to the cashier who served them, smiling, um, offering them help, saying hello and saying goodbye. And they mark us on every single area of the store. And then we do, um, accompanied shops, so on a quite regular basis one of the managers in the store will simply ask a customer if they mind if we walk around with them while they do their shopping and then we make a note of comments they make about their shopping experience.

UNIT 22

7 Listening page 105

L = Lewis Bronze; I = Interviewer

- **L:** We do have a typical customer. Our typical customer is, um, the teacher in a classroom faced with delivering some aspect of the National Curriculum to a group of children that could be aged anything from four to 11. That's a typical customer. We have a dedicated customer relations team, we have a freephone helpline, which is always available, er, for teachers to ring up during the day with their comments or questions or criticisms. We send every subscribing school an email bulletin every week with … which lists all the new material that's gone into the service. Um, and we have a sophisticated support network that … can … rack up problems on the technical side from the telephone support to talking to a … a trained engineer possibly sending an engineer out to the school … In terms of attracting new business, um, we have business development managers that are based around the country. We have, I think, eight currently, serving different parts of the country, and it's their job to develop relationships with the schools in their area and to focus on the parts of their territory where we judge the opportunities are the best in a given period.
- **I:** And how do you manage, how do you measure customer satisfaction?
- **L:** Well, we have a very simple mechanism for doing that; as I said earlier, we're a subscription service, so if they don't renew, they're not happy.
- **I:** And do they have, um, a way of registering any dissatisfaction or problems presumably?
- **L:** Yes, we pride ourselves on encouraging dialogue between Espresso and our customers, and they can talk to us over the telephone and via email; in fact, part of the site is broadcast, er, each week, contains comments and reviews sent in by children. We often have suggestions from teachers about new material we could be developing, and then we do develop it and put it in the site.

8 Listening page 106

I = Interviewer; J = Jane Milton

- **I:** How do you go about finding new customers?
- **J:** We cold-call, we send a brochure normally and then phone afterwards. But probably at the moment, about 40% of our new work enquiries, people approaching us, come from our website, which was not really why I set the website up. I set the website up so that when people wanted to see examples of our work, I could refer them to it. But I imagined that I'd have already established a relationship with them, but actually some of my biggest jobs have come from people finding us on the web.
- **I:** What for you is the key to good customer relations?
- **J:** I think we're always honest and up-front. We quote people for work, and if it takes much longer than we expected it to take, then we stand by that quote and we just have to swallow that cost and be better at estimating another time, but if it takes much less time, we would go back to them and tell them and discount the job, so I think we're very fair with people and we build long-term relationships with them. We've a lot of small clients who initially made very little money for us 'cause they had very li…, they only needed help with tiny bits of things, but then they respected that we gave them that help, and as they've got bigger, they've given us more and more work.
- **I:** And how would you deal with a dissatisfied customer?
- **J:** We're very lucky because I've never had one, and I think a lot of that is initial communication being good and setting up that initial communication, and when we are given a job, either we ask clients to give us a brief, a written brief, and if they can't do that, then I would give them one and get them to confirm it and so we're absolutely clear before we start on anything exactly what's expected of us. I think because of that, we rarely have … have any problems, and if we do, they're small, we know about them because of the relationship we've got with the person and we would clear them up there and then.

UNIT 23

9 Listening page 111

- **Sloane:** By the way, Jolan, we really must write to BDD about their late delivery. It caused us a lot of problems.
- **Jolan:** Would you like me to write to them, John?
- **Sloane:** If you could. I've got quite a lot on my plate for the next few days.
- **Jolan:** OK. What would you like me to say?
- **Sloane:** Well, they sent me a letter the other day saying that we are a valued, long-standing client. Look, here it is. I think we should remind them that that's what they said. See if it's true.
- **Jolan:** OK. But what are we complaining about? The documents arrived late, didn't they?
- **Sloane:** Five days late, and we specifically asked them to deliver them because in the letter it said that they would be delivered in 12 hours. I could have done it quicker myself.
- **Jolan:** Of course!
- **Sloane:** And then you should point out what the results of this late delivery were.
- **Jolan:** Very embarrassing – at least for me.
- **Sloane:** Sure, since we had the meeting set up to sign the contract, and you had to phone them to postpone it.
- **Jolan:** That's right. Do you think they'll take any notice of our complaint?
- **Sloane:** They'll have to, otherwise we'll stop doing business with them. You can tell them that, too. I mean, their deliveries must be problem-free from now on.
- **Jolan:** OK, John. I'll put all that in a letter. At least that will make me feel better about what's happened!
- **Sloane:** Thanks, Jolan.

UNIT 24

10 Listening page 112

1   … there's really no substitute for actually going there; in my experience, if you're thinking about launching your product abroad, you really must visit the country beforehand to get a feel for the place. It's no good relying on anecdotes or things other people have told you – you've got to go there yourself, otherwise you may be in for some nasty surprises. I remember …

2   … well, as it happens, we employed an agency to find the offices. In retrospect, I think we could probably have done it ourselves more cheaply, but it has turned out very well and saved us a lot of hassle, because at the time the management team was seriously understaffed, and it's not worth taking on staff just for a job like that. Anyway, we're very happy with the result, I must say, and …

3   … We spent ages trying to find the right company for the job. In actual fact, the firm we employed to finish off the design work gave us no end of trouble, and after about six months, we had to terminate the contract and find someone else. Firstly, we found that they couldn't manage our software. Then next we had endless difficulties making ourselves understood – the language barrier was such a problem. It just wasn't worth the money we hoped we were saving. And another thing that we found really frustrating about the whole situation …

4   … It really is absolutely vital to make sure you're talking to the right person. Just to give you one instance: a few years ago we were trying to get a large car manufacturer interested in one of our products and we'd done all the usual things – we'd visited their stand at a trade fair, we'd sent them samples accompanied by all sorts of literature, but we still hadn't made contact with the right man, that is, the man whose job it was to take the final decisions …

5   … and it's very clear and concise – of enormous use to any manager. Quite early on, in the first chapter, I think, he makes several points. The first is this: you should always involve staff as soon as possible in any decisions. If people feel involved, they are usually very ready to accept new ideas and new ways of working. On the other hand, if people are excluded from the decision-making process, they may feel enormous resentment and become unco-operative. His next point is to make sure that you fully research all the options …

11 Listening page 113

Woman: So, Bill, you were going to talk to us about how your company manages its communications with customers.

Bill: Yes, well, my company makes plastic components for the electronics industry, so in actual fact we have a quite limited number of customers. So, firstly, I have to say the Internet is one of our main ways of communicating on a daily basis. Our clients send their requirements and specifications, and we design and produce to meet those specifications. And another thing is that we tend to work together with our customers on quite big projects. They outsource work to us, so when that happens, we have lots of meetings at lots of different levels – management level for deciding prices, how we're going to work together, structuring the project, then design and technical teams work together on the actual product and our part in it. Then I have to say that we try to keep on friendly terms with the key people in our client companies, so we managers socialise quite a lot when we can. Just to give you one instance, my finance director plays golf with the head of R&D in one of our client companies once or twice a month. I often have dinner with my opposite numbers. We find that way we have a much stronger relationship than just a commercial one. In my experience, it's no good thinking that you can keep personal relationships out of business. They're essential.

Woman: Thanks, Bill. How does that compare with your experience, Eileen?

EXAM SKILLS AND EXAM PRACTICE

12 Listening Paper Part 4, Skills Exercise 1b

I = Interviewer; F = Frances

I: Frances, I'm interested in how you know whether your customers are happy or not.

F: Well, I suppose I've got two types of customer really: the outlets – the hairdressers and beauty salons who buy my products – and the end users – you know, the people who actually buy the products from the outlets. These people tend to tell their hairdresser or beauty therapist more or less how they feel. I mean, I don't get a market researcher going round or anything like that, but at least I do send out a questionnaire twice a year to the outlets for them to fill in, so I do have a sort of semi-formal system. And it works quite well. I mean, people tell me what they think, you know.

I: Do you have any typical difficulties with your customers?

F: Um, well, I suppose there are a few who take their time paying, but they're the minority really. And I'm pretty understanding. I mean, we've all had cashflow problems from time to time, and if you're understanding, you know, people get over them. Most people, though, are pretty decent and pay straight out, cash on the nail. Then there are the types – especially older men – who expect my products to make them look 30 years younger than they are, which is a bit unrealistic. Actually though, the main problem is that the market is highly seasonal. Something you wouldn't expect, but people only seem to worry about their appearance at the beginning of the summer when they're thinking of going to the beach.

I: And how do you go about winning new customers?

F: People tell each other, basically. I have a website of course. Everyone has to have one of those nowadays. I've never used things like junk mail or advertising because really they're not cost-effective in my line of work, so basically I rely on selling a good product and letting the news get round on the grapevine.

I: But do you get any customers at all from your website?

13 Listening Paper Part 4

Section 1: questions 33 to 38

You will hear a discussion between Brian, the managing director of a company, and Judy, its finance director, about premises for a new head office.

For questions 33 to 38, circle one letter, A, B or C, for the correct answer.

You will hear the discussion twice.

You have 20 seconds to read the questions.

Now you will hear the discussion.

B: Well, Judy, now that we've both had a chance to visit the two buildings, let's compare notes. Do you think either of them would be suitable for our new head office?

J: I rather liked the location of the Carter House, Brian. About three kilometres from the town centre, but still within the built-up district, and mostly surrounded by housing. It seemed a very pleasant area.

B: … and not far from open country. Yes, I think that was very much in its favour. I could imagine working there. And it's in a reasonable state of repair, isn't it? Though it'll certainly need *some* work to make it suit our requirements. It's a bit small, but we could build onto it.

J: Don't you think we could get away with removing some walls, to turn two or three small rooms into one bigger one? Then we can use the existing space more efficiently.

B: Good idea. Anyway, there's space for an extension, if we decide we need it in the future.

J: We need to consider access, though. We don't want to have problems with that.

B: Mm. It wouldn't be difficult to reach the place from the motorway, which will help with deliveries, as well as staff getting to and from work.

J: I didn't like the fact that the only way into the car park was near a bend in the road. It might be worth changing that, to approach the car park from the other side of the building.

B: Yes, that might be better. Did you have time to talk to the agent about the price?

J: Yes, I did. The asking price is one and three quarter million. But the agent hinted that the company that owns it would be prepared to come down to one and a half. My guess is that if we made an offer in the next couple of weeks, we could get it for one and a quarter million. I really don't think it's worth more than that.

B: But do you think they'd accept that?

J: The agent gave me the impression that the owners want to complete the sale as soon as possible. Apparently one of their subsidiaries is planning to construct a new shopping centre in the town, and the holding company is trying to raise as much of the finance as they can from their assets, to avoid having to borrow it all from the bank and pay interest.

B: That certainly seems to work in our favour! Well, it's worth taking this further.

J: What do you think should be the next step? Our Board members will want to have a look at the building before we purchase it, won't they?

B: Yes, but I think time is the most important factor here. I'll get onto the agent straight away and put in an offer. We can always withdraw it if the directors decide against it. If the owners accept it, I'll brief the Board next week and fix up a visit for them. Then we'll be in a strong position to go ahead with the purchase.

J: Good idea.

Now you will hear the discussion again

Section 2: questions 39–44

You will hear a radio interview with a man called Gary Waters about how advertising agencies can win new business.

For questions 39 to 44, circle one letter, A, B or C, for the correct answer.

You will hear the interview twice.

You have 20 seconds to read the questions.

Now you will hear the interview.

I = Interviewer; G = Gary

I: With me tonight is advertising executive Gary Waters to talk about planning an advertising campaign. Gary, how does it start?

G: Say a company wants us to plan a campaign for a new product – it could be in magazines, on TV – whatever. We have regular clients, of course, but a lot of work comes from people who've seen work of ours and like it. Usually they call us first, and at this stage it's really exploratory, to see if you're on the same wavelength – we don't usually get into a discussion of money yet. Next, they send a written brief, outlining what they want, and we agree on a date to present our proposal to the company. That presentation's really important, because it'll help them decide whether or not to give us the job. So we must have good ideas and present them convincingly.

I: How do you get ideas for your proposal?

G: I may do some background research and play with a few ideas, but I make sure I have a preliminary meeting with the client – usually their marketing manager. That's when I pick up the image they have of the product, any problems they might be having, what they're really looking for and what pressures they're under – say from their competitors. I need to get a feel for the company itself – that's actually more important than the product, and that's when the campaign usually takes shape in my mind.

I: What do you do next?

G: I put together a team. That way we get far better ideas than by working separately. Once we've got an idea we're happy with, we work on it till we know exactly how we see the campaign. Then we start planning the presentation we're going to give the client. That's an oral presentation, followed up by a written proposal package, but we prefer to do *that* part of the proposal individually. A lot of agencies write both the presentation and the back-up as team efforts, but the danger is that you can end up with a mixture of styles, which would make both your work and your agency seem disorganised.

I: Do you write out the presentation in full?

G: Some people do, but it's much more effective not to. I plan it carefully, and just write down key words to remind me of the points I want to cover. That way, I can talk to the client in a much more natural way than if I'm reading aloud. I can also keep an eye on how they're responding, and modify the presentation if I see I'm losing them.

I: Do you ever get asked difficult questions?

G: Oh yes. We always practise giving the presentation to colleagues, to make sure everything's clear, and the people listening try to anticipate the clients' questions by asking as many as they can think of – particularly difficult ones. That way, we're hardly ever taken by surprise when we present to the clients.

I: Finally, Gary, what's the secret of an effective presentation?

G: Some people like to make it funny, but I think it's important to keep it clear, short and simple. People can't usually concentrate for longer than about 20 minutes, and you can't cover everything in that time, anyway, so the detail can go in the written proposal package.

I: Gary Waters, many thanks.

Now you will hear the interview again.

Section 3: questions 45–50

You will hear a radio news item about Ben Miller being appointed as the new European Chairman of GTR, a big advertising group.

For questions 45 to 50, circle one letter, A, B or C, for the correct answer.

You will hear the news item twice.

You have 20 seconds to read the questions.

Now you will hear the news item.

First some marketing news: Ben Miller, former Creative Director with American advertising group Jackson Media, is expected to move to the GTR marketing group in the newly created role of European Chairman. The surprise move follows the launch of his own agency, Hudson, in the US earlier this year, in partnership with Susie Thomas. Miller confirms that he quit Hudson last week, but declined to comment on his new job. It's understood that he has yet to sign the contract.

Inside sources at GTR suggest that Ben Miller won't be welcomed by everyone in the group. This appointment is unsettling, especially since it comes at a time when GTR is still in a state of transition. The company was only created last year, as a result of a merger of three European and North American agencies, so it sorely needs stability and clear vision. It's felt by certain key GTR staff that the decision to appoint Miller was taken at the group's New York headquarters, without any discussion with senior management of the European division, whom Miller is expected to join in London.

Miller's move to GTR will reunite him with the man he used to report to at Jackson Media, Mark West. In fact, West recruited Miller to join him in Jackson's Manhattan office, having done business with him some time previously. West is now President and Chief Operating Officer of GTR.

West was ousted from Jackson Media at the beginning of last year, after investigations into the agency's finances by the US Securities and Exchange Commission, and Ben Miller left the company soon afterwards. Apparently, Miller didn't get on with West's successor, and when he left, he took some of Jackson Media's biggest clients with him, which gave Miller's own agency, Hudson, a good start.

Hudson finds itself in trouble now that Miller has left. The agency was recently responsible for an advertising campaign on behalf of Yellowstone, the American food and drinks giant, and was expecting to pick up further business from the client. The initial deal was down to Yellowstone's seven-year relationship with Miller, built up while he was at Jackson Media. Yellowstone had subsequently moved their business to another agency, but Miller picked them up when he founded Hudson this year.

Commentators are surprised at Miller's move, not only because it means leaving his own newly emerging agency, but also because there were rumours that he had been approached by the chairman of another big marketing agency, Outward Signs. It's thought that Outward Signs was interested in acquiring Hudson from Miller and his partner, with a view to strengthening their own position. The agency is now expected to look elsewhere.

Now for news of the manufacturing industry.

Now you will hear the interview again.

14 Speaking Test Part 2, Skills Exercise 2b

Well, I'm going to talk this evening about what is important when setting up a new business. Firstly, it may depend on the type of business you are thinking of starting up, but if it's a small business with just one or two employees, management experience is not absolutely essential. What is far more important is knowledge of the product. For example, if you're going to open a clothes shop, you should have some experience of working in a clothing outlet and know a lot about clothes.

Another important thing is a knowledge of the market. You should know who your competitors will be, and you will have already identified your target customers and perhaps even spoken with some of them before launching your business. So you will feel reasonably confident that someone is going to buy your product. I mean, you don't want to invest your life savings in a business, only to find that it doesn't interest anyone!

A further point is that you must have a reasonable working knowledge of finance, so that you can produce a sales forecast. You should estimate your costs and make a cashflow prediction. This way, you'll be able to persuade a bank to give you a loan or overdraft.

But, to conclude, the most important thing is interest in the product and your customers.